Peru

WORLD BIBLIOGRAPHICAL SERIES

General Editors:

Robert G. Neville (Executive Editor)
John J. Horton   Ian Wallace
Hans H. Wellisch   Ralph Lee Woodward, Jr.

John J. Horton is Deputy Librarian of the University of Bradford and currently Chairman of its Academic Board of Studies in Social Sciences. He has maintained a longstanding interest in the discipline of area studies and its associated bibliographical problems, with special reference to European Studies. In particular he has published in the field of Icelandic and of Yugoslav studies, including the two relevant volumes in the World Bibliographical Series.

Ian Wallace is Professor of Modern Languages at Loughborough University of Technology. A graduate of Oxford in French and German, he also studied in Tübingen, Heidelberg and Lausanne before taking teaching posts at universities in the USA, Scotland and England. He specializes in East German affairs, especially literature and culture, on which he has published numerous articles and books. In 1979 he founded the journal *GDR Monitor*, which he continues to edit.

Hans H. Wellisch is Professor emeritus at the College of Library and Information Services, University of Maryland. He was President of the American Society of Indexers and was a member of the International Federation for Documentation. He is the author of numerous articles and several books on indexing and abstracting, and has published *The Conversion of Scripts* and *Indexing and Abstracting: an International Bibliography*. He also contributes frequently to *Journal of the American Society for Information Science, The Indexer* and other professional journals.

Ralph Lee Woodward, Jr. is Chairman of the Department of History at Tulane University, New Orleans, where he has been Professor of History since 1970. He is the author of *Central America, a Nation Divided*, 2nd ed. (1985), as well as several monographs and more than sixty scholarly articles on modern Latin America. He has also compiled volumes in the World Bibliographical Series on *Belize* (1980), *Nicaragua* (1983), and *El Salvador* (1988). Dr. Woodward edited the Central American section of the *Research Guide to Central America and the Caribbean* (1985) and is currently editor of the Central American history section of the *Handbook of Latin American Studies*.

VOLUME 109

Peru

John R. Fisher

Compiler

CLIO PRESS

OXFORD, ENGLAND · SANTA BARBARA, CALIFORNIA
DENVER, COLORADO

British Library Cataloguing in Publication Data
Fisher, John
  Peru – (World bibliographical series; v. 109)
  1. Peru. Bibliographies
  I. Title II. Series
  016.985

ISBN 1–85109–100–9

Clio Press Ltd.,
55 St. Thomas' Street,
Oxford OX1 1JG, England.

ABC-CLIO,
130 Cremona Drive,
Santa Barbara,
CA 93117, USA.

Designed by Bernard Crossland.
Typeset by Columns Design and Production Services, Reading, England.
Printed and bound in Great Britain by
Billing and Sons Ltd., Worcester.

THE WORLD BIBLIOGRAPHICAL SERIES

This series, which is principally designed for the English speaker, will eventually cover every country in the world, each in a separate volume comprising annotated entries on works dealing with its history, geography, economy and politics; and with its people, their culture, customs, religion and social organization. Attention will also be paid to current living conditions – housing, education, newspapers, clothing, etc.– that are all too often ignored in standard bibliographies; and to those particular aspects relevant to individual countries. Each volume seeks to achieve, by use of careful selectivity and critical assessment of the literature, an expression of the country and an appreciation of its nature and national aspirations, to guide the reader towards an understanding of its importance. The keynote of the series is to provide, in a uniform format, an interpretation of each country that will express its culture, its place in the world, and the qualities and background that make it unique. The views expressed in individual volumes, however, are not necessarily those of the publisher.

VOLUMES IN THE SERIES

1 *Yugoslavia*, John J. Horton
2 *Lebanon*, Shereen Khairallah
3 *Lesotho*, Shelagh M. Willet and David Ambrose
4 *Rhodesia/Zimbabwe*, Oliver B. Pollack and Karen Pollack
5 *Saudi Arabia*, Frank A. Clements
6 *USSR*, Anthony Thompson
7 *South Africa*, Reuben Musiker
8 *Malawi*, Robert B. Boeder
9 *Guatemala*, Woodman B. Franklin
11 *Uganda*, Robert L. Collison
12 *Malaysia*, Ian Brown and Rajeswary Ampalavanar
13 *France*, Frances Chambers
14 *Panama*, Eleanor DeSelms Langstaff
15 *Hungary*, Thomas Kabdebo
16 *USA*, Sheila R. Herstein and Naomi Robbins
17 *Greece*, Richard Clogg and Mary Jo Clogg
18 *New Zealand*, R. F. Grover
19 *Algeria*, Richard I. Lawless
20 *Sri Lanka*, Vijaya Samaraweera
21 *Belize*, Ralph Lee Woodward, Jr.
23 *Luxembourg*, Carlo Hury and Jul Christophory
24 *Swaziland*, Balam Nyeko
25 *Kenya*, Robert L. Collison

26 *India*, Brijen K. Gupta and Datta S. Kharbas
27 *Turkey*, Merel Güçlü
28 *Cyprus*, P. M. Kitromilides and M. L. Evriviades
29 *Oman*, Frank A. Clements
31 *Finland*, J. E. O. Screen
32 *Poland*, Richard C. Lewański
33 *Tunisia*, Allan M. Findlay, Anne M. Findlay and Richard I. Lawless
34 *Scotland*, Eric G. Grant
35 *China*, Peter Cheng
36 *Qatar*, P. T. H. Unwin
37 *Iceland*, John J. Horton
39 *Haiti*, Frances Chambers
40 *Sudan*, M. W. Daly
41 *Vatican City State*, Michael J. Walsh
42 *Iraq*, A. J. Abdulrahman
43 *United Arab Emirates*, Frank A. Clements
44 *Nicaragua*, Ralph Lee Woodward, Jr.
45 *Jamaica*, K. E. Ingram
46 *Australia*, I. Kepars
47 *Morocco*, Anne M. Findlay, Allan M. Findlay and Richard I. Lawless
48 *Mexico*, Naomi Robbins

49 *Bahrain*, P. T. H. Unwin
50 *The Yemens*, G. Rex Smith
51 *Zambia*, Anne M. Bliss and J. A. Rigg
52 *Puerto Rico*, Elena E. Cevallos
53 *Namibia*, Stanley Schoeman and Elna Schoeman
54 *Tanzania*, Colin Darch
55 *Jordan*, Ian J. Seccombe
56 *Kuwait*, Frank A. Clements
57 *Brazil*, Solena V. Bryant
58 *Israel*, Esther M. Snyder (preliminary compilation E. Kreiner)
59 *Romania*, Andrea Deletant and Dennis Deletant
60 *Spain*, Graham J. Shields
61 *Atlantic Ocean*, H. G. R. King
63 *Cameroon*, Mark W. DeLancey and Peter J. Schraeder
64 *Malta*, John Richard Thackrah
65 *Thailand*, Michael Watts
66 *Austria*, Denys Salt with the assistance of Arthur Farrand Radley
67 *Norway*, Leland B. Sather
68 *Czechoslovakia*, David Short
69 *Irish Republic*, Michael Owen Shannon
70 *Pacific Basin and Oceania*, Gerald W. Fry and Rufino Mauricio
71 *Portugal*, P. T. H. Unwin
72 *West Germany*, Donald S. Detwiler and Ilse E. Detwiler
73 *Syria*, Ian J. Seccombe
74 *Trinidad and Tobago*, Frances Chambers
76 *Barbados*, Robert B. Potter and Graham M. S. Dann
77 *East Germany*, Ian Wallace
78 *Mozambique*, Colin Darch
79 *Libya*, Richard I. Lawless
80 *Sweden*, Leland B. Sather and Alan Swanson
81 *Iran*, Reza Navabpour
82 *Dominica*, Robert A. Myers
83 *Denmark*, Kenneth E. Miller
84 *Paraguay*, R. Andrew Nickson
85 *Indian Ocean*, Julia J. Gotthold with the assistance of Donald W. Gotthold
86 *Egypt*, Ragai, N. Makar
87 *Gibraltar*, Graham J. Shields
88 *The Netherlands*, Peter King and Michael Wintle
89 *Bolivia*, Gertrude M. Yeager
90 *Papua New Guinea*, Fraiser McConnell
91 *The Gambia*, David P. Gamble
92 *Somalia*, Mark W. DeLancey, Sheila L. Elliott, December Green, Kenneth J. Menkhaus, Mohammad Haji Moqtar, Peter J. Schraeder
93 *Brunei*, Sylvia C. Engelen Krausse, Gerald H. Krausse
94 *Albania*, William B. Bland
95 *Singapore*, Stella R. Quah, Jon S. T. Quah
96 *Guyana*, Frances Chambers
97 *Chile*, Harold Blakemore
98 *El Salvador*, Ralph Lee Woodward, Jr.
99 *The Arctic*, H.G.R. King
100 *Nigeria*, Robert A. Myers
101 *Ecuador*, David Corkhill
102 *Uruguay*, Henry Finch with the assistance of Alicia Casas de Barrán
103 *Japan*, Frank Joseph Shulman
104 *Belgium*, R.C. Riley
105 *Macau*, Richard Louis Edmonds
106 *Philippines*, Jim Richardson
107 *Bulgaria*, Richard J. Crampton
108 *The Bahamas*, Paul G. Boultbee
109 *Peru*, John R. Fisher

Contents

INTRODUCTION xi

THE COUNTRY AND ITS PEOPLE 1

GEOGRAPHY 6
General 6
Maps and atlases 8

TOURISM AND TRAVEL GUIDES 10

EXPLORATION AND TRAVELLERS' ACCOUNTS 12
Colonial 12
From independence to 1900 15
20th century 19

FLORA AND FAUNA 24

ARCHAEOLOGY AND PREHISTORY 28
General 28
Pre-Inca 31
Inca 33

HISTORY 38
General 38
The Spanish conquest (1524-48) 39
The colonial period (1548-1821) 42
Independence (1821-24) 51
The republican period (1824- .) 53

POPULATION 65

IMMIGRATION AND INTERNAL MIGRATION 69

ANTHROPOLOGY 75

LINGUISTICS 84

Contents

RELIGION 92

SOCIAL CONDITIONS 97

GOVERNMENT AND POLITICS 102

FOREIGN RELATIONS 111

THE ECONOMY 115
General 115
Trade 119
Industry and mining 121
Agriculture 124

TRANSPORT AND COMMUNICATIONS 129

LABOUR MOVEMENT AND TRADE UNIONS 131

STATISTICS 134

ENVIRONMENT 136

EDUCATION 139

SCIENCE AND TECHNOLOGY 141

LITERATURE 143
General 143
Novels and poetry in translation 145

FOLKLORE 148

MUSIC AND THEATRE 150

ART AND ARCHITECTURE 151

FOOD AND FOOD POLICY 153

LIBRARIES AND ARCHIVES 155

MASS MEDIA 157
General 157
Newspapers and periodicals 158

REFERENCE WORKS 160

BIBLIOGRAPHIES 162

Contents

INDEX OF AUTHORS 167

INDEX OF TITLES 173

INDEX OF SUBJECTS 187

MAP OF PERU 195

ix

Introduction

When compared by objective criteria with its South American neighbours, modern Peru emerges as a country of, at best, middle-ranking importance. With a land area of almost 500,000 square miles, it is the third largest country in the subcontinent after Brazil and Argentina, although almost half of its inhabitants live in the narrow coastal strip, 1,400 miles long, which embraces only 11 per cent of the national territory. Its population is estimated (in 1989) at 21 million inhabitants; the most recent census, that of 1981, counted 17 million, increasing annually at a rate of 2.5 per cent. This makes it the fourth most populous country in South America, after Brazil, Argentina and Colombia. Other indices are much less impressive: Peru has the highest infant mortality rate (99 per 1,000) and overall mortality rate (10 per 1,000) of all countries in the region other than Bolivia. Peru's literacy rate (79 per cent) is lower than those of all other South American countries except Brazil and, predictably, Bolivia. Peru occupies the same lowly position, third from bottom with respect to per capita income, its estimated figure of US $1,040 being approximately double those for both Bolivia and Guyana, but a long way behind that of the next lowest country, Colombia. When these statistics and other demographic and economic indices are aggregated to form a 'physical quality of life index', Peru scores 65 on a scale rising to 100, with only the unfortunate Bolivia (39) behind it and Uruguay (86) and Argentina (85) far ahead.

In global economic terms, too, Peru is of middling significance. Its 1986 foreign debt of 15 billion dollars, although large in relation to the country's inability to service it, let alone repay it, places it relatively low in the Latin American debtors' league. Moreover, president Alán García's radical statements on the imperialist rôle of the International Monetary Fund (IMF) and the parasitical nature of foreign banks have not been translated into debt repudiation, a factor which has averted serious conflict with international financial institutions, although at the cost of denting the short-lived domestic popularity accruing from his initially loud stance. The country has been cushioned from some of the worst effects of inflation and balance of payment problems, which have affected South America as a whole in the 1980s, by the relatively unorthodox domestic economic policies pursued by García since he took office in July 1985, and by its enviable position as an exporter of oil. Furthermore, with petroleum and other minerals, including copper, zinc, silver and lead, accounting for approximately two-thirds of its exports in the 1980s, Peru has avoided over-dependence upon a single commodity and has thus been somewhat better placed than agricultural exporters to withstand the adverse effects of the significant shift in the terms of international trade against producers of primary products.

Internationally, Peru has not provoked serious problems for the world system for over a century. It enjoys relatively good relations, with the US, despite the expropriation of a number of large US corporations in the 1970s and a brief flirtation with Cuba and the Eastern bloc; with Japan, a major investor in mining and industrial enterprizes; and with Western Europe, notwithstanding some British resentment at what was perceived as over-enthusiastic support for Argentina during the Falklands War. Cowed by successive military defeats at the hands of Chile in the 19th century, it has maintained cordial relations with its powerful southern neighbour in the 20th century, only obtaining territorial compensation for the loss of Arica from Ecuador, which it defeated in a brief war in 1940.

Politically, too, relative moderation has tended to characterize modern Peru. Although it produced, in the 1920s, Latin America's most original Marxist thinker before Che Guevara, in the person of Jose Carlos Mariategui, and, in Victor Raul Haya de la Torre, a truly inspirational organizer of the emerging working class and the disaffected lower-middle class, threats in that decade to the oligarchic control of political life were stifled by a combination of repression and the co-opting of potential opponents. Populism flickered in the 1930s, as did pro-Axis sympathies, but both trends were over-shadowed internationally by parallel developments in Argentina and Brazil. The small size of the Peruvian working class, the exclusion of the rural masses from political life by the literacy qualification, the economic attractions of collaboration with the US during World War II, and the readiness of the army to intervene in politics to prevent the Aprista Party from taking power combined to preserve a relatively stable political structure during the 1940s. Towards the end of that decade and through the 1950s, the military continued to conspire against the Apristas, even when the latter had ceased to support real revolution in Peru. Indeed, the renewed intervention of the military in politics in 1968, with the collapse of the first presidency of Fernando Belaúnde amidst financial scandal, rural unrest, and political confusion, was initially interpreted as an old-style attempt to shore up the established political system in the face of pressure from below for drastic changes in economic, political and social structures.

In fact, the period of military rule, which lasted from 1968 to 1980, was characterized, particularly during its most radical phase, until 1975, by a determination not to resist change but to impose it, from above, upon a demoralized oligarchy, a bemused peasantry (which wanted land rather than co-operatives), and confused foreign interests, which were unprepared for revolutionary militarism. This process provoked a dramatic upsurge of research into and writing on Peru by social scientists, coinciding with a dynamic and fairly optimistic political climate. Their interest survived the internal coup within the military leadership to remove from office Juan Velasco Alvarado in 1975. Scholarly attention shifted after 1975, first, to post-mortems upon Velasco's radical reforms, and, second, to analyses of the policies of his successor, general Francisco Morales Bermúdez. It also persisted into the 1980s as, following the military's decision to return to barracks, the old Aprista leader Haya de la Torre was allowed to preside over the constituent assembly which produced a new constitution in 1979, under which, to the amazement of many observers, more than half of the electorate voted for the return to the presidency of the same Belaúnde who had been ousted in 1968. Since Belaúnde's inauguration in 1980, democracy has survived in Peru, under the first constitution to extend the franchise to all adults, despite the perils of the debt crisis, the inauguration in 1985 of the country's first Aprista president, Alán García, and the latter's inability to fulfill his radical election promises. It has survived against a background of rampant inflation, general economic weakness, and an upsurge in political violence which, according to official figures, claimed 12,613 lives between 1980 and 1988.

Why is this relatively poor, and, until recently, politically unexciting South American country better known, to both academics and to the general public, than the majority of its richer, more powerful, and allegedly more important neighbours? Why, in 1988, did more than 12,000 British tourists visit the country, together with tens of thousands more from the US and other European countries, despite the danger of attacks upon foreigners by supporters of the 'Shining Path' (Sendero Luminoso) guerrilla movement?

One answer is that they went to see a country whose physical beauty and diversity can be only partially appreciated from photo-graphs and films, and whose unprepossessing national capital, Lima, is more than compensated for by fascinating colonial cities such as Arequipa and by the even more impressive Cuzco, where magnificent hispanic buildings stand upon superb Inca foundations. Above all, they are attracted by a country where indigenous social, racial and cultural forces have survived, despite centuries of repression, to help create a unique social structure reflecting both Indian and European-style values.

In the colonial period, in general, the notion of a dual society, embracing an indigenous as well as a Spanish élite, had been acceptable to many whites. They recognized that Peru's prestige in South America rested not only upon the wealth of its mines and the political privileges granted by the Spanish crown to its viceregal court, but also upon the comparative cohesion of native social organization, which enabled a relatively small number of Spaniards and their descendants to impose themselves in the place of the Incas at the apex of a complex socio-economic pyramid with Indian foundations.

During the late colonial period, Peru's whites, who constituted only thirteen per cent of the viceroyalty's population, displayed divided attitudes towards the Indian majority (fifty-eight per cent) and to the substantial numbers of *mestizos* (twenty-two per cent) who tended to identify with their Indian mothers rather than their Spanish fathers. The majority of whites were horrified by a major Indian uprising in 1780, the rebellion of Túpac Amaru, which both protested against the increasing socio-economic exploitation of the Indian population, and, invoking Inca legitimacy, vaguely held out the possibility of an independent Peru, based upon racial equality. During the subsequent independence period and in the 1830s, white separatists in the highlands attempted to recruit Indian support for regional political movements designed to break the dominance of Lima and the coast over the interior of Peru. The failure of these movements ensured that, from the 1840s, political and economic power resided in the hands of a small, outward-looking, coastal élite.

Throughout the 19th century and for most of the first half of the 20th century, Peru's political élite, drawn exclusively from the white minority of mainly Spanish descent, attempted to deny the country's Indian identity and to create a republic which looked outwards, culturally and economically, to the US and Western Europe rather than inland to the highlands. Foreign travellers who visited Peru in the 19th century to marvel at its Inca remains frequently commented upon the fact that the inhabitants of Lima were unwilling even to visit the interior of the country, despite, or because of, the fact that the nation's fascination for the foreigner depended less upon Peru's export of *guano* and nitrates to Europe than upon its rich historical and cultural traditions. The minority of Peruvians who had acquired political authority with the establishment of the republic in 1824, a process which many of them had initially resisted in favour of continued rule from Spain, came increasingly to regard all Indians as their inferiors, as part of a subordinate rural proletariat, to be squeezed economically, socially and culturally, with the expansion of capitalist agriculture into the highlands.

Today, after the experiences of revolutionary militarism in the 1970s, and genuine mass participation in politics in the 1980s, it is impossible for the remnants of that oligarchy to turn back the political and social clock to the time when the masses of the population were denied political participation. What the future holds for Peru is uncertain. To a certain extent, the problems which it will face in the 1990s are common to South America as a whole. However, the intrinsic importance and interest of Peru lies less in its capacity to serve as a model for other countries than in its uniqueness. It is that singularity, and its rich cultural diversity which have made Peru the most fascinating country in South America, and one about which much has been written.

About the bibliography

The modest aims of this bibliography are to provide new enthusiasts with an introduction to the rich published sources available for the study of Peru, and to draw the attention of those who already know the country to the most significant works published during the last two decades. The University of Liverpool library, in which the bulk of the research for this bibliography has been undertaken, contains no less than 3,110 books with 'Peru' in their titles, a point which enables the compiler both to record his thanks to the library staff for their assistance, and to stress the point that this is a *selective* bibliography. The primary criterion employed in the selection of material, including many items which do not embrace 'Peru' within their titles, has been to provide details of works which will be of interest to and relevance for the non-specialist English-speaking reader. A related aim has been to concentrate upon relatively recent publications, except, obviously, in the section dealing with exploration and travellers' accounts, which contains a substantial number of classic works of the 19th century. Elsewhere, works published more than twenty years ago are included only if they are of enduring significance, and works in Spanish appear only if they are of particular importance and/or if they relate to topics for which the English-language coverage is thin.

Within each section works are ordered alphabetically by title. Place names and proper nouns are cited consistently in the annotations, but, in the interests of accurate bibliographic reference, are left in their original forms in all titles. Thus, for example, 'Cuzco' is sometimes referred to in titles as 'Cusco', particularly in recent Spanish-language works. Another minor complication is that Peruvian authors tend to be inconsistent about the use of the maternal surname on the title pages of their works. The majority cite both paternal and maternal surnames, some use the matronymic in some works but not in others, and a few abbreviate it to a capital letter. Again in the interests of bibliographical accuracy, names are cited as they appear in the respective works (for example, 'Rogger Mercado U.').

Some of the sections into which the bibliography is divided ('Literature', for example) are relatively self-contained. Others embrace works which other compilers might have classified under different headings, but judicious use of the indexes and the application of common-sense by the reader will overcome any problems. Cross-referencing has been avoided, partly because the compiler considers it unnecessary, but primarily because, in a broad sense, the majority of works on modern Peru are of relevance to all other items. For example, many of the titles in the section on religion are of anthropological interest, and vice versa. Similarly, works on agriculture and internal migration are generally relevant to social conditions. The overall policy has been to locate items in the sections which, on balance, appear to be most appropriate. For example, a work in which the discussion of religion is secondary to the broader analysis of indigenous culture, world view and social organization will appear under 'Anthropology', whereas one which, although of anthropological interest, concentrates upon religious beliefs and practices in their own right will be found in the 'Religion' section. The perennial problem of determining when history ends and politics begins has been resolved in this case by taking 1930 (the year which witnessed the end of the eleven-year presidency of Augusto Leguía) as the point of division. Nevertheless, some works primarily on the post-1930 period include earlier material, and some items which deal mainly with the period before 1930 extend their coverage beyond that date. Consequently, readers with historical interests should also scan the 'Government and Politics' section, and would-be social scientists should also refer to 'History'. All works which are exclusively bibliographical are included in the section entitled 'Bibliographies', even when they deal specifically with material for which there is a separate disciplinary section in this work.

Acknowledgements

The compiler wishes to record his gratitude to his Liverpool colleagues James Higgins, who drafted a number of the entries in the literature section, and Penny Harvey, who provided valuable advice on works relating to anthropology, linguistics and religion. Any errors or omissions in those sections are, of course, his own responsibility. Compilation of the bibliography coincided with his tenure as Dean of the Faculty of Arts in Liverpool, the principal benefit of which was that the manuscript was patiently and expertly typed by the Faculty Secretary, Sandie Murphy, despite the heavy burden of routine office work at a particularly busy period of the academic year. Robert Neville of Clio Press was understanding when other responsibilities delayed the compilation process. Last, but not least, thanks are due to the compiler's wife, Ann, who agreed to forego a summer holiday in 1989 to enable him to complete the manuscript.

John Fisher
Liverpool
August 1989

The Country and its People

1 **Amazon task force.**
Peter Dixon, foreword by Edward Heath, MP.   London: Hodder &
Stoughton, 1984. 191p. map.
In 1982, a British combined services expedition used a specially designed hovercraft to
explore the forbidding terrain of the River Apurimac, the source tributary of the
Amazon. This account of their travels, and of their attempts to provide medical
assistance and fresh water for 'some of the poorest people in the world' (Foreword),
makes good reading. The book contains many excellent photographs.

2 **The Andean republics: Bolivia, Chile, Ecuador, Peru.**
William Weber Johnson.   New York: Time-Life Books, 1968. 2nd ed.
160p. 2 maps. bibliog.
Organized thematically rather than by country, this extremely well-illustrated volume
provides a straightforward, useful introduction to the history and social structures of
the Andean republics.

3 **Inside South America.**
John Gunther.   London: Hamish Hamilton, 1967. 610p. 5 maps. bibliog.
The sections on Peru in this excellent, well-informed general survey of South America
(p. 321-88) begin with a description of 'El Señor Presidente', Fernando Belaúnde
Terry, with whom the author had lunch. He predicted, inaccurately, as it turned out,
that the army was not likely to throw him out of office 'not merely because it regards
Belaúnde highly, but . . . because it considers itself to be an instrument of order and
"constitutional" continuity'.

4 **The land and people of Peru.**
George Pendle.   London: Adam & Charles Black, 1966. 96p. map.
The introduction to this pleasant, though perhaps naïve, general survey was written at
a time when Lima, then with a population of a mere two million (less than half today's
figure) could still be described as 'South America's most impressive capital'.

1

The Country and its People

5 **Lands of the Andes: Peru and Bolivia.**
   Thomas Russell Ybarra.   New York: Coward-McCann, 1947. 273p.
Although this is not a travel guide as such, it was written to provide background information for would-be visitors from the United States. The author's intention was to describe 'the parts of Peru and Bolivia and the things in them that, I think, have the strongest attraction for foreigners in general and can be seen by them without undue hardship'. Both countries, he suggested, could be 'done' comfortably in eight weeks.

6 **Latin America and the Caribbean: a handbook.**
   Edited by Claudio Véliz.   London: Anthony Blond, 1968. 840p. maps.
   bibliog.
The history of republican Peru until the mid 1960s is outlined in one chapter of this weighty tome (Frederick B. Pike, p. 111-25). There are also chapters on the fishing industry (Gerard Eliott, p. 646-51) and the Indians of the Andes (Andrew Pearse, p. 690-95). There are many references to Peru in the general chapters on institutions and contemporary arts.

7 **Nineteenth century South America in photographs.**
   H. L. Hoffenberg.   New York: Dover Publications, 1982. 152p.
The evocative photographs of Peru in this fascinating collection include selections from the work of the brothers Aquiles and Eugenio Courret (active 1863-73), Emilio Garreaud (active 1856-59) and Villroy L. Richardson (active 1859-77); there are also a number of anonymous contributions. The first photograph in the collection shows a panorama of Lima in 1882, seen ominously from a gun emplacement, from which a large cannon, surrounded by shells, points towards the city centre.

8 **The old and the new Peru.**
   Marie Robinson Wright.   Philadelphia, Pennsylvania: George Barrie,
   1908. 456p. map.
Subtitled 'a story of the ancient inheritance and the modern growth and enterprise of a great nation', this somewhat uncritical work, dedicated to the president of the time, José Pardo y Barreda, contains a superb collection of photographs of Peru in the first decade of the 20th century.

9 **Paisajes natural y cultural del Perú.** (Natural and cultural sketches of
   Peru.)
   Leonidas Castro Bastos.   Lima: Editorial Universo, 1971. 251p.
Physical features, ecology and descriptions of selected cities (including Tumbes, Piura, Lima, Arequipa and Cuzco) receive roughly equal treatment in this survey.

10 **Le Pérou.** (Peru.)
   Olivier Dollfus.   Paris: Presses Universitaires de France, 1967. 126p.
   bibliog. (Que sais-je?).
This pocket-sized volume is a compendium of facts, some useful, some merely interesting, on Peru in the 1960s.

11 **Peru.**
Victor Alba. Boulder, Colorado: Westview, 1977. 245p. bibliog.
This is a lively, general description of the country, written by a prominent Spanish journalist, which covers its geography, history, economy, society and culture.

12 **Peru.**
C. Reginald Enock. London: T. Fisher Unwin, 1908. 320p. map.
The contents of this solid, serious work are best summed up by its subtitle: 'its former and present civilisation, history and existing conditions, topography and natural resources, commerce and general development'. Its aim was 'to set forth the past and present conditions of Peru in a manner which may be of value practically, whilst retaining the interest and colour which have always tinged our imaginings of this fascinating land' (Preface). On balance, this aim was realized.

13 **Peru.**
Grace Halsell. London: Macmillan, 1969. 138p. bibliog.
This lightweight, but readable volume was published at a time of relative optimism about the country's future, when, 'political leaders [were] making wider use of television and radio to carry their messages . . . to the formerly isolated Andeans and the presently alienated youth, to the workers and the intellectual. . .' (Conclusion).

14 **Peru.**
Sir Robert Marett. London: Ernest Benn, 1969. 288p. map. bibliog.
This is a sympathetic general survey by a former British Ambassador to Peru (1963-67), who also served in the British Embassy between 1948 and 1952. The work is enlivened by the author's personal reminiscences of key political figures of the mid-20th century, including Victor Raúl Haya de la Torre, Manuel Odría and Fernando Belaúnde Terry.

15 **Peru.**
Ronald Jerome Owens. London: Oxford University Press, 1963. 195p. 3 maps. bibliog.
This serious, well-researched study was published under the auspices of the Royal Institute of International Affairs. It provides a general coverage of the country's historical development, society, economy and culture.

16 **Peru: a country study.**
Edited by Richard F. Nyrop. Washington, DC: American University, 1981. 3rd ed. 302p. 4 maps. bibliog. (Area Handbook Program of the Foreign Area Studies of the American University).
As with other volumes in the series, this updated edition of the 1972 contribution concentrates upon historical antecedents, and on the cultural, political and socio-economic characteristics of the modern period.

3

The Country and its People

17 Peru: a cultural history.

Henry F. Dobyns, Paul L. Doughty. New York: Oxford University Press, 1976. 336p. 6 maps. bibliog.

A deliberate bias in favour of provincial society and the 'common people' is displayed in this wide-ranging, stimulating analysis of Peruvian cultural history.

18 Peru from the air.

George Robbins Johnson, Raye Roberts Platt. New York: American Geographical Society, 1930. 159p. (Special Publications, no 12).

The 150 aerial photographs in this superb collection were taken between 1928 and 1930 by lieutenant Johnson in his official capacity as chief photographer of the Peruvian Naval Air Service. They are divided into three groups, covering, respectively: the coast; Mollendo, Arequipa and the Colca Valley; and the Chanchamayo-Ucayali Valleys.

19 Peru in 1906 and after, with a historical and geographical sketch.

Alexander Garland. Lima: La Industria, 1908. 353p.

Prepared and published with the support of the president of Peru in 1908, José Pardo, this evocative study was designed to provide 'persons desirous of being acquainted with the Peru of today' with 'the necessary data for the due appreciation of its progress during the last ten years'. Its photographs are excellent.

20 Peru in four dimensions.

David A. Robinson. Lima: American Studies, 1964. 424p. 16 maps. bibliog.

This solid general account of the Peru of the early 1960s was inspired 'over a period of years of residence' there by the author's awareness of the lack of a 'comprehensive book' to provide 'facts and figures' about the country (Preface).

21 Peru in pictures.

David Alfred Boehm. London: Oak Tree, 1966. 64p.

This brief, but stimulating, volume contains a wealth of photographs on the land, history, government and business, and the people.

22 Peru of the twentieth century.

Percy Falcke Martin. London: Arnold, 1911. 348p.

Unlike many other works of this period, this book ignores 'Ancient Peru' – the author suggests that 'the list of works upon the land of the Incas is so ample that the market may be considered as sufficiently, if not over, supplied' – in favour of a general, readable survey of resources, industry, mining, agriculture and trade. It gives detailed information about the official programmes then underway to improve road and railway communications.

23 Peruvians of today.

William Belmont Parker. New York: Kraus Reprint, 1967. 616p.

This reprint of a work originally published in Lima in 1919 under the auspices of the Hispanic Society of America contains biographies of some 130 'representative

Peruvians': diplomats, statesmen, authors, lawyers, clergymen, planters, physicians, engineers, teachers, soldiers, sailors, merchants, explorers and geographers. Perhaps predictably, the first biographical sketch is of the then president of Peru, Augusto B. Leguía.

24 The 20 Latin Americas.

Marcel Niedergang, translated by Rosemary Sheed. Harmondsworth, England: Penguin, 1971. vol. 2. 387p.

First published in French in 1962, but revised for the English edition, this general introduction provides a somewhat lyrical account of Peru's cultural diversity (p. 87-136).

25 The Upper Amazon.

Donald Ward Lathrap. London: Thames & Hudson, 1970. 256p. maps. bibliog.

This outstanding survey of the cultural history and ethnography of the Upper Amazon suggests that sedentary communities are at least as old there as they are in the Central Andes; it demonstrates, however, that most of them had their origins in the Central Amazon Basin, rather than in the highlands.

Geography

General

26 **The Andes of southern Peru: geographical reconnaissance along the seventy-third meridian.**
Isaiah Bowman. London: Constable, 1920. 336p.
This pioneering work on the human and physical geography of Peru, arising from the Yale Peruvian Expedition of 1911, is almost as interesting as a human study, for what it reveals of the author's supercilious attitudes towards Peruvians, as for its insights into the nature of Peruvian society.

27 **Catálogo de nombres geográficos del Perú.** (A catalogue of geographical names in Peru.)
Ministerio de Guerra. Lima: Instituto Geográfico Militar, 1979. 164p.
Organized by departments, this catalogue provided details of the geographical co-ordinates of settlements, and of their height above sea level.

28 **The central Andes.**
Clifford T. Smith. In: *Latin America: geographical perspectives*. Edited by Harold Blakemore, Clifford T. Smith. London; New York: Methuen, 1983, 2nd ed. p. 253-324. 11 maps. bibliog.
This extensive chapter provides a wide-ranging and readable account of the physical, social and economic geography of Bolivia, Ecuador and Peru. It is particularly detailed and informative on Peru.

29 **Diccionario geográfico del Perú.** (Geographical dictionary of Peru.)
César García Rosell. Lima: Editorial Minerva, 1972. 167p.
This dictionary is a handy work of reference for place names.

30 **Geografía del Perú: las ocho regiones naturales del Perú.** (Geography of
Peru: the eight natural regions of Peru.)
Javier Pulgar Vidal. Lima: Peisa, 1987. 9th ed. 244p. maps. bibliog.

In this revised and amplified version of a standard work, first published in 1967, Dr.
Pulgar sustains his thesis that Peru, conventionally divided by geographers into three
principal regions (coast, mountains, jungle) consists of eight natural regions, running
west to east.

31 **Geografía del Perú: manual.** (The geography of Peru: a manual.)
Jose Pareja P.S. Lima: Librería Internacional del Perú, 1955. 238p.

Although very traditional in its structure and approach, this work is still useful,
particularly for the physical geography of Peru.

32 **Geografía general del Perú: síntesis.** (A general geography of Peru: a
synthesis.)
Carlos Peñaherrera del Aguila. Lima: Editorial Ausonia, 1969. 312p.

Although this book is described as a first volume, it appears that no subsequent
volume(s) were published. It provides a sound survey of Peru's physical geography.

33 **Latin America**
Preston E. James, C. W. Minkel. New York: John Wiley, 1986. 5th
ed. 578p. maps. bibliog.

The chapter on Peru (p. 334-56) in this outstanding survey, the first edition of which
appeared in 1942, provides an excellent introduction to its geography. There is also a
valuable general introduction, and a concluding discussion of 'problems and prospects'.

34 **Le Pérou: introduction géographique a l'étude du developpement.** (Peru:
geographical introduction to the study of development.)
Olivier Dollfus. Paris: Institut des Hautes Etudes de l'Amerique
Latine, 1968. 355p. 2 maps. bibliog.

The principal focus of this valuable French study is the human geography of Peru, with
particular reference to the obstacles to development provided by the country's physical
features.

35 **Perú: una nueva geografía.** (Peru: a new geography.)
Emilio Romero. Lima: Studium, [n.d.] 2 vols. maps. bibliog.

Although the date of publication is not shown, this work is relatively recent (probably
1981) and may be recommended as an up-to-date general geographical survey.

36 **El Perú 1821-1960: división política completa.** (Peru 1821-1960: complete
political division.)
Lima: Gráfica Moderna Editores, 1960. 136p. 24 maps.

This anonymous work provides details of changes in the country's administrative and
departmental structure since independence. The material is organized by departments,
and includes in each case a sketch map, a note of the area, the population (as in 1958)
and a listing of provinces and their districts.

37 **Los pueblos del Perú.** (The settlements of Peru.)
Primitivo Sanmarti.   Lima: Imprenta y Librería de San Pedro, 1905.
336p.

This gazetteer is somewhat disorganized, but it contains a useful index of place names, and provides supporting data on altitudes, distances and population. Although the population figures are outdated, the other geographical information is of enduring relevance.

38 **Síntesis geográfica del Perú.** (Geographical synthesis of Peru.)
Carlos Peñaherrera del Aguila.   Rio de Janeiro: Instituto Pan-Americano de Geografía e Historia, Comissão de Geografía, 1966. 119p.
bibliog.

This is a neat, pocket-sized summary, providing simple information about physical, social and economic geography.

39 **Síntesis geográfica general del Perú.** (General geographical synthesis of Peru.)
Francisco Cebreros.   Lima: Sociedad Geográfica de Lima, 1971. 141p.
maps.

A map of each department and basic statistical and geographical data are included in this useful summary, designed primarily, according to the prologue, to meet the needs of public servants.

40 **Toponimia quechua del Perú.** (Quechua place-names of Peru.)
Max Espinoza Galarza.   Lima: Cosesa, 1973. 469p.

A discussion of the Quechua language and of Inca remains precedes an alphabetical list of place names. Each entry is accompanied by a brief description of the location and characteristics of the place.

41 **Visión geopolítica del Perú.** (Geo-political vision of Peru.)
Fernando Morote Solari.   Lima: Studium, 1984. 109p.

Dedicated to 'my compatriots who believe in a grandiose future for Peru', this slightly unusual book covers issues such as maritime rights and Peruvian claims to a presence in the Antarctic.

Maps and atlases

42 **Atlas del Perú.** (Atlas of Peru.)
Andres López Dominovich.   Lima: Librería e imprenta 'Guía Lascano', 1964. 68p.

This simple, but useful atlas, designed for school and college use, contains a series of general maps and one for each of the country's twenty-four departments.

43 **Atlas histórico geográfico y de paisajes peruanos.** (An atlas of history,
geography, and Peruvian scenery.)
Instituto Nacional de Planificación, Asesoría Geográfica. Lima:
Presidencia de la República, 1970. 738p.

This major atlas has separate sections on historical cartography, thematic cartography,
individual departments, and frontiers. A final section contains photographs from
different regions. The majority of its maps are on a scale of 1:5,000,000.

44 **Latin American history: a teaching atlas.**
Cathryn L. Lombardi, John V. Lombardi, K. Lynn Stonier. Madison,
Wisconsin: University of Wisconsin Press, 1983. 104 maps.

This work, produced for the Conference on Latin American History of the United
States, contains a number of useful outline maps of modern Peru. It is particularly
helpful for boundary disputes.

45 **Lima: guía de calles.** (Lima: street plan.)
Lima: La Guía Amarilla Lima 2000, 1984. 5th ed. 152p.

This is a simple, effective, booklet-sized street plan of Lima. The map of the city is
divided into thirty-one separate plans (scale 1:25,000) appended to the main text,
which comprises a series of indexes to places of interest, districts and streets.

46 **Mapa planimétrico de imagenes de satélite.** (A planimetric map of
satellite images.)
Lima: Instituto Geográfico Nacional, 1987.

The whole of Peru is covered by this superb set of ninety-five satellite maps, each
measuring sixty by eighty-three cm, and on a scale of 1:250,000.

47 **Mapa vial del Perú.** (A road map of Peru.)
Lima: Lima 2000 SA (Tierra Verlag), 1987.

Provincial and department boundaries, and national parks are shown on this road map,
with no contours, measuring ninety-five by sixty-eight cm.

48 **Perú: carta nacional.** (Peru: national map.)
Lima: Instituto Geográfico Militar, 1968-71.

Each of the five sheets in this set measures eighty by sixty-three cm.

49 **República del Perú: mapa político.** (Republic of Peru: political map.)
Lima: Instituto Geográfico Militar, 1971.

There are eight sheets in this set of maps. Each measures sixty-eight by eighty-seven
cm.

Tourism and Travel Guides

50 **Arequipa artística y monumental.** (Artistic and monumental Arequipa.)
Luis Enrique Tord. Lima: Banco del Sur del Perú, 1987. 205p. bibliog.
This superbly illustrated guide to the architectural beauties of the southern city of
Arequipa, and its surrounding province, is particularly valuable for its photographs and
descriptions of churches.

51 **Calendario turístico.** (Tourist calendar.)
Augusto Vásquez Ayllón. Lima: Editorial Monterrico, [n.d.] 256p.
The date of publication of this ubiquitous guide is not given. However, its context
suggests it is of relatively recent origin. It is crammed with useful information.

52 **Crónicas del Cuzco.** (Chronicles of Cuzco.)
Luis Enrique Tord. Lima: Delfos Ediciones, 1978. 121p.
This illustrated guide to the ancient city of Cuzco contains many colour photographs of
its convents and churches.

53 **Fodor's South America.**
Edited by Robert C. Fisher, Leslie Brown. London: Hodder &
Stoughton; New York: McKay, 1987. 640p. maps. (Fodor's Travel
Guides).
The chapter on Peru in this sophisticated travel guide is of enduring value. Its co-
author, C. N. Griffis, was at one time editor and publisher of *Peruvian Times*, now
superseded by *Andean Times* (1975- . monthly).

54 **Gran guía turística del Perú.** (Great tourist guide to Peru.)
Carlos Hernando Caceda, Victor H. Orzero Villegas. Lima: Delfar,
1986. 382p. map.
Compiled by two well-known journalists, one of whom, Orzero, died before actual

10

publication, this guide suggests a number of individual tours, including three to the Amazon region grouped under the heading 'Towards the exotic'.

55 **Guide to Peru: handbook for travelers.**
Gonzalo de Reparaz. Lima: Ediciones de Arte Rep, [n.d.] 6th ed. 318p.

As is often the case with works produced in Peru, there is no indication in this book of date of publication. The context suggests the late 1970s. It remains a handy, practical guide for travellers, which provides a considerable amount of tourist-level historical and cultural information.

56 **Itinerario general del Perú.** (General itinerary of Peru.)
S. Briceño y Salinas. Lima: Imprenta Nacional, 1921. 405p.

This curious work provides details of distances between settlements, and is organized by departments.

57 **Machupicchu, Cuzco-Perú.**
Democrito Ribeiro Ibañez. Lima: Swiss Foto, 1977. 36p.

This is a simple but attractive annotated colour guide, with thirty photographs of Peru's best-known archaeological site.

58 **Perú: el libro del viajero.** (Peru: the book of the traveller.)
Adriana Alarco de Zadra. Lima: Editorial Universo, 1978. 288p.

Like most travel books, this has dated in some respects, but it is still a very useful pocket guide for the tourist.

59 **South American survival: a handbook for the independent traveller.**
Maurice Taylor. London: Wilton House Gentry, 1977. 272p. 91 maps.

The chapter on Peru in this excellent guide (p. 105-28) deals briefly with its physical setting, history, society and economy. The bulk of it is devoted to descriptions of a number of specific itineraries and towns. The majority are of enduring relevance, with the exception of those of Ayacucho, which foreign travellers should now avoid because of its serious security problems. The general chapters dealing with currencies, preliminary preparations, climate and related matters are also of relevance.

60 **South American handbook.**
Edited by Ben Box, Joyce Candy. Bath, England: Trade & Travel Publications, 1924- . annual.

Updated every year, this outstanding travel guide rightly proclaims itself to be the 'best guide for vacation and business travellers'. The section on Peru in the latest edition (1990, p. 711-853) gives, as ever, accurate, up-to-date and sensible advice and information. The handbook's introductory quotation from Francis Bacon is particularly appropriate for Peru: 'Travel, in the younger sort, is a part of education; in the elder, a part of experience. He that travelleth into a country before he hath some entrance into the language, goeth to school, and not to travel'.

Exploration and Travellers' Accounts

Colonial

61 Colonial travelers in Latin America.
Edited by Irving A. Leonard.   New York: Knopf, 1972. 235p.

Extracts, translated into English, from the writings about Peru of Antonio Vázquez de Espinosa (1615) Amadée F. Frezier (1712-14), and of an anonymous traveller (1600-15), are printed in this compendium.

62 Compendium and description of the West Indies.
Antonio Vázquez de Espinosa, translated by Charles Upson Clark. Washington, DC: Smithsonian Institution Press, 1942. 862p.

A Carmelite friar, Vázquez de Espinosa travelled widely in Peru in the early-17th century. His account of his travels, originally written about 1620, contains a wealth of geographical detail.

63 Los cronistas del Perú (1528-1650) y otros ensayos. (The chronicles of Peru and other essays.)
Raúl Porras Barrenechea, edited by Franklin Pease.   Lima: Banco de Crédito del Perú, 1986. 964p.

This monumental work contains the major writings of Porras (1897-1960) on the chronicles of Peru of the 16th and early-17th centuries.

64 **Discourse and political reflections on the kingdom of Peru.**
Jorge Juan, Antonio de Ulloa, translated by John J. TePaske, Besse A.
Clement. Norman, Oklahoma: University of Oklahoma Press, 1978.
326p.

Written in 1749, but not published until 1826, this damning indictment of administrative, fiscal, judicial and social maladministration in 18th-century Peru is best described by its subtitle: 'government, special regimen of their inhabitants, and abuses which have been introduced into one and another, with special information on why they grew up and some means to avoid them'. The authors were two young Spanish naval officers, sent by Philip V to act as 'watchdogs' over a French scientific expedition, which spent ten years in Ecuador and Peru. This confidential report on maladministration was circulated widely among royal bureaucrats in Madrid, and became the basis for a number of imperial reforms introduced in Peru in the second half of the 18th century.

65 **Ensayo político sobre el reino de la Nueva España.** (Political essay on the kingdom of New Spain.)
Alexander von Humboldt. México: Editorial Porrua, 1966. 696p. 8
maps.

This famous Prussian traveller entered Peru in 1802 from Ecuador via the headwaters of the Amazon. Although he went no further south than Lima and Callao (from where he sailed for Mexico), he keenly sought economic data as he travelled through northern Peru. His account of the mining centre of Hualgayoc – which he believed to be capable of becoming 'a second Potosí' – is incorporated into this major work on New Spain (p. 406). The edition cited, a revision of the first Spanish edition (Paris, 1822), is the most accessible; a number of 19th-century editions are also available.

66 **Extracts from a journal written on the coasts of Chile, Peru, and Mexico in the years 1820, 1821, 1822.**
Basil Hall. Edinburgh: Archibald Constable; London: Hurst &
Robinson, 1824. 2 vols. map.

Hall, a captain in the British navy, was stationed off the coast of Peru during the crucial period when José de San Martín, accompanied by an army brought from Chile, attempted to secure the viceroyalty's emancipation from Spain. His account of his observations, and of his meetings with the principal political figures, including San Martín and the Spanish viceroy, is fascinating.

67 **El lazarillo: a guide for inexperienced travelers between Buenos Aires and Lima 1773.**
Concolocorvo (pseud.), translated by Walter D. Kline. Bloomington,
Indiana: Indiana University Press, 1965. 315p.

The probable author of this pseudonymous work was Alonso Carrio de la Vandera, appointed inspector of the postal routes between Buenos Aires and Lima in 1771. The racy, humourous narrative only partially conceals an ironic and satirical critique of provincial maladministration in the late colonial period.

68 **Narrative of a visit to Brazil, Chile, Peru and the Sandwich Islands during the years 1821 and 1822.**
Gilbert Farquhar Mathison.   London: Charles Knight, 1825. 478p. map.

Unlike many travellers of this early period, Mathison was rather unimpressed with what he saw in South America: 'the prospect which South America displays is far less brilliant than the friend of humanity would desire, or than the generality of persons appear willing to believe'. He does appear, however, to have admired the costumes of the Peruvian women, several of which are depicted in his plates.

69 **Narrative of services in the liberation of Chili, Peru and Brazil from Spanish and Portuguese domination.**
Thomas Cochrane, Earl of Dundonald.   London: James Ridgway, 1859. 2 vols.

After his expulsion from the British navy for connivance in a stock exchange fraud, Cochrane offered his services as a naval officer to the fledgling republic of Chile. He commanded the Chilean navy from 1819 to 1822, and, in that capacity, carried José de San Martín's army to Peru. He resigned his command in 1822, following disagreements with San Martín over payment for his sailors, and subsequently became an admiral in the Brazilian navy (1823-25). In this gripping account of his career, published a year before his death, he provides a great deal of detail about Peru and Peruvians in 1820-22.

70 **The present state of Peru.**
Joseph Skinner.   London: Richard Phillips, 1805. 487p.

The chapters in this beautifully illustrated work cover geography, topography, natural history, mineralogy, commerce, customs and manners of the inhabitants, the state of literature, and missionary travels in eastern Peru. In fact, all are unacknowledged translations from a journal, the *Mercurio Peruano*, published in Lima in the 1790s. In view of the fact that the originals were written by the outstanding intellectuals of late colonial Peru, the work is of enduring value.

71 **Relaciones de viajes de los siglos XVII y XVIII.** (Accounts of travels of the 17th and 18th centuries.)
Edited by Ruben Vargas Ugarte.   Lima: Publicaciones del Instituto de Investigaciones Históricas, 1947. 381p. (Biblioteca Histórica Peruana, V).

This volume contains extracts from the travel journals of Juan de Montemayor (Mexico to Lima, 1617), an unnamed exiled Jesuit (Lima to Cádiz, 1767), and five Capuchin nuns (Madrid to Lima, 1710-22).

72 **Travels from Buenos Ayres by Potosi to Lima.**
Anthony Zachariah Helms.   London: Richard Phillips, 1807. 92p.

Helms, a native of Hamburg, sailed from Cádiz for Buenos Aires in 1789, as a member of a mining mission. Led by the Swede Thaddeus von Nordenflycht, this had been recruited by the Spanish crown to modernize the mining and refining of silver in Peru. Travelling overland from Buenos Ayres (sic) by way of Potosí, he eventually reached Peru early in 1790, remaining there for nearly two years until being granted permission

14

to resign his commission because of 'nostalgia' for his homeland. On his return to Europe, he wrote this embittered account of his experiences in Peru, where, he believed, the mine owners and officials entrusted with the control of the industry were 'entirely destitute of mineralogical knowledge'.

73   **A voyage to Peru; performed by the Conde of St Malo, in the years 1745, 1746, 1747, 1748 and 1749.**
     René Courte de la Blanchardière.   London: R. Griffiths, 1753. 173p.
The English version of this travel account, unlike the French original of 1751, has an appendix 'containing the present state of the Spanish affairs in America, in respect to mines, trade and discoveries'.

74   **A voyage to South America.**
     Jorge Juan, Antonio de Ulloa, translated by J. Adams.   New York: Knopf, 1967. 245p.
Almost entirely the work of Ulloa (who later became governor of the Peruvian mercury-mining town of Huancavelica), this is an abridged version of the famous account of the expedition (1735-44) of the French Academy of Sciences to measure an arc of the meridian near the equator, the first Spanish version of which was published in Madrid in 1748.

75   **A voyage to the South Sea, and along the coasts of Chili and Peru, in the years 1712, 1713 and 1714.**
     Amadée F. Frézier.   London: J. Bowyer, 1717. 335p.
During the War of the Spanish Succession (1700-13), Spain's new Bourbon king, Philip V, granted permission for the first time for French ships to enter the Pacific ports of South America. Frézier's accounts of his voyages and explorations (1712-14) make fascinating reading. He is especially informative on social and economic conditions, and the contraband trade.

From independence to 1900

76   **Cuzco: a journey to the ancient capital of Peru; with an account of the history, language, literature, and antiquities of the Incas. And Lima: a visit to the capital and provinces of modern Peru; with a sketch of the viceregal government, history of the republic, and a review of the literature and society of Peru.**
     Clements R. Markham.   London: Chapman & Hall, 1856. 412p. map.
After meeting W. H. Prescott, the famous narrator of the conquests of Mexico and Peru, Markham made his first trip to Peru in 1852. This work neatly juxtaposes a description of Cuzco and Inca civilization and an account of Lima and modern Peruvian society, thereby underlining the national schizophrenia which afflicted the

15

country throughout the 19th century. In his subsequent career, as president of both the Hakluyt Society and the Royal Geographical Society, Markham edited twenty volumes of early accounts of travels in the Americas, many of them relating to the conquest of Peru.

77 **Insecurity of British property in Peru. Imprisonment of a British subject. Contempt of British authority. Bad faith and fraud in the administration of the law. Persecution endured in the attempt to obtain justice. An appeal to the representatives of the British nation by Henry de Wolfe Carvell.**
Henry de Wolfe Carvell.   London: Chapman & Hall, 1863. 70p.

The title says it all. Much to the dismay of British subjects who suffered wrongs, real and imagined, during times of civil strife in 19th-century Peru, successive governments, and the navy, invariably resisted appeals for armed intervention on their behalf. Nevertheless, works such as this succeeded in depicting Peru as an unsafe location for British travellers and businessmen.

78 **Journal of a passage from the Pacific to the Atlantic, crossing the Andes in the northern provinces of Peru, and descending the river Marañon, or Amazon.**
Henry Lister Maw.   London: John Murray, 1829. 486p.

A lieutenant in the British navy, Maw took particular interest in the possibilities of utilizing Peru's rivers for navigable communication with the Atlantic.

79 **A journey across South America from the Pacific Ocean to the Atlantic Ocean.**
Paul Marcoy (pseud.).   London: Blackie, 1873. 2 vols. 12 maps.

The principal value of this work by the famous French traveller and artist (real name Laurent Saint-Cricq), who crossed from the coast of Peru to the Atlantic via the Amazon lies in his descriptions and in the 600 engravings drawn by E. Riou, many of which depict members of the Indian tribes of the upper Amazon region.

80 **Journey from Buenos Ayres, through the provinces of Cordova, Tucuman, and Salta, to Potosi, thence by the deserts of Caranja to Arica, and, subsequently, to Santiago de Chili and Coquimbo, undertaken on behalf of he Chilian and Peruvian Mining Association in the years 1825-26.**
Joseph Andrews.   London: John Murray, 1827. 2 vols.

The prolonged title says most of what needs to be noted about this work. It provides a good description of the port of Arica, now in Chile, emphasizing its continuing importance as the principal Pacific outlet for Bolivian silver after independence.

81 **Melbourne, and the Chincha islands; with sketches of Lima, and a voyage round the world.**
George Washington Peck.   New York: Charles Scribner, 1854. 294p. maps.

Behind this rather convoluted title lies an interesting travel book by an accomplished author, journalist, artist and music critic. About half of it (p. 141- 284) refers to South America, and the descriptions of Callao and Lima are extensive.

82 **The memoirs of General Miller in the service of the republic of Peru.**
John Miller.   London: Longman, Rees, Orme, Brown & Green. 1828. 2 vols.

The outstanding military memoir of Peruvian independence is this account of the exploits of William Miller, prepared by John Miller from his brother's journals and recollections. William, who had fought in Spain during the Peninsular War, had an illustrious career in South America as a volunteer fighting with the patriot forces; after independence he was appointed governor of Potosí and, subsequently, marshal of Peru. His account of the struggle for independence has an inevitable anti-Spanish flavour, given that its aim was 'to paint in true colours the merit, the valour, the constancy, and the natural benevolence, of the Peruvian, Chileno, and Argentine peasantry and soldiery, who possess these good qualities in spite of the many vices resulting from Spanish contagion and misrule'. His brilliant account of the 1824 battle of Ayacucho, which ended Spanish rule in Peru, possesses an almost poetic quality.

83 **Narrative of a journey across the cordillera of the Andes, and of a residence in Lima and other parts of Peru, in the years 1823 and 1824.**
Robert Proctor.   London: Hurst & Robinson, 1825. 374p.

Proctor travelled to Peru as agent for the first British loan, and took particular interest in the economic conditions prevailing during the country's final transition to independence.

84 **Narrative of a journey from Lima to Para, across the Andes and down the Amazon.**
William Smyth, Frederick Lowe.   London: John Murray, 1836. 305p.

The value of this book by two officers in the British navy is twofold. First, they provide detailed accounts of the Pachita, Ucayali and Amazon rivers, as they explore the possibility of navigable communication from Peru to the Atlantic by this means; second, they describe in considerable detail the social and economic conditions of the central Peruvian highlands, which they traversed in 1834 on their way to the remote eastern jungles. Their conclusions make gloomy reading: 'the most horrid and barbarous murders escape investigation' because of 'the hands of justice being too weak to interfere'.

85 **Naval adventures during thirty-five years service.**
William Bowers.   London: Richard Bentley, 1833. 2 vols.

Written from the standpoint of a British naval officer observing the transition of Chile and Peru to independence, this work contains much material on San Martín's attempts to emancipate Peru from Spanish rule.

86 **Our artist in Peru. Leaves from a sketch book of a traveller during the winter of 1865-6.**
George Washington Carleton.   New York: Carleton, 1866. 50p.
This pleasant collection contains fifty sketches, preceded by a brief introductory essay.

87 **Peru as it is: a residence in Lima, and other parts of the Peruvian republic, comprising an account of the social and physical features of that country.**
Archibald Smith.   London: Richard Bentley, 1839. 2 vols.
This work provides a very detailed account of Peru's principal silver mining centre, Cerro de Pasco, in the 1830s. It was in this period that production began to rise after the dislocation caused by the wars of independence.

88 **Peru: incidents of travel in the land of the Incas.**
Ephrain George Squier.   London: Macmillan. 1877. 599p. map.
During his service as US commissioner to Peru (1863-65), Squier took particular interest in its Inca remains. He had worked as an archaeologist on native remains in the US before embarking on a diplomatic career.

89 **Peru in the guano age: being a short account of a recent visit to the guano deposits with some reflections on the money they have produced and the uses to which it has been applied.**
Alexander James Duffield.   London: Richard Bentley, 1877. 151p.
Although employed in Peru as a mining chemist, Duffield took a keen interest in and wrote two books about 'the guano age' of which this is the best. By the time he wrote, commercial attention had already shifted from this natural fertilizer deposited on islands off the Peruvian coast to the nitrate plains of the Atacama desert. Confusion and rivalry over the frontiers in this area of Peru, Chile and Bolivia were the principal cause of the subsequent War of the Pacific (1879-83).

90 **The Peruvians at home.**
George R. Fitzroy Cole.   London: Kegan Paul & Trench, 1844. 277p.
This description of Peru's 'most important towns and sights' was written by a businessman who spent over two years there in the 1870s.

91 **Sixteen years in Chile and Peru from 1822 to 1839.**
Thomas Sutcliffe.   London: Fisher, 1841. 563p.
This account is particularly detailed on Chile, where the author held several military and administrative positions, including that of governor of the island of Juan Fernández. However, it also contains material on Peru, whose disorder is compared unfavourably with Chile's political tranquility.

92 **South America and the Pacific: comprising a journey across the pampas and the Andes, from Buenos Ayres to Valparaiso, Lima and Panama.**
Peter Campbell Scarlett.   London: Henry Colburn, 1838. 2 vols. maps.
A career diplomat, who served in various South American locations, the author

travelled overland to Peru in the 1830s. His work contains interesting plans and statements for establishing steam navigation along the west coast of South America (a goal to be realized, in fact, in 1840).

93   Travelling impressions in, and notes on, Peru.

Felix Seebee.   London: Eliot Stock, 1901. 196p.

The principal interest of this volume lies in its eye-witness account of the bloody Chilean capture of Lima in January 1881.

94   Travels in various parts of Peru.

Edmond Temple.   London: Henry Colburn & Richard Bentley. 1830.
2 vols.

Temple travelled widely in Peru and Bolivia as agent for the Potosí, La Paz and Peruvian Mining Association, which collapsed in 1826. His jaundiced report of his travels attacked both ignorant shareholders and irresponsible local political leaders. Uncounsciously anticipating the formation in 1836 of the Peru-Bolivia Confederation, he observed: 'Bolivia is probably not destined to remain an independent state; its geographical position, as well as its most prudent policy, seems to demand a junction with Lower Peru'.

20th century

95   Adventures in Peru.

Cecil Herbert Prodgers.   London: John Lane, 1924. 250p.

The author seems to have been an old-style adventurer and traveller. He recommends Peru and Bolivia as countries which 'besides offering great scope for people who have their heads screwed on the right way, also hold out inducements to sufferers who have found European medical methods ineffectual' (Preface). A note records that he died while the book was in press. Although written from a somewhat blinkered perspective, the work is lively and informative.

96   The Andes and the Amazon: life and travel in Peru.

C. Reginald Enock.   London: T. Fisher Unwin, 1908. 2nd ed. 379p.

A fellow of the Royal Geographical Society, who travelled widely in Peru in the early-20th century, Enock succeeded in preserving the prejudices of his Victorian predecessors about its Spanish, Catholic past, and the belief of his contemporaries in the importance of economic growth and modernization on the Anglo-Saxon model. He writes, 'The Republic of Peru . . . has endured its baptism of sword and priestcraft. But the Peruvian . . . is losing some of the evil conditions which were grafted upon his country by his progenitors. The three main causes which have dominated the community to their hurt have been political methods, militarism, and clericalism; but these are now giving way to the principles of fair government which the inexorable march of civilisation demands'.

97 **Across South America: with an account of a journey from Buenos Aires to Lima by way of Potosi, with notes on Brazil, Chile and Peru.**
Hiram Bingham. Boston, Massachusetts; New York: Houghton Mifflin, 1911. 405p. maps.

In the course of this epic journey of exploration the author discovered the Inca ruins at Machu Picchu, thereafter known, somewhat misleadingly as 'the lost city of the Incas'. In fact, it was only one, albeit magnificent, garrison settlement, rather than the Incas' last refuge.

98 **The condor and the cows.**
Christopher Isherwood. London: Methuen, 1949. 195p.

This famous writer travelled through Colombia, Ecuador, Peru, Bolivia and Argentina in 1947-48, keeping a detailed diary of his impressions. Those of Peru (p. 101-40) are perceptive, as are his general remarks about expatriates: '. . . the foreigner just cannot help being bossy . . . Deep down in his heart he is apt to have a slight sense of grievance. He has come to this country – it isn't home and he is sometimes lonely and uncomfortable – and he feels, in his wistful, less reasonable moments, that he has made a sacrifice. He would like just a little gratitude. Now and then he gets it' (p. 91).

99 **Family in Peru.**
John Sykes. London: Anthony Blond, 1962. 221p.

This novelist's account of his travels in Peru some thirty years ago is articulate and incisive. It describes a country with deep social, political and racial divisions, in which the author's first contacts among the 'Lima élite' regarded the Andean Indian as 'sub-human'.

100 **Golden wall and mirador: travels and observations in Peru.**
Sacheverell Sitwell. Clevelend, Ohio; New York: World Publishing Company, 1961. 286p.

To a certain extent this book resembles its 19th-century predecessors, in that it reveals almost as much of the peculiar attitudes and behaviour of its author as it does of the country under his scrutiny. A visit to the magnificent Inca fortress of Ollontay-Tambo (sic) got no further than the railway station, 'and here we got down from our train, for it was intended that we should visit the Inca ruins, but we were too tired and breathless to attempt this'. The splendours of Cuzco were clouded by disappointment at the inefficacity of cardamine tablets at such a high altitude. The photographs are admirable.

101 **El hombre del Marañon: vida de Manuel Antonio Mesones Muro.** (The man of the Marañon: life of Manuel Antonio Mesones Muro.)
José Mejía Baca. Lima: Sanmarti, 1943. 149p.

Mesones Muro (1862-1930) explored widely in the Marañon river region until his death. Although this book is something of a hagiography, it serves the purpose of reminding the reader that much basic exploratory activity was undertaken by Peruvians themselves in the late-19th and early-20th centuries.

102 **Hacia el pais de las orquideas.** (Towards the land of the orchids.)
César E. Ferreyros.   Lima: Torres Aguirre, 1944. 114p.
This account of travel and exploration in eastern Peru, 'the land of the orchids', provides a good impression of the difficulties of communication in the region.

103 **Heirs of the Incas: a book about Peru.**
Carroll Kinsey Michener.   London: Methuen, 1926. 213p.
This book begins by displaying an anti-Argentina bias – 'The world has heard overmuch of Buenos Aires . . . Buenos Aires, this observer has it, is the silk hat crowning a nude man'. The intention is to make the point that 'the essential South America' is not 'a cosmopolitan centre, with its aping of things European' but the country of Peru where 'a new race' was formed from 'the fusion of Spaniard and Indian, consanguinary and sociological'.

104 **Inca land: explorations in the highlands of Peru.**
Hiram Bingham.   Cambridge, Massachusetts: Riverside, 1922. 365p.
As director of the Peruvian expeditions organized by Yale University and the National Geographic Society in 1909, 1911, 1912 and 1915, Bingham was the most authoritative and respected traveller and explorer of early-20th century Peru. This volume summarizes the results of his four journeys into the interior of southern Peru in search of Inca remains. It contains many interesting photographs.

105 **Incas and other men: travels in the Andes.**
George Woodcock.   London: Faber & Faber, 1959. 268p. map.
A Canadian resident, Woodcock travelled widely in Peru during the late 1950s. Apart from the usual descriptions of life in the Andes, he offers some interesting observations on the easing of the dictatorship of Manual Odría.

106 **In the wilds of South America: six years of exploration in Colombia, Venezuela, British Guiana, Peru, Bolivia, Argentina, Paraguay, and Brazil.**
Leo E. Miller.   London: T. Fisher Unwin, 1921. 428p. map.
As a field-naturalist from the American Museum of Natural History, Miller took part in seven expeditions to South America (1911-16) for the purpose of collecting birds and mammals, studying the fauna, and making 'all possible observations regarding the flora, topography, climate, and human inhabitants of the regions visited'. He visited Peru in 1916, sailing down to the coast of Mollendo, and inland by train to Lake Titicaca via Arequipa and Puno (p. 265-78). The material on Peru is useful, despite its brevity.

107 **Keep the river on your right.**
Tobias Schneebaum.   London: Jonathan Cape, 1970. 184p.
The author travelled widely in eastern Peru in 1955 as a Fulbright fellow, achieving some minor notoriety when the US embassy there concluded incorrectly that he had been killed by the Indians. Although falling far short of a proper anthropological study, his account of life at a jungle mission station is serious and informative.

108 Llama land: east and west of the Andes in Peru.
Anthony Dell. London: Geoffrey Bles, 1927. 248p.

The tone of this work is light-hearted; it begins 'When I told my friends I was going to Peru they became flippant. The most staid and serious immediately quoted limericks about young men of Peru who had nothing to do and sent snakes to the zoo'. Behind this lies a serious, attractive account of Peru in the 1920s.

109 Peruvian adventure.
Will Brown. London: Robert Hale, 1958. 191p.

The author visited Peru in 1957 with two other Cambridge medical students – Piers and Sydney – to carry out experiments on mouse genetics at high altitudes. One of the photographs shows 'Piers being revived with oxygen at Tuctu'.

110 Peruvian pageant.
Blair Niles. London: John Murray, 1937. 355p. map.

This 'very personal story of a journey in time' combines a sympathetic account of personal travel by an author seeking background information for her historical novel with a series of stories about Peruvian history. It includes many amateurish but interesting photographs.

111 The Putumayo: the devil's paradise.
Walter E. Hardenburg. London: T. Fisher Unwin, 1912. 347p. map.

This account of a young American engineer's travels down the Putumayo in 1907-08 was the first major revelation of the atrocities committed against the Indians of the upper Amazon by the Peruvian Amazon Rubber Company of Julio César Arana. Its publication followed the despatch in 1910 of Roger Casement from his post as consul-general in Rio de Janeiro to investigate accusations of maltreatment. Although there was a major public outcry in Britain following the publication of both this book and Casement's report in 1912, the company carried on with its rubber-gathering until put out of business by Malayan competition.

112 A search for the apex of America: high mountain climbing in Peru and Bolivia including the conquest of Huascaran, with some observations on the country and people below.
Annie S. Peck. New York: Dodd, Mead, 1911. 370p. map.

There is not much that needs to be added by way of explanation to the title. The physical description is detailed, and supported by many photographs.

113 Silent highways of the jungle.
George Miller Dyott. London: Chapman & Dodd, 1924. 2nd ed. 320p. map.

A British geographer, Dyott travelled into the remote parts of the interior of Peru on the eastern slope of the Andes at the instigation of the country's president Agustin B. Leguía, with a view to ascertaining the feasibility of aerial transport into potentially rich areas which could not be reached by either railways or roads. At one stage in his travels, the author was abandoned in the forest by a companion called Muñoz, who escaped before Dyott was able to 'put an ounce of lead through his villainous head'. Fortunately, Dyott survived to inform the authorities in Lima of what had occurred: 'Some months later, in London, I received notification that Muñoz, on arrival in

Iquitos, had been given a sound thrashing by Mr J. W. Massey of the Booth Steamship Company, and that he (Muñoz) had then retired to jail for an extended period'. On his release, Mr R. C. Sharpe of the Commercial Bank of Spanish America 'thinking he needed yet another thrashing . . . promptly administered it'.

114 Three worlds of Peru.
Frances Toor.   New York: Crown Publishers, 1949. 239p. bibliog.
After a residence of twenty-five years in Mexico, the author travelled widely in Peru throughout 1948. Her account is strong on geographical and social description, but says relatively little about politics. It contains seventy-three excellent photographs, a number of them by Martín Chambi of Cuzco.

115 Two against the Amazon.
John Brown.   London: Hodder & Stoughton, 1952. 224p.
This account of a somewhat amateurish scientific expedition to identify the true source of the Amazon, undertaken in the late 1940s by two upper-class Englishmen depressed by life in peace-time Britain – 'I was bullied by income-tax inspectors and ignored by housing officials. It was difficult to move about the world and the pound was no longer the international currency' (p. 13) – is incredibly and unintentionally amusing. The tone is set even before they reach Peru: 'Cartagena was our port of call in the republic of Colombia, and I am sorry to say I did not even know what country it was in until this trip' (p. 34). It continues in similar vein: 'Dried llama and *pisco*, or *tamales* and *aguardiente* may be all right for the Indians, but don't order them . . . or they may ship you back stiff as a board, by the next boat' (p. 188). The book is highly recommended as a typical manifestation of British insensitivity and bad taste.

116 Up the Amazon and over the Andes.
Violet O. Cressy-Marcks, introduced by Admiral Sir William E. Goodenough.   London: Hodder & Stoughton, 1932. 336p. 3 maps.
'A traveller in many lands', to quote from the brief introduction to this book by the President of the Royal Geographical Society, Cressy-Marcks sailed up the Amazon to Iquitos in 1930, and from there by river and land to Ocopa, Huancayo, Lima and Cuzco. Both the style and the sentiments expressed are inevitably dated, but the insight into physical and social conditions in the interior of Peru in this period is quite profound.

117 Viajes por el Perú centro y sur. (Travels through central and southern Peru.)
Luis J. Benoit.   Lima: Editorial P.T.C.M., 1947. 121p. 12 maps.
This handsome, well-illustrated travelogue describes a round trip by road from Lima to the Chilean frontier by way of the *sierra* (taking in Huancayo, Ayacucho, Cuzco, Puno and Arequipa), returning by the coastal route. The photographs are excellent.

118 Wanderings in the Peruvian Andes.
A. M. Renwick.   London; Glasgow: Blackie, 1939. 225p.
This is a serious, scholarly work describing the varied travels among the Andean valleys and the 'immeasurable forests beyond the mountains', of an individual who served thirteen years as head of the Anglo-Peruvian College in Lima. The thirty-six photographs include a number taken by the famous Cuzco photographer of the 1920s, Martín Chambi.

Flora and Fauna

119 **Amazon jungle: green hell to red desert? An ecological discussion of the environmental impact of the highway construction program in the Amazon basin.**
R. J. A. Goodland, M. S. Irwin.   Oxford: Elsevier, 1975. 155p.

Peruvian Amazonia remains relatively unspoiled. This discussion of landscape management, or the lack of it, in Brazil provides a warning of the threat to its ecology from economic development.

120 **Atlas of plant life.**
H. Edlin.   London: Aldus Books, 1973. 128p.

This general survey of plant life contains a chapter on South America, within which there are a number of references to Peru.

121 **Biogeography and ecology in South America.**
Edited by Ernst Josef Fittkau, J. Illies, H. Klinge, G. H. Schwabe, H. Sioli.   The Hague: Junk, 1968-69. 2 vols. (Monographiae Biologicae, 18-19).

As with similar works, the organization of the material in this collection of essays on the fauna and insects of South America is by theme rather than country. There are frequent references to Peru in the chapters dealing with mammals, birds, fresh-water fish, molluscs, fossils and coleoptera.

122 **The birds of Chile and adjacent regions of Argentina, Bolivia and Peru.**
A. W. Johnson, colour plates by J. D. Goodall.   Buenos Aires: Platt Establecimientos Gráficos, 1965. 397p. map. bibliog.

As the title indicates, the principal focus in this work is upon the birds of Chile. However, since they are ignorant of national boundaries, there is also considerable coverage of the bird life of southern Peru. The painted colour illustrations and black-and-white photographs are helpful and attractive.

123 **Birds of the ocean: a handbook for voyagers. Containing descriptions of all the sea-birds of the world with notes on their habits and guides to their identification.**
Wilfrid Backhouse Alexander. London: Putnam, 1955. 282p.
This general guide to the sea-birds of the world contains many references to the rich bird life encountered off the long Pacific coastline of Peru.

124 **Butterflies of the world.**
H. L. Lewis. London: Harrap, 1973. 312p.
The organization in this superbly illustrated work is by species, thirteen of which are encountered in South America. Cross-referencing to the descriptive text identifies those which are found in Peru.

125 **The flight of the condor: a wildlife exploration of the Andes.**
Michael Alford Andrews. London: Collins and the British Broadcasting Corporation, 1982. 158p. 4 maps. bibliog.
Produced to accompany a series of three television programmes, this lavishly illustrated work on the plant and animal life of the Andes deals with both the making of the films and the richly varied wildlife of the area from Cape Horn to the Equator.

126 **A forgotten river: a book of Peruvian travel and botanical notes.**
Christopher Sandeman. London: Oxford University Press, 1939. 299p. map.
This volume describes a journey of three months duration down the Huallaga river, from its source near Cerro de Pasco, some 14,000 feet above sea level, to the tropical riverside town of Yurimaguas, 580 feet above sea level, where it becomes navigable by steamer to Iquitos. The author returned to the Pacific coast through the remote Balsapuerto-Moyobamba region. His principal interest was in the rich plant life of these areas, and he modestly describes his findings as 'botanical jottings'.

127 **The great mountains and forests of South America.**
Paul Fountain. London: Longmans, Green, 1902. 306p.
The principal purpose of the journey to South America, undertaken in 1884, which Fountain recounts in this book was to study bird life and to make a collection of specimens. Although he deals with his principal findings in Chile and Peru in a specific chapter, entitled 'Mountain and valley in Chili and Peru' (p. 264-81), his introductory and concluding remarks are also of relevance for Peruvianists.

128 **A guide to the birds of South America.**
Rodolphe Meyer de Schauensee. Edinburgh: Oliver & Boyd, 1970. 470p. bibliog.
Aimed at both the professional and amateur ornithologist, this illustrated guide to the incredibly rich bird fauna of South America complements the author's earlier one-volume listing: *The species of birds of South America and their distribution* (Narberth, Pennsylvania: Livingston, 1966).

129 **Notes of a botanist on the Amazon & Andes.**
Richard Spruce, edited and condensed by Alfred Russel Wallace.
London: Macmillan, 1908. 2 vols. 7 maps.
Spruce spent fifteen years (1849-64) in northern Brazil, Peru and Ecuador on behalf of a syndicate of British botanists, collecting more than 7,000 species of flowering plants, together with ferns, mosses, lichens and fungi. He returned to England in poor health in 1864, and died in poverty in 1893. Eventually his friend Wallace, who had himself travelled widely in Amazonia in the 1850s with Henry Walter Bates, collected and edited Spruce's extensive notes for publication.

130 **Oceanic birds of South America: a study of species of the related coasts and seas, including the American quadrant of Antarctica, based upon the Brewster-Sanford collection in the American Museum of Natural History.**
Robert Cushman Murphy.   New York: American Museum of Natural History, 1936. 2 vols. bibliog.
The oceanic birds of Peru are covered by this standard work of reference, although the arrangements of its contents is by species rather than country.

131 **Orchids of Peru.**
Charles Schweinfurth.   *Fieldiana: Botany*, vol. 30, nos. 1-4 (1958-61), 1026p.
This massive contribution to the journal series of botanical reports produced by the Chicago Natural History Museum is definitely for the serious scientist rather than the 'coffee-table' browser.

132 **Plant hunters in the Andes.**
Thomas Harper Goodspeed.   New York: Farrar & Rinehart, 1941. 429p. 3 maps.
This book describes in great detail the findings of two plant hunting expeditions sent to Peru and Chile in 1935-36 and 1938-39 by the University of California Botanical Garden.

133 **Relación histórica del viage que hizo a los reynos del Perú y Chile el botánico D. Hipólito Ruiz en el año de 1777 hasta el de 1788, en cuya época regresó a Madrid.** (Historical account of the journey undertaken to the kingdoms of Peru and Chile by the botanist Hipólito Ruiz in the year 1777 until that of 1778, when he returned to Madrid.)
Hipólito Ruiz, edited by Jaime Jaramillo-Arango.   Madrid: Real Academia de Ciencias Exactas, Físicas y Naturales, 1952. 2 vols. maps.
The first of these superbly illustrated volumes, derived from Ruiz' papers in the British Library, presents the botanical findings of an expedition to Peru which was sponsored by the crown. The second volume contains several botanical and zoological indices. An English version of the text, (minus the illustrations) translated by B. E. Dahlgren, was published in 1940, entitled *Travels of Ruiz, Pavon, and Dombey in Peru and Chile (1777-1788)* (Washington, DC: Field Museum of Natural History).

134 South America and Central America: a natural history.

Jean Dorst.   London: Hamish Hamilton, 1967. 298p.

This general survey of the natural history of Latin America is superbly illustrated. It has a separate chapter (p. 190-213) on the Peruvian highlands, entitled 'Icy land beneath a tropical sun', and there is also detailed coverage of Peru (and Chile) in the chapter on deserts, 'Arid coasts and teaming seas' (p. 214-35).

135 South American zoo.

Victor Wolfgang Von Hagen.   London, Glasgow; Collins, 1947. 183p.

Although designed to introduce children to the faunal natural history of South America, this work might also be of some interest to adults seeking an easy way into the subject.

136 South America: the green world of the naturalists.

Edited by Victor Wolfgang Von Hagen.   London: Eyre & Spottiswoode, 1951. 398p. map.

This selection of extracts from the accounts of their travels in South America by naturalists is organized chronologically. Those of relevance for Peru include the ornithological descriptions of the cayuco by Frank Michler Chapman (p. 346-49) and of the guanay (or cormorant) by Robert Cushman Murphy (p. 357-77).

137 Travels in Peru and India while superintending the collection of chinchona plants and seeds in South America, and their introduction into India.

Clements R. Markham.   London: John Murray, 1862. 572p. maps.

The chinchona tree, from whose bark quinine is derived, is native to Peru. During the colonial period and the 19th century its 'Jesuit bark', as it was commonly known, was exported in large quantities to Europe. This account of a successful mission to collect plants and seeds for introduction of the species into India contains a considerable amount of interesting information on Peruvian plant life in general.

138 A wanderer in Inca land.

Christopher Sandeman.   London: Phoenix House, 1948. 192p. map.

Sandeman travelled widely in Peru (1938-46), collecting specimens of the country's rich plant life for the Herbaria of Kew Gardens and Oxford University. The eighty-nine photographs, each accompanied by a page of description, in this attractive volume include a number of animals, birds and plants.

Archaeology and Prehistory

General

139 The ancient American civilizations.
Friedrich Katz.   London: Weidenfeld & Nicolson, 1969. 386p. 3 maps. bibliog.

One of the virtues of this excellent survey is that it provides a general context for the consideration of the prehistory of the Andean region by means of chapters on the origins of the native population of the Americas, and the birth of agriculture. Three of its fourteen chapters deal exclusively with the Andean region.

140 The ancient civilizations of Peru.
J. Alden Mason.   Harmondsworth, England: Penguin, 1969. rev. ed. 335p. 2 maps. bibliog.

Although inevitably somewhat dated, this revised version of a work first published in 1957 remains a sound general introduction to the history of Peru, from earliest times until the Spanish conquest.

141 Ancient Peruvian textiles.
Ferdinand Anton.   London: Thames & Hudson, 1987. 236p. map. bibliog.

This is a beautifully illustrated volume; 112 of the 302 illustrations are in colour. It is divided both thematically, with chapters on 'Gods, spirits, and beasts' and 'From naturalism to abstraction', and to an extent chronologically, with specific discussion of both the Chavín culture and the Inca empire.

142 **Andean culture history.**
Wendell C. Bennett, Junius B. Bird. London: Robert Hale, 1965.
236p.

This English edition of a work first published in 1949 (New York: American Museum of Natural History) is of fundamental historiographical importance, although, of course, many of its findings have been qualified in the light of later research. The general sections were written by Bennett, while Bird dealt specifically with techniques used to produce ceramics, metalwork and textiles.

143 **Atlas of ancient America.**
Michael Coe, Dean Snow, Elizabeth Benson. Oxford: Equinox, 1986.
240p. 56 maps. bibliog.

The specific section on South America (p. 153-206) in this combined atlas and descriptive account of pre-conquest America both North and South is concerned primarily with Peru.

144 **The civilizations of ancient America.**
Edited by Sol Tax. New York: Cooper Square, 1967. 2nd ed. 328p.
bibliog.

Originally presented at the XXIXth International Congress of Americanists (New York) in 1949 and first published in 1951, this outstanding collection of papers is of enduring importance. The ten essays on the central Andes (p. 195-268) include contributions from Gordon Willey, Samuel Lothrop, Richard Schaedel, Adrian Digby and John Rowe.

145 **Introducción al Perú.** (Introduction to Peru.)
Hermann Buse. Lima: Colegio Militar 'Leoncio Prado', 1965. 393p.

A general account of the development of archaeology in Peru precedes a discussion of specific prehistoric sites.

146 **The making of the past: the New World.**
Warwick M. Bray, Earl H. Swanson, Ian S. Farrington. Oxford:
Elsevier, 1975. 151p.

This general account of the early history of the New World, as revealed by modern science-based archaeology, is particularly useful for its discussions of Machu Picchu, and Inca architecture and engineering.

147 **Monuments of civilization: the Andes.**
Enrico Guidoni, Roberto Magni. London: Cassell, 1977. 189p. map.
bibliog.

Illustrated by many colour photographs, this attractive volume concentrates upon the Inca empire (p. 105-75), but also provides a useful discussion of the early Andean cultures which preceded it.

148 **The origins and development of the Andean state.**
Edited by Jonathan Haas, Sheila Pozorski, Thomas Pozorski.
Cambridge, England: Cambridge University Press, 1987. 188p. bibliog.
The fifteen papers in this volume examine the emergence of the first formal political systems in the Andean region in the beginning of the second millenium BC, and follow the political development of Andean societies up through the formation and collapse of empires immediately preceding the arrival of the Spaniards.

149 **Past worlds: the Times atlas of archaeology.**
Edited by Elizabeth Wyse, Barry Winkleman. London: Times Books, 1988. 319p.
The section dealing with the New World (p. 204-34) provides excellent coverage of Peruvian civilizations from 4000 BC to the Spanish conquest.

150 **The peoples and cultures of ancient Peru.**
Luis G. Lumbreras, translated by Betty J. Meggers. Washington, DC: Smithsonian Institution Press, 1974. rev. ed. 248p. bibliog.
This revised edition of a work, published in Spanish in 1969 (Lima: Moncloa-Campodonico), by one of the country's most influential archaeologists, is intended primarily for students seeking a panoramic view of Central Andean archaeology. The fact that less than one-tenth of its contents is devoted to the Inca empire ('Tawantisuyu') underlines for the general reader the point that the Incas were merely the last in a long line of pre-conquest civilizations.

151 **Peru.**
G. H. S. Bushnell. London: Thames & Hudson, 1963. rev. ed.. 216p. map. bibliog.
Divided chronologically, and illustrated by seventy-one black-and-white plates, this survey provides the general reader with an authoritative introduction to Peruvian prehistory, from the arrival of man to the fall of the Inca empire.

152 **Peru before Pizarro.**
George Bankes. Oxford: Phaidon, 1977. 208p. bibliog.
Extensively illustrated with almost 200 photographs (both colour and black-and-white) and line drawings, this work provides an excellent introduction to pre-Columbian Peru for the general reader.

153 **Peru before the Incas.**
Edward P. Lanning. Englewood Cliffs, New Jersey: Prentice-Hall, 1967. 216p. 14 maps. bibliog.
This is a lively and readable account of the evolution of the older Peruvian civilizations by an anthropologist who undertook extensive field work in the period 1956-63.

154 **Peruvian prehistory: an overview of pre-Inca and Inca society.**
Edited by Richard W. Keatinge. Cambridge, England: Cambridge University Press, 1988. 364p. 6 maps. bibliog.
The thirteen contributors to this volume – eleven of them from the United States –

provide a general overview of the state of Peruvian archaeology, emphasizing the research findings of the last forty years. The work is divided chronologically into three main parts, followed by a concluding section on the often neglected tropical forest region of eastern Peru.

155 The pre-Columbian mind.
Francisco Guerra. London; New York: Seminar, 1971. 335p. map. bibliog.

Based primarily upon the somewhat subjective accounts of Indian social behaviour compiled by 16th-century Spanish chroniclers, this fascinating volume discusses the aberrant nature of sexual drives, drugs affecting behaviour, and attitudes towards life and death in pre-Columbian America. Peru is not dealt with separately, but references to it are found under most of the vices itemized in the index.

156 South American Indian art.
Frederick J. Dockstader. London: Studio Vista, 1967. 222p. 2 maps. bibliog.

Complemented by 250 photographs, the majority of them in colour, this introduction to prehistoric art of America discusses Peru within a general South American context.

157 Textiles of ancient Peru and their techniques.
Raoul d'Harcourt, edited by Grace G. Denny, Carolyn M. Osborne, translated by Sadie Brown. Seattle, Washington: University of Washington Press, 1962. 302p. bibliog.

This amplified and revised version of a pioneering work first published in French, entitled *Les textiles anciens et leurs techniques* (Paris: Les Editions d'art et d'histoire, 1934) is a fundamental work of reference. It is organized according to weaving techniques rather than geography or chronology.

158 The weavers of ancient Peru.
M. S. Fini. London: Tumi, 1985. 64p. map.

Compiled as a catalogue of an exhibition of Peruvian textiles held at the Commonwealth Institute, London, in 1985, this well-illustrated work provides a simple but sound introduction to the history of Peruvian textiles.

Pre-Inca

159 Ancient burial patterns of the Moche Valley, Peru.
Christopher B. Donnan, Carol J. Mackey. Austin, Texas; London: University of Texas Press, 1978. 412p. 9 maps. bibliog.

This volume provides a scholarly account of the excavation, since 1969, of a series of pre-Columbian burial sites in the Moche Valley, whose location in the arid coastal strip of northern Peru has preserved objects and remains of up to 3,500 years old.

160 **Culturas precolombinas: Nazca.** (Pre-Columbian cultures: Nazca.)
Arturo Jiménez Borja, James W. Reid, Javier Ferrand Moscati.
Lima: Banco de Crédito del Perú, 1986. 204p. bibliog.

The most attractive feature of this superb survey of the Nazca civilization, which flourished on the southern coast of Peru nearly 2,000 years ago, is its collection of high-quality colour photographs of textiles, pottery and gold objects.

161 **The desert kingdoms of Peru.**
Victor Wolfgang Von Hagen. London: Weidenfeld & Nicolson, 1965.
191p. 3 maps. bibliog.

For some 1,500 years the Mochicas and the Chimús were the dominant tribes in northern Peru, falling to a full-scale Inca invasion only seventy years before the arrival of the Spaniards. This survey provides a sound, general account of their environment, crafts and social organization.

162 **Early ceremonial architecture in the Andes.**
Edited by Christopher B. Donnan. Washington, DC: Dumbarton
Oaks Research Library and Collection, Library of Congress, 1985.
289p. bibliog.

This is a collection of thirteen papers presented at a 1982 symposium on early ceremonial architecture in the highlands and on the coast of central Peru between 2400 and 200 BC.

163 **Life, land and water in ancient Peru.**
Paul Kosok. New York: Long Island University Press, 1965. 264p.
bibliog.

Based upon study of the ancient irrigaton systems of the coastal area of northern Peru, this volume both describes excavation techniques and underlines the fundamental importance of control of water for the emergence and survival of the Chimú empire.

164 **Lines to the mountain gods: Nazca and the mysteries of Peru.**
Evan Hadingham. New York: Random House, 1987. 307p. bibliog.

The Nazca lines – the profusion of geometric designs on the stony desert of southern Peru – have provoked much interest and many theories among both professional archaeologists and amateur interpreters. This well-illustrated study links them to similar features found in California and the Midwest of the United States, suggesting that their common thread is the basic theme of shamanism: the solitary priest who communicated directly with mountain spirits or their animal representatives by drawing their images.

165 **The Mochica: a culture of Peru.**
Elizabeth P. Benson. London: Thames & Hudson, 1972. 164p. 2
maps. bibliog.

The most fascinating of the north-coast cultures in Peruvian prehistory is that of the Mochica, who left one of the richest legacies of artifacts in all the Andes. Using Mochica remains from the first millenium BC for clues to their beliefs and customs, this book discusses their origins, social organization, religion, architecture and production.

166 **The mystery of the Nasca lines.**
Tony Morrison, foreword by Maria Reiche.   Woodbridge, England:
Nonesuch Expeditions, 1987. 154p.

The Nazca lines themselves come under detailed scrutiny in this work, in which the author deliberately adopts the local usage 'Nasca' rather than the commonly accepted 'Nazca'. However, the principal focus in this interesting volume is the career of the German-born Reiche, who has studied them since 1941.

167 **The Nazca lines: a new perspective on their origin and meaning.**
Johan Reinhard.   Lima: Editorial Los Pinos, 1985. 60p. bibliog.

This persuasive study analyses the desert geoglyphs in terms of mountain fertility concepts found widely throughout the Andes. It suggests that they were created as part of religious practices designed primarily to guarantee the fertility of crops.

168 **Prehistoric hunters of the high Andes.**
John W. Rick.   London; New York: Academic Press, 1980. 360p.
bibliog.

This book represents a pioneering attempt to reconstruct the life of a highland community in the high Andes during the early post-Pleistocene period when the *vicuña* was first domesticated.

Inca

169 **An analysis of Inca militarism.**
Joseph Bram.   Seattle, Washington: University of Washington Press,
1966. 2nd ed. 85p. bibliog.

This study analyses the principal Spanish chronicles of the conquest of Peru, in order to reconstruct the relationship in the Inca empire between warfare and social and political institutions.

170 **Anthropological history of Andean polities.**
Edited by John Victor Murra, Nathan Wachtel, Jacques Revel.
Cambridge, England: Cambridge University Press, 1986. 383p.

The seventeen essays in this collection, written by scholars from the Andean countries, Europe and the United States, combine the perspectives of archaeology, anthropology and history to present a complex view of Andean societies over various millenia. The majority deal with the impact of the Inca state on different regions and ethnic groups, and with the transformations wrought through the colonial presence.

171 **L'art inca et ses origines: de Valdivia a Machu Picchu.** (Inca art and its origins: from Valdivia to Machu Picchu.)
Henri Stierlin. Fribourg, Switzerland: Edition du Seuil, 1986. 2nd ed. 224p.

The Incas tend to be regarded by archaeologists and historians as a people less concerned with beauty than with efficiency. This modern study examines their art, as expressed in textiles, ceramics and buildings, and relates it to that of earlier civilizations in Peru.

172 **Aspects of Inca architecture: description, function and chronology.**
Ann Kendall. Oxford: British Archaeological Reports, 1985. 448p. (BAR International Series, 242).

Originally presented as a doctoral thesis in 1974, this study describes field work on the later periods of Cuzco prehistory. See, too, the same author's more general work, *Everyday life of the Incas* (London: Batsford, 1979).

173 **The ceque system of Cuzco: the social organization of the capital of the Inca.**
R. T. Zuidema. Leiden, The Netherlands: E. J. Brill, 1964. 265p. bibliog.

In this complex but indispensable monograph it is afgued that sightlines radiating from the Temple of the Sun in Cuzco formed part of a network extending throughout the Inca empire, which co-ordinated planting, irrigation and state ritual with calendrics and astronomy.

174 **Empire of the Inca.**
Burr Cartwright Brundage. Norman, Oklahoma: University of Oklahoma Press, 1985. 396p. bibliog.

This paperback edition of a work first published in 1963 is reliable and well written. It is somewhat dated in its preoccupations with the Inca élite, and its neglect of the ordinary Indian.

175 **The economic organization of the Inka state.**
John V. Murra. Greenwich, Connecticut, 1980: JAI. 214p. bibliog.

Originally presented in 1955 as a thesis at the University of Chicago, Murra's outstanding analysis of Inca economic organization circulated widely among anthropologists and ethnohistorians until he finally agreed in 1977 to the publication of what he described as 'a personal document . . . a communication between the author and his psychotherapist'. Spanish editions appeared in 1977 and 1978, before this, the first English-language edition.

176 **Hatunqolla: a view of Inca rule from the Lake Titicaca region.**
Catherine J. Julien. Berkeley, California: University of California Press, 1983. 286p. 3 maps. bibliog.

Drawing upon both archaeological and historical evidence, this study concentrates upon the nature of Inca rule in the area on the frontier between modern Peru and Bolivia.

177 **Highway of the sun.**
Victor Wolfgang Von Hagen.   London: Travel Book Club, [n.d.]
264p. 4 maps. bibliog.

In 1952 the American Geographical Society supported the 'Inca highway expedition', designed to explore the road system of Inca Peru. Much of what it 'discovered' was already known to archaeologists. Nevertheless, the description of its activities makes lively and interesting reading.

178 **The Inca and Aztec states 1400-1800: anthropology and history.**
Edited by George A. Collier, Renato I. Rosaldo, John D.Wirth.   New York: Academic Press, 1982. 475p. 5 maps. bibliog.

The sixteen papers in this volume were read at conferences in Stanford in 1978 and Princeton in 1979. The first, by Pedro Carrasco, attempts to draw a comparative model of the political economy of the Aztec and Inca states. The largest section, containing six papers, examines Inca state administration and colonization, and three further papers examine the indigenous response to the Spanish conquest of Peru.

179 **Inca architecture.**
Graziano Gasparini, Louise Margolies, translated by Patricia J. Lyon.
Bloomington, Indiana: Indiana University Press, 1980. 350p. map.
bibliog.

The Spanish version of this book was published in Venezuela in 1977; the English version is identical, except for an updated bibliography. One of its qualities, apart from its clarity of expression and its profuse illustrations, is that it combines 20th-centry observations of Inca remains with 16th-century eye-witness accounts of Spanish chroniclers.

180 **The Incas.**
Alfred Métraux.   London: Studio Vista, 1965. 192p.

This compact volume provides a sound introduction to the principal features of Inca civilization.

181 **The Incas and their industries.**
Henry Van Den Bergh.   London: Routledge, 1934. 2nd ed. 48p.

This brief, pioneering work discusses weaving and pottery, and also pays some attention to the technological aspects of Inca warfare.

182 **Inkawasi the new Cuzco.**
John Hyslop.   Oxford: British Archaeological Reports, 1985. 147p.
bibliog. (BAR International Series, 234).

This volume provides a solid contribution to the archaeology of southern Peru during the Inca period, and is based upon a detailed excavation of the unique remains of the city of Inkawasi.

183 **The land of the Incas.**
Hans Silvester, Jacques Soustelle. London: Thames & Hudson, 1977. 74p. map.

Soustelle's brief introduction complements Silvester's superb collection of seventy-four colour photographs, showing both Inca monuments and the Indian inhabitants of Cuzco and its region in the 20th century.

184 **Lords of Cuzco: a history and description of the Inca people in their final days.**
Burr Cartwright Brundage. Norman, Oklahoma: University of Oklahoma Press, 1967. 458p. 3 maps. bibliog.

This is a history of the city of Cuzco and its rulers from the immediate pre-Conquest period until the 1570s.

185 **Monuments of the Incas.**
John Hemming. Boston, Massachusetts: Little & Brown, 1982. 228p. 4 maps. bibliog.

Over 200 excellent black-and-white photographs illustrate this very clear discussion of Inca building techniques, within which there is specific discussion of major monuments, including Sacsahuamán, Machu Picchu and Ollantaytambo.

186 **On the royal highways of the Inca: civilizations of ancient Peru.**
Heinrich Ubbelohde-Doering, translated by Margaret Brown. London: Thames & Hudson, 1967. 311p. map.

The author directed excavations at various Peruvian sites (1931-32, 1937-39, 1953-54, 1962-63), paying particular attention to the archaeological material of the 15th century in the Cuzco region. This volume, which focuses upon the 'almost incomparable highway system' of the Incas, describes his findings. It is illustrated by over 300 black-and-white photographs.

187 **Peru under the Incas.**
Cottie Arthur Burland. London: Evans Brothers, 1967. 144p. (Life in Ancient Lands).

A contribution to the series edited by Edward Bacon, this deceptively straightforward summary of Inca society is lively and well informed.

188 **Power and property in Inca Peru.**
Sally Falk Moore. Westport, Connecticut: Greenwood, 1973. 2nd ed. 190p. bibliog.

The focus in this imaginative study, first published in 1958, is upon law and government in Inca Peru, with particular reference to land law, taxation, inheritance and criminal law. There is also an interesting discussion of historiography and of the reliability of the 16th- and 17th-century chronicles, which continue to provide the springboard for most attempts to reconstruct Inca society.

189 **Realm of the Incas.**
Victor W. Von Hagen.   London: New English Library, 1961. 2nd ed.
223p. bibliog.

A prolific writer about Peru provides a readable, lively description of the Incas,
copiously illustrated with line drawings and photographs.

190 **A socialist empire: the Incas of Peru.**
Louis Baudin, edited by Arthur Goddard, translated by Katherine
Woods.   Princeton, New Jersey: Van Nostrand, 1961. 442p. map.
bibliog.

This classic work, first published in French as *L'empire socialiste des Inka* (Paris:
Institut d'Ethnologie, 1928) provides a highly complimentary account of the 'utopian'
aspects of Inca society. See, too, the same author's *Daily life in Peru under the last
Incas* (London: Allen & Unwin, 1961).

191 **A totalitarian state of the past: the civilization of the Inca empire in
ancient Peru.**
Rafael Karsten.   Helsingfors, Finland: Societas Scientarum Fennica,
1949. 288p.

Although there is some discussion of archaeology in this study, its principal focus is
upon the political and sociological organization of Inca Peru, and its intellectual life.
Its principal conclusion is that 'the rule of the Incas was stern and rigorous but just'.

192 **Vilcabamba: lost city of the Incas.**
Gene Savoy.   London: Robert Hale, 1970. 239p. 6 maps.

'Without any formal training in archaeology or anthropology but with the astoundingly
keen intuition of a natural-born explorer' (Cover copy), Savoy, a former journalist, led
an expedition in 1964-65 which discovered the Inca city of Vilcabamba, north west of
Cuzco. This readable account describes his exploits.

193 **The world of the Inca.**
Bertrand Flornoy, translated by Winifred Bradford.   New York:
Vanguard, 1956. 212p. bibliog.

Originally written in French, this account of Inca Peru is curiously organized in that its
solid discussion of the expansion of the Inca empire is preceded by a brief narrative
account of its collapse in face of the Spanish conquest.

194 **The world of the Incas: a socialistic state of the past.**
Otfrid von Hanstein, translated by Anna Barwell.   London: George
Allen & Unwin, 1924. 189p.

The principal, perhaps the only, merit of this simplistic work is that it demonstrates
how a European idealist of the 1920s attempted to use the history of the Inca as a peg
upon which to hang his theories about mankind's innate potential for benevolence.

History

General

195 **The Andean past: land, societies, and conflicts.**
Magnus Mörner.   New York: Columbia University Press, 1985. 300p.
13 maps. bibliog.
Sweden's outstanding historian of Latin America examines the historical evolution
during the last 450 years of the three countries (Bolivia, Ecuador and Peru), which
now occupy the territory which once made up the Inca empire. He pays particular
attention to themes such as social development and human adaptation to the physical
environment.

196 **Historia del indigenismo cuzqueño: siglos XVI-XX.** (History of
indigenismo in Cuzco 16th-20th centuries.)
José Tamayo Herrera.   Lima: Instituto Nacional de Cultura, 1980.
394p. bibliog.
In Cuzco, the ancient Inca capital, and its region, the white population has tended to
display a greater willingness than its counterparts on the coast to embrace and take
pride in Peru's Indian past. This fascinating study both describes the phenomenon of
indigenismo, which emerged most clearly in intellectual circles in the early-20th
century, and analyses its origins.

197 **The kingdom of the sun: a short history of Peru.**
Luis Martín.   New York: Charles Scribner, 1974. 288p. map. bibliog.
This lively and well-informed history, organized chronologically and laying particular
stress upon cultural clashes and changes during the last 400 years, is aimed at the
general reader.

198 **The modern history of Peru.**
Fredrick B. Pike. London: Weidenfeld & Nicolson, 1967. 386p.
2 maps. bibliog.
After an introductory chapter on the late colonial period, this work is concerned
primarily with the political history of the republic. It argues that the frequency of
'revolutions' since independence disguises the essential continuity and moderation of
political development.

199 **Peru: a short history.**
David P. Wehrlich. Carbondale, Illinois: Southern Illinois University
Press, 1978. 434p. 5 maps. bibliog.
Although it provides a general coverage of the history of Peru from prehistoric times
until 1976, this work concentrates upon the period since 1914, and deals in particular
depth with the military revolution of 1968 and its aftermath. The bibliography is
excellent. It is a suitable work for both the student and the general reader.

The Spanish conquest (1524-48)

200 **The conquest of the Incas.**
John Hemming. London: Macmillan, 1970. 641p. 6 maps. bibliog.
Thoroughly grounded in the published chronicles of contemporary Spanish commentators, this book provides a highly readable and convincing narrative of the conquest of
Peru, from the arrival there of Francisco Pizarro through to the execution in 1572 of
the last independent Inca emperor, Túpac Amaru. It concludes with a fascinating
account of modern searches for Vilcabamba, the remote jungle city which provided
Túpac Amaru and his family with the base for the retention of a reduced, but still
significant Inca state for nearly forty years after Pizarro's 1533 entry into Cuzco.

201 **Coricancha (garden of gold): being an account of the conquest of the
Inca empire.**
A. F. Tschiffely. London: Hodder & Stoughton, 1943. 220p. map.
Intended for popular consumption, this study of the conquest, based upon the better-
known chronicles, stresses the drawbacks of the Inca system and the benefits, religious
and material, which the Spanish conquest provided for Europe as a whole.

202 **La découverte et la conquête du Pérou d'après les sources originales.**
(The discovery and conquest of Peru from the original sources.)
Albert García. Paris: Klincksieck, 1975. 778p. map. bibliog.
Although hardly light reading, this dense volume provides a very thorough guide to the
original published sources, the 'chronicles', that are available for the study of the
discovery and conquest of Peru. The detailed map of the routes of Francisco Pizarro,
Diego de Almagro and Bartolomé Ruiz is especially useful, as is the chronological
table (p. 725-32).

203 The discovery and conquest of Peru.
Agustín de Zárate, translated by J. M. Cohen.   Harmondsworth, England: Penguin, 1968. 279p. 3 maps.

Although he did not reach Peru until 1544, eleven years after the Spanish capture of Cuzco, Zárate, a treasury official, succeeded in compiling, on the basis of information received from participants in the conquest, what is generally considered by historians to be the best early account of the discovery and conquest of the Inca empire.

204 Dogs of the conquest.
John G. Varner, Jeannette J. Varner.   Norman, Oklahoma: University of Oklahoma Press, 1983. 238p. bibliog.

Presents a curious but readable study of the use, by the Spanish conquerors, of man-eating mastiffs and greyhounds, in skirmishes and battles with Indians who resisted their advances. The authors quote extensively from the eye-witness accounts of chroniclers.

205 Fall of the Inca empire and the Spanish rule in Peru: 1530-1780.
Philip Ainsworth Means.   New York: Gordian, 1964. 2nd ed. 351p. bibliog.

First published in 1931 and thoroughly researched from 16th-century chronicles, this volume presents an account of the conquest which emphasizes both the positive aspects of Inca civilization and the exploitative nature of the colonial system constructed by the Spanish conquerors.

206 Francisco Pizarro: el marqués gobernador. (Francisco Pizarro: the marquis-governor.)
José Antonio de Busto Duthurburu.   Madrid: Ediciones Rialp, 1966. 280p. bibliog.

The career of Pizarro (1477-1541), the principal conqueror of Peru, is traced systematically, from his humble origins in Extremadura, where he was born, to his murder in his palace in Lima.

207 History of the conquest of Peru.
William H. Prescott, edited by Victor Wolfgang Von Hagen.   New York: Mentor, 1961. rev. ed. 416p.

Prescott's pioneering, narrative history of the conquest of Peru, first published in 1847, was a work of enormous historiographical importance. This partly abridged and revised edition retains the flavour and excitement of the original.

208 The Inca concept of sovereignty and the Spanish administration in Peru.
Charles Gibson.   New York: Greenwood, 1969. 2nd ed. 146p. map. bibliog.

The basic theme addressed in this articulate, incisive monograph is the transition from Inca to Spanish sovereignty in early colonial Peru at the upper, dominant level of indigenous society.

209 **The men of Cajamarca: a social and biographical study of the first conquerors of Peru.**
James Lockhart. Austin, Texas: University of Texas Press, 1972. 496p. map. bibliog.

The 168 Spaniards, led by Francisco Pizarro, who seized the Inca emperor, Atahualpa, at the town of Cajamarca in northern Peru, in November 1532, became overnight men of power and wealth; beforehand many of them had been relatively obscure individuals. The study analyses their backgrounds, their motives, their characteristics and their subsequent careers. An individual biography, ranging from a few lines for the most obscure to many pages for the best documented figures, is provided for each man.

210 **El nombre del Perú.** (The name of Peru.)
Raúl Porras Barrenechea. Lima: Villanueva, 1968. 99p.

According to Porras, the invented name 'Peru', which the Spaniards gave to the Inca empire, first reached Europe in 1534, with the arrival in Sevilla of Hernando Pizarro. In this articulate study, he combines an examination of its literary diffusion with a general discussion of the process of conquest.

211 **Relation of the discovery and conquest of the kingdoms of Peru.**
Pedro Pizarro, translated by Philip Ainsworth Means. New York: Cortés Society, 1921. 2 vols. bibliog.

Born in Toledo (1515), Pedro Pizarro travelled to America with his uncle, Francisco Pizarro, (1530). He served as a cavalryman during the conquest of Cuzco (1533), and was both a witness of and a participant in the subsequent civil war between Pizarrists and Almagrists. He subsequently settled in the southern city of Arequipa, where he completed this important chronicle in 1571; he died there in 1602. The work was first published (in Spanish) in 1844.

212 **The vision of the vanquished: the Spanish conquest of Peru through Indian eyes, 1530-1570.**
Nathan Wachtel, translated by Ben Reynolds, Sian Reynolds. Hassocks, England: Harvester, 1977. 328p. map. bibliog.

As soon as it first appeared in French as *La vision des vaincus: les indiens du Pérou devant la conquête espagnol, 1530-1570* (Paris: Gallimard, 1971), this work was recognized as a major contribution to the history of the Spanish conquest. Using native sources – some initially oral, others, like that of Guamán Poma, written – it succeeds in explaining the native view of the Spanish invasion and conquest.

The colonial period (1548-1821)

213 **The African slave in colonial Peru.**
Frederick P. Bowser.   Stanford, California: California University
Press, 1974. 439p. map. bibliog.

In Peru, as in other parts of Spanish America, Negro slaves were present in small numbers in the first half of the 16th century, becoming more numerous and important in the second half, partly in response to the development of plantations, and partly because of increased crown resistance to the enslavement of Indians. This monograph examines the origins, the importance and the nature of Negro slavery in the early colonial period.

214 **Bourbons and brandy: imperial reform in eighteenth-century Arequipa.**
Kendall W. Brown.   Albuquerque, New Mexico: University of New
Mexico Press, 1986. 319p. 3 maps. bibliog.

Arequipa was not only the third most important city in colonial Peru (after Lima and Cuzco) but also the centre of viticulture, producing both wines and brandies. Behind the somewhat superficial title of this monograph there lies a serious study of the effects upon the local economy of the Bourbon imperial reforms of the last quarter of the 18th century.

215 **The cabildo in Peru under the Hapsburgs.**
John Preston Moore.   Durham, North Carolina: Duke University
Press, 1954. 309p. map. bibliog.

The municipal council, or *cabildo*, was the only organ of government in colonial Peru, and elsewhere in Spanish America, which gave representation and experience to local inhabitants. This study analyses the Spanish origins of the institution and its transplantation to Peru. A subsequent volume by the same author carries the analysis through the 18th and early-19th centuries, when the *cabildos*, deliberately revived by the crown in the search for better local government, were aroused from the decadence of the late Hapsburg period. The second work is entitled *The cabildo in Peru under the Bourbons* (Durham, North Carolina: Duke University Press, 1966).

216 **Chronicle of colonial Lima: the diary of Josephe and Francisco Mugaburu, 1640-1697.**
Edited and translated by Robert Ryal Miller.   Norman, Oklahoma:
University of Oklahoma Press, 1975. 342p.

Josephe de Mugaburu, a Spanish sergeant stationed in the viceregal palace in Lima, where he had an opportunity to observe official reactions to principal events kept a diary from 1640 to 1686; his son, Francisco, continued it for a further decade. It provides a fascinating insight into matters such as commodity prices, crime and punishment, medical services, Negro slavery and attitudes towards Peru's Indian population.

217 **Commercial relations between Spain and Spanish America in the era of free trade, 1778-1796.**
John Fisher. Liverpool, England: Centre for Latin American Studies, University of Liverpool, 1985. 155p. bibliog. (Monograph, 13).

In 1778, the Spanish crown finally dismantled the vestiges of the old colonial commercial system, which had granted Callao, the port of Lima, a monopoly of South American trade with Spain. This monograph examines not only the motives of the free trade legislation of that year but also, by means of a detailed analysis of some 7,000 ships' registers, the results of the new system for the economies of both the mother country and its colonies. Particular attention is paid to trade between Peru and Spain.

218 **Conquest and agrarian change: the emergence of the hacienda system on the Peruvian coast.**
Robert G. Keith. New Haven, Connecticut: Harvard University Press, 1977. 176p. 3 maps. bibliog.

For both economic and social reasons, including the needs of the viceregal capital for food, and the heavy mortality among the coastal Indian population, large Spanish-owned estates were established early in the colonial period on the Peruvian coast. This detailed monograph clearly explains the process.

219 **Crisis and decline: the viceroyalty of Peru in the seventeenth century.**
Kenneth J. Andrew. Albuquerque, New Mexico: University of New Mexico Press, 1985. 287p.

Historians of Europe have tended to assume that Spain's decline in the 17th century was both caused by, and provoked, economic and demographic recession in America. The present study, based upon a detailed scrutiny of fiscal records, shows that this century was, in fact, a period of general growth in the Peruvian economy. However, the bulk of treasury receipts were retained in the viceroyalty, particularly to pay for its defence, instead of being remitted to Spain.

220 *Curas* **and social conflict in the** *doctrinas* **of Cuzco, 1780-1814.**
David Cahill. *Journal of Latin American Studies*, vol. 16 (1984), p. 241-76.

The Cuzco region of southern Peru witnessed large-scale indigenous insurgency in both 1780 and 1814. This article examines the relationship between social discontent in rural areas and the struggle for economic and political authority between parish priests (*curas*) and local administrators appointed by the crown.

221 **Daughters of the conquistadores: women of the viceroyalty of Peru.**
Luis Martín. Albuquerque, New Mexico: University of New Mexico Press, 1983. 354p. bibliog.

This volume analyses the part played in colonial society by women of pure Spanish or mixed Spanish-Indian descent; Negro and Indian women are excluded as are the lower classes in general, who tended not to leave written records. It is particularly detailed on convent life and those marital problems brought to the notice of religious tribunals. Although a scholarly work, it is lively and interesting, and likely to appeal to the general reader.

222 **Demographic collapse: Indian Peru, 1520-1620.**
Noble David Cook. Cambridge, England: Cambridge University Press, 1981. 310p. maps. bibliog.

With few exceptions, the indigenous population of coastal Peru and of the low-lying areas of the northern islands was almost entirely wiped out during the century after the conquest, to be replaced by Europeans, Africans, and migrants from other regions. In the highlands there was also a severe downward spiral, but not to the point of collapse. This important monograph explains and details these trends, providing in the process the most authoritative estimates available of the size of Peru's pre-conquest population.

223 **Early trade and navigation between Mexico and Peru.**
Woodrow W. Borah. Berkeley, California: University of California Press, 1954. 170p. map. bibliog.

Officially, inter-colonial trade which might compete with that of Spain was prohibited in the Hapsburg period. In reality, as this pioneering work indicates, economic necessity prevailed over bureaucratic restrictions, and Peru built up a thriving trade with Mexico. Its principal exports were silver and mercury, with Mexican woollens and Asian silks featuring as prominent imports.

224 **Flowers for the king: the expedition of Ruiz and Pavon and the flora of Peru.**
Arthur R. Steele. Durham, North Carolina: Duke University Press, 1964. 378p. bibliog.

By means of a detailed scrutiny of a botanical expedition to Peru, sponsored by the crown in the second half of the 18th century, this book throws much light upon late colonial intellectual life in general in the viceroyalty.

225 **Franciscan beginnings in colonial Peru.**
Antonine Tibesar. Washington, DC: Academy of American Franciscan History, 1953. 162p. bibliog.

Peru was of secondary importance, after New Spain, to the Franciscan order. Nevertheless some of its members arrived there as early as 1531, and the order went on to found a major convent in Lima, and, more significantly, to undertake evangelization in central Peru from the 1570s. This volume provides a reliable account of the order's activities in the 16th century as a whole.

226 **Francisco de Toledo, fifth viceroy of Peru, 1569-1581.**
Arthur F. Zimmerman. Caldwell, Idaho: Caxton, 1938. 307p. 2 maps. bibliog.

Toledo was the key viceroy in the establishment of the Spanish colonial system in Peru. Surprisingly, this is still the only biography of him in English, and even in Spanish nothing of significance has been produced for over fifty years.

227 **Government and society in colonial Peru: the intendant system 1784-1814.**
John Fisher. London: Athlone, 1970. 289p. map. bibliog.

Between 1777 and 1785, the Spanish crown undertook a thorough examination and reorganization of the internal administration of the viceroyalty of Peru. The focus for this monograph is the new system of provincial administration by intendants, introduced in 1784. Detailed attention is given to their work in promoting economic growth, overseeing the collection of taxation, and attempting to mitigate the socio-economic exploitation of Peru's indigenous population by the élite of landowners and mineowners.

228 The Huancavelica mercury mine.

Arthur P. Whitaker. Cambridge, Masachusetts: Harvard University Press, 1941. 150p. map. bibliog.

Throughout the colonial period, the bulk of American silver was produced not by smelting, which was suitable only for high-grade ores, but by amalgamation with mercury. Peru possessed the only significant source of American mercury at Huancavelica, where deposits were mined from 1564. This brief monograph is unreliable in its discusssion of mercury production in the late colonial period, but otherwise provides a very sound account of the history and the organization of mercury production and distribution.

229 Huarochirí: an Andean society under Inca and Spanish rule.

Karen Spalding. Stanford, California: Stanford University Press, 1984. 384p. bibliog.

This is an important work of scholarship, concerned with the interaction in central Peru during the colonial period between traditional Andean social and economic structures, and the institutions imposed upon native communities by the Spanish conquerors.

230 The Incas under Spanish colonial institutions.

John H. Rowe. *Hispanic American Historical Review*, vol. 37 (May 1957), p. 155-99.

Inevitably this article has been superseded in some respects by recent research findings, which tend to stress the ability of the indigenous population to cope with and modify attempted exploitation. It remains, however, a good introduction to the topic of how the Spaniards attempted to use pre-conquest mechanisms to exploit native labour.

231 El Inca: the life and times of Garcilaso de la Vega.

John Grier Varner. Austin, Texas: University of Texas Press, 1968. 413p. bibliog.

The famous chronicler of the Incas and the conquest of Peru, Garcilaso de la Vega (1539-1616), was born in Cuzco, the son of a Spanish conqueror and an Indian woman of royal blood. Although he never returned to Peru, after his departure for Spain at the age of twenty, and died at Córdoba, his great work *Royal commentaries of the Incas*, the first part of which was published in 1609, succeeded in depicting the Incas as a noble people, on a par with their conquerors. This volume charts his life, his work and his times in great detail.

232 **Landowners in colonial Peru.**

Keith A. Davies.   Austin, Texas: University of Texas Press, 1985. 237p. 2 maps. bibliog.

An intricate study of land tenure in and around the southern Peruvian city of Arequipa, from its foundation in 1540 until the late-17th century, is provided in this research monograph.

233 **Language, authority and indigenous history in the "Comentarios reales de los Incas".**

Margarita Zamora.   Cambridge, England: Cambridge University Press, 1988. 209p. bibliog.

In this brief, incisive study, Professor Zamora analyses the significance of the famous *Royal commentaries* of Garcilaso de la Vega, not only as an historical work in its own right but also as a contribution to renaissance thinking on the concept of history, and the uncertainty about the nature of the American Indian.

234 **Letters and people of the Spanish Indies: the sixteenth century.**

Edited by James Lockhart, Enrique Otte.   Cambridge, England: Cambridge University Press, 1976. 267p. bibliog.

In this volume, the editors present a translated selection of letters written by Spanish officials, merchants, and above all ordinary settlers, with a view to creating a panorama of 16th-century Spanish American settler society. Of the thirty-eight letters in the collection, eight were written by settlers in Peru, and a ninth was written by Hernando Pizarro (half-brother of Francisco) in 1545, from his prison in Spain.

235 **Lima: la ciudad y sus monumentos.** (Lima: the city and its monuments.)

Jorge Bernales Ballesteros.   Sevilla: Escuela de Estudios Hispano-Americanos, 1972. 387p. bibliog.

Founded on 6 January 1535 (hence its name 'City of the Kings'), Lima, the capital of the viceroyalty of Peru, was the richest, most powerful city in Spanish America in the 16th and 17th centuries (Mexico City overtook it in the 18th century). This well-illustrated volume describes and examines the architectural vestiges of its colonial pre-eminence, paying particular attention to its churches and convents.

236 **Lords of the land: sugar, wine and Jesuit estates of colonial Peru, 1700-1767.**

Nicholas P. Cushner.   Albany, New York: State University of New York Press, 1980. 225p. 3 maps. bibliog.

Throughout Spanish America, the Jesuit order acquired and exploited large landed estates, the profits from which were used in part for its missionary and educational work. This detailed analysis of the development, functioning and distribution of the products of the twenty-three large estates in coastal Peru that were owned by the order until its expulsion in 1767 is a major contribution to the study of Peru's economic and agricultural history.

237　**La lutte contre les religions autochtones dans le Pérou colonial: "l'extirpation de l'idolatrie" entre 1532 et 1660.** (The struggle against autochtonous religions in colonial Peru: "the extirpation of idolatry" between 1532 and 1660.)
Pierre Duviols.　Paris: Institut Francais d'Etudes Andines, 1971. 428p. bibliog.

The frequency in the early colonial period of both anti-idolatry campaigns among native peoples, led by the clergy, and of protest movements against colonialism, organized by native religious leaders, demonstrates that the rapid evangelization of Peru was superficial. These phenomena are examined in a detailed monographic study, which draws its evidence from both published and unpublished primary sources.

238　**Maritime defence of the viceroyalty of Peru (1600-1700).**
Peter T. Bradley.　*Americas*, vol. 36 (1979), p. 155-75.

In the 17th century, Peru was under constant pressure to defend its coastline against first Dutch intruders and later English and French buccaneers and traders. This article provides a clear and thorough account of both the problems encountered in defending a lengthy coastline and of the overriding importance of protecting the treasure fleet from foreign predators.

239　**Le marquis et le marchand: les luttes de pouvoir au Cuzco (1700-1730).** (The marquis and the merchant: struggles for power in Cuzco [1700-1730].)
Bernard Lavallé.　Paris: Centre National de la Recherche Scientifique, 1987. 184p. map.

A personal struggle in Cuzco between the marquis of Valleumbroso, an eminent member of the city's creole aristocracy, and an upwardly-mobile Spanish immigrant is used as a convenient base for a general discussion about the emergence of a distinctive 'American' consciousness in the city by the beginning of the 18th century.

240　**The military and society in colonial Peru 1750-1810.**
Leon G. Campbell.　Philadelphia, Pennsylvania: American Philosophical Society, 1978. 254p. bibliog.

Historians of 19th-century Spanish America have tended to look for the origins of militarism in the political and administrative structures of the late colonial period. This study examines this and related issues in a wide-ranging discussion of the reorganization of Peru's defences, against both external and internal threats, in the second half of the 18th century.

241　**Miners of the red mountain: Indian labor in Potosí, 1545-1650.**
Peter Bakewell.　Albuquerque, New Mexico: University of New Mexico Press, 1985. 213p. 2 maps. bibliog.

Potosí was the most important mining centre of South America during the colonial period. This work is a meticulous analysis of the origins and development of free and forced labour systems there.

History. The colonial period (1548-1821)

242 **Los ministros de la audiencia de Lima (1700-1821).** (The ministers of the *audiencia* of Lima [1700-1821].)
Guillermo Lohmann Villena. Sevilla: Escuela de Estudios Hispano-Americanos, 1974. 200p.

The *audiencia* of Lima was Peru's supreme civil and criminal court in the colonial period, and it also exercized important administrative functions. This detailed analysis of its membership, built around brief biographies of 158 judges who held office in the period 1700-1821, demonstrates that in the last fifty years of the colonial period the Spanish crown deliberately discriminated in favour of men born in Europe when making appointments. Exclusion from high office thus became one of the key grievances of prominent Peruvians.

243 **Nueva corónica y buen gobierno.** (New chronicle and good government.) Felipe Guamán Poma de Ayala, edited by Franklin Pease. Caracas: Biblioteca Ayacucho, 1980. 2 vols.

In 1912, Richard Pietschmann revealed to the scientific community the manuscript of Felipe Guamán Poma de Ayala which he had discovered four years earlier in the Royal Library of Copenhagen. Little is known about its Indian author other than that he was born in central Peru shortly after the conquest, and that he completed his exotic pictorial history at the end of the 16th century. It was both a critique of the colonial system and a complex history of the Andean past. It is a work of fundamental importance to historians, anthropologists and ethno-historians. This is the best available edition.

244 **Peru's Indian peoples and the challenge of Spanish conquest: Huamanga to 1640.**
Steve J. Stern. Madison, Wisconsin: University of Wisconsin Press, 1982. 295p. 3 maps. bibliog.

Taking as its geographical focus the central Peruvian town and province of Huamanga (modern Ayacucho), this innovative study looks beyond the immediate conquest to examine the ways in which the Indian peoples of Peru adjusted to their subjugation. It demonstrates that Indian resistance and adaptation gradually forced the conquerors and their heirs to modify their modes of exploitation.

245 **Politics of a colonial career: José Baquíjano and the audiencia of Lima.**
Mark A. Burkholder. Alburquerque, New Mexico: University of New Mexico Press, 1980. 184p. map. bibliog.

In the last quarter of the 18th century, the Spanish crown reverted to a deliberate policy of appointing peninsular-born Spaniards to senior administrative posts in Peru. Although this development probably improved the efficiency of government, it did so at the cost of alienating wealthy American-Spaniards (creoles), who were denied access to high office. This microscopic analysis of the quest for judicial office of an ambitious Peruvian illustrates these trends. In fact, Baquíjano finally secured appointment as a judge in Lima in 1797, after nearly three decades of trying. During the subsequent independence period he emerged as a loyalist, critical of many features of Spanish rule, but unwilling to support an armed struggle for independence.

246 **The Potosí mita, 1573-1700: compulsory Indian labor in the Andes.**
Jeffrey A. Cole.   Stanford, California: Stanford University Press.
206p. 2 maps. bibliog.

The *mita* system, devised by viceroy Francisco de Toledo in the 16th century, required
Indian communitites to provide conscript workers on a rotation basis for work in the
mines of Potosí. This monograph concentrates upon the institutional and administrative framework of the system, known as the *mita*, rather than upon the details of the
social and labour conditions faced by the workers in Potosí.

247 **Potosí y Huancavelica: bases económicas 1545-1640.** (Potosí and
Huancavelica: economic foundations 1545-1640.)
Gwendolyn Ballantine Cobb.   La Paz, Bolivia: Academia Boliviana de
la Historia, 1977. 204p. bibliog.

The economic structure of Spanish South America in the colonial period depended
upon the silver of Potosí, and the latter upon the mercury produced at the Peruvian
town of Huancavelica, without which the silver could not be refined. This pioneering
work, derived from research done in the 1940s, demonstrates the effects of this
relationship upon both internal and international trading patterns.

248 **Provincial patriarchs: land tenure and the economics of power in
colonial Peru.**
Susan E. Ramírez.   Albuquerque, New Mexico: University of New
Mexico Press, 1986. 471p. bibliog.

Capitalist agriculture soon developed in colonial Peru, to provide its expanding
Spanish population with the foodstuffs and other commodities to which they had been
accustomed in Europe. This detailed study examines the development of the great
estate, or hacienda, in northern Peru, the centre of sugar production, from the late-
16th century. It makes an important contribution to both social and economic history.

249 **Rebellions and revolts in eighteenth century Peru and Upper Peru.**
Scarlett O'Phelan Godoy.   Cologne, GFR: Bohlau Verlag, 1985. 345p.
map. bibliog.

Dr. O'Phelan, a Peruvian historian writing in English, provides a synthetic view of no
less than 140 revolts and disturbances which occurred in Peru and Bolivia in the period
1700-83. Her conclusion is that the majority of protests, including the great rebellion
initiated by Túpac Amaru in 1780, were anti-fiscal in character.

250 **Scholars and schools in colonial Peru.**
Luis Martín, Jo Ann Guerin Pettus.   Dallas: Southern Methodist
University, School of Continuing Education, 1973. 206p. bibliog.

Extracts from primary sources concerning schools and colleges, and the writings of
individual thinkers, teachers and scientists of the colonial period, form the core of this
unusual and interesting volume.

251 **Silver mines and silver miners in colonial Peru, 1786-1824.**
John Fisher.   Liverpool, England: Centre for Latin American Studies,
University of Liverpool, 1977. 150p. map. bibliog. (Monograph, 7).

In 1776, the Spanish crown transferred Upper Peru (modern Bolivia) from the viceroyalty of Peru to the new viceroyalty of the Río de la Plata, governed from Buenos Aires. Since Upper Peru until that date was responsible for sixty per cent of Peru's silver production, the bulk of it at Potosí, historians tended to assume that the administrative reorganization, coupled with commercial reform two years later, condemned Peru to economic decline in the late colonial period. This revisionist work undermines this thesis, demonstrating – on the basis of a detailed study of production records – that output at mining centres elsewhere in Peru, notably at Cerro de Pasco, increased significantly in the last quarter of the 18th century, and more than compensated for the loss of Potosí.

252 **Spanish Peru, 1532-1560: a colonial society.**
James Lockhart. Madison, Wisconsin: University of Wisconsin Press, 1968. 285p. map. bibliog.

Making detailed and imaginative use of the records of Spanish notaries active in Peru in the three decades immediately after the capture of Atahualpa by Pizarro, this book analyses the creation of a Spanish, mainly urban society. This society was divided primarily according to occupational, and social, status into groups such as merchants, artisans, professionals and sailors, etc. The concluding chapters deal briefly with the rôles of Negroes and Indians as appendages to Spanish society.

253 **Tales of Potosí: Bartolomé Arzans de Orsua y Vela.**
Edited by R. C. Padden, translated by Frances M. López-Morillas. Providence, Rhode Island: Brown University Press, 1975. 209p. bibliog.

From its discovery in 1546 until the late-18th century, the great silver-mining centre of Potosí, now in Bolivia, formed part of the viceroyalty of Peru, and was of fundamental importance to its economic and social infrastructures. Early in the 18th century Bartolomé Arzans wrote the history of the city from its foundation until 1736, the year of his death. This translation of his tales vividly recreates the prestige and power of Potosí, particularly in the 17th century, when it was the largest city in the Spanish world.

254 **Túpac Amaru II – 1780.**
Edited by Alberto Flores-Galindo. Lima: Retablo de Papel, 1976. 323p. bibliog.

In 1780, southern Peru was convulsed by a major indigenous uprising, led by a community leader, José Gabriel Condorcanqui, who assumed the name of the country's last independent Inca emperor. Historians disagree about the significance of the movement, which survived until 1783, although Túpac Amaru was executed in Cuzco in 1781. Peruvians have tended to depict it as a multi-racial bid for independence, while others favour the view that it was a reformist protest against local maladministration. These and related issues emerge clearly from this collection of essays, edited by one of Peru's outstanding young historians.

Independence (1821-24)

255 **Bolívar and the war of independence.**
Daniel Florencio O'Leary, translated and edited by R. F. McNerney.
Austin, Texas: University of Texas Press. 386p. 7 maps.

This abridged version of O'Leary's memoirs provides detailed coverage of the Colombian-Peruvian dispute over possession of Guayaquil, Bolívar's campaigns in Peru in 1823-24, and the upsurge of opposition to him once the royalists had been defeated (p. 203-321). The discussion of his earlier campaigns in Venezuela and Peru also contains frequent references to Peru.

256 **The "detached recollections" of General D. F. O'Leary.**
Edited by R. A. Humphreys. London: Athlone, 1969. 66p. 2 maps.

As aide de camp to Bolívar from 1820, O'Leary was closely involved in his campaigns in Peru. O'Leary travelled with him to Lima in 1823, arriving safely, despite the fact that the Colombian ship carrying them, the *Chimborazo*, 'took fire from the negligence of the cook one afternoon'. His notes provide useful insights into Bolívar's personality and Peruvian attitudes towards independence.

257 **The emergence of the republic of Bolivia.**
Charles Wolfgang Arnade. New York: Russell & Russell, 1970.
rev. ed. 269p. bibliog.

From 1809, when the viceroy of Peru sent Peruvian forces into Upper Peru to quell insurgency, until 1825, when the independent republic of Bolivia was formed, the history of these two countries was inextricably linked. The majority of Bolivians would probably have preferred union with Peru to a separate independence, but this was ruled out by Simón Bolívar, who did not wish to see a strong southern Andean state which might challenge the hegemony of Colombia. This excellent analysis, first published in 1957, covers these themes, and is also authoritative on dissension within the royalist army during the final phases of the independence period in Peru.

258 **The fall of the royal government in Peru.**
Timothy E. Anna. London: University of Nebraska Press, 1980.
291p. bibliog.

This work provides a scholarly analysis, based upon extensive archival research, of the final years of Spanish rule in Peru, as seen by first royalist and, from 1821, revolutionary forces in control of Lima, the national capital. It says relatively little about political and military events elsewhere in the viceroyalty.

259 **Fidelismo y separatismo del Perú.** (Fidelity and separatism of Peru.)
Carlos Daniel Valcárcel. *Revista de Historia de América*, vols. 37-38 (1954), p. 133-62.

Peru was the most conservative and royalist of Spain's American possessions in the early-19th century. The varied reasons for the lack of enthusiasm among its political and social élite for taking up arms to gain independence are clearly outlined in this article.

260 **Historiografía de la independencia del Perú.** (Historiography of the independence of Peru.)
José A. de la Puente Candamo.   *Revista de Historia de América*, vol. 59 (1965), p. 280-93.

The literature concerning Peruvian independence and the interpretations of the process are discussed in this well-informed survey.

261 **Imperialism, centralism and regionalism in Peru, 1776-1845.**
John Fisher.   In: *Region and class in modern Peruvian history*. Edited by Rory Miller. Liverpool, England: Institute of Latin American Studies, University of Liverpool, 1987, p. 21-34. (Monograph, 14).

This discussion of the relationship between regional rivalries within Peru and national identity before, during and after the country's transition to independence in 1824 also examines the reasons for the collapse of the Peru-Bolivia Confederation of 1836-39.

262 **La independencia en el Perú.** (Independence in Peru.)
Heraclio Bonilla (et al.)   Lima: Instituto de Estudios Peruanos, 1981. 2nd ed. 240p. bibliog.

This partially revised edition of an iconoclastic work, first published in 1972, challenges the then military's government's official insistence that the declaration of independence from Spain in 1821 had united all races and classes behind the national cause. It argues that the white élite opted for independence as a means of preserving, rather than destroying, the traditional society and institutions of the colonial period.

263 **Lord Cochrane: critic of San Martín's Peruvian campaign.**
James C. Carey.   *Americas*, vol. 18 (1962), p. 340-51.

A major factor in San Martín's failure to confront the royalist forces in Peru in open battle was dissension among his own forces, a notable feature of which was the unwillingness of his naval commander, Cochrane, to obey his instructions. Cochrane, for his part, was critical of San Martín's indecisiveness, as this article clearly demonstrates.

264 **The Peruvian church at the time of independence in the light of Vatican II.**
Antonine Tibesar.   *Americas*, vol. 26 (1970), p. 349-75.

Behind this somewhat unusual title there lies an interesting general survey of the importance, wealth and attitudes of the Peruvian church at the end of the colonial period. It examines relationships between its leaders, notably the last Spanish archbishop of Lima, Bartolomé María de las Heras, and the insurgents in 1820-21.

265 **Revolución y contrarrevolución en México y el Perú: liberalismo, realeza y separatismo (1800-1824).** (Revolution and counter-revolution in Mexico and Peru: liberalism, royalism and separatism [1800-1824].).
Brian R. Hamnett.   Mexico: Fondo de Cultura Economica, 1978. 454p. bibliog.

Peru and Mexico were the most conservative and royalist areas of Spanish America during the independence period, and in each viceroyalty the struggles which eventually brought them independence in 1821-24 were essentially civil wars. This book is primarily a political study, concentrating upon the rôles played by Peruvian and Mexican liberals, who believed that constitutional reforms might be secured within the context of continuing Spanish rule.

266 **San Martín, the liberator.**
John Callan James Metford. Westport, Connecticut: Greenwood, 1971. 2nd ed. 154p. 2 maps.
Whereas excellent biographies of Simón Bolívar abound, there is no good, modern treatment of San Martín. This brief work, first published in 1950, provides a useful introduction to his career, with some specific consideration of the reasons for the failure of his mission to emancipate Peru.

267 **Simón Bolívar.**
Gerhard Masur. Albuquerque, New Mexico: University of New Mexico Press, 1969. rev. ed. 572p. 2 maps. bibliog.
This monumental work, the first edition of which appeared in 1948, remains the best biography in English on Bolívar. It provides detailed coverage of the 1822 dispute between Colombia and Peru over possession of Guayaquil, and of Bolívar's campaigns in Peru.

268 **The Spanish American revolutions, 1808-1826.**
John Lynch. New York: Norton, 1986. 2nd ed. 448p.
First published in 1973, this outstanding synthesis of the complex processes whereby the Spanish empire in America collapsed in the first quarter of the 19th century has an excellent section (Chapter 5) about Peru. Its late colonial history is also referred to frequently in the introductory chapters on the background to independence.

The republican period (1824- .)

269 **Arequipa y el sur andino: ensayo de historia regional (siglos XVIII-XX).**
(Arequipa and the Andean south: an essay in regional history [18th-20th centuries].)
Alberto Flores-Galindo. Lima: Editorial Horizonte, 1977. 194p. bibliog.
During the first half of the 19th century, Arequipa vied with Cuzco for primacy in southern Peru, surging ahead in the second half as a result of rapid commercial and economic growth. Thereafter it gave a lead to the southern departments, including Puno and parts of Bolivia, in preserving regional identity in face of the centralization of power in Lima. This sophisticated study briefly examines the late colonial origins of southern regionalism, and its principal features in the 19th and 20th centuries.

History. The republican period (1824- .)

270 **Bandits and politics in Peru: landlord and peasant violence in Hualgayoc 1900-30.**
Lewis Taylor.   Cambridge, England: Centre of Latin American Studies, University of Cambridge, 1986. 140p.

This detailed study of local level political behaviour and power structures in the department of Cajamarca shows that the central government of Peru was relatively weak in the first three decades of the 20th century. It also demonstrates the complexity of landlord–peasant relations, which were characterized by both hostility and alliances, and depended upon local and personal factors.

271 **British consular reports on the trade and politics of Latin America, 1824-1826.**
Edited by R. A. Humphreys.   London: Royal Historical Society, 1940. 385p. map. bibliog.

The detailed report on the state of Peru in 1826, submitted on 27 December of that year to George Canning by the first British consul, Charles Milner Ricketts, is an essential point of departure for understanding the problems of the new republic (p. 107-206). Like the parallel reports on other countries, which provide useful comparative data, it concentrates upon the potential for British economic and commercial penetration.

272 **Business imperialism 1840-1930: an inquiry based on British experience in Latin America.**
Edited by D. C. M. Platt.   Oxford: Clarendon, 1977. 449p. 3 maps.

This wide-ranging volume examines a number of British business connections with Latin America before 1930, in banking, insurance, public utilities, import and export, coffee, nitrates, meat, *guano* and railways. The businesses are compared and conclusions reached on the points of influence, power, and control throughout the chain which links producer to consumer, investor to contractor and entrepreneur. Two of the eleven essays deal specifically with Peru: in 'Antony Gibbs & Sons, the *guano* trade and the Peruvian government, 1842-1861', W. M. Mathew suggests that Gibbs and the Peruvian government had complementary interests (p. 337-70); Rory Miller presents a similar argument for the late-19th and early-20th centuries in 'British firms and the Peruvian government, 1885-1930' (p. 371-94).

273 **The conflict between indigenous and immigrant commercial systems in the Peruvian central sierra, 1900-1940.**
Fiona Wilson.   In: *Region and class in modern Peruvian history.* Edited by Rory Miller. Liverpool, England: Institute of Latin American Studies, University of Liverpool, 1987, p. 125-61. map. (Monograph, 14).

This paper takes changes in transport and exchange relations in the central Andean province of Tarma as a point of departure for the analysis of the interplay between the region's integration into the national economy and internally generated dynamics of change.

274 **The defence of community in Peru's central highlands: peasant struggle and capitalist transition, 1860-1940.**
Florencia E. Mallon.   Princeton, New Jersey: Princeton University Press, 1983. 384p. 6 maps. bibliog.

This wide-ranging inter-disciplinary study of a relatively restricted region, in the central highlands of Peru, Oroya-Huancayo, focuses upon peasant resistance to capitalist penetration of the countryside during the late-19th and early-20th centuries. It is essential background reading for those interested in agrarian reform since the 1940s.

275 **Dictators Gamarra, Orbegoso, Salaverry, and Santa Cruz.**
Andrew N. Cleven.   In: *South American dictators during the first century of independence.* Edited by A. Curtis Wilgus. Washington, DC: George Washington University Press, 1937, p. 289-333.

The complex political manoeuvres and instability of the first twenty years after independence are clearly outlined in this series of biographical sketches of the most important early presidents of Peru. It is argued that politics were determined almost entirely by personalism and opportunism, rather than by issues of principle.

276 **Don Nicolás de Piérola: una época de la historia del Perú.** (Don Nicolás de Piérola: an epoch in the history of Peru.)
Alberto Ulloa y Sotomayor.   Lima: Imprenta-Editorial Minerva, 1981. 2nd ed. 495p.

Piérola served as president of Peru from 1895 to 1899. He came to the post as one of the country's most colourful and controversial figures, noted for his dogmatism and irresponsibility in his quest for power. In office, however, he was honest, efficient and successful in initiating almost two decades of unusually stable government. First published in 1949, this biography is serviceable and reliable.

277 **Earning a living in Hualgayoc, 1870-1900.**
Lewis Taylor.   In: *Region and class in modern Peruvian history.* Edited by Rory Miller. Liverpool, England: Institute of Latin American Studies, University of Liverpool, 1987, p. 103-24. 2 maps. (Monograph, 14).

This study of the impact of agrarian modernization upon rural society in the northern sierra of Peru during the late-19th century helps to penetrate much of the obscurity of peasant life.

278 **An essay on the Peruvian cotton industry, 1825-1920.**
W. S. Bell.   Liverpool, England: Centre for Latin American Studies, University of Liverpool, 1985. 99p. bibliog. (Working Paper, 6).

This pioneering attempt to provide a framework for understanding the development of the cotton industry in Peru in the century after independence contains useful data on production and trade.

279 **An essay on the Peruvian sugar industry 1880-1920.**
Bill Albert. Norwich, England: School of Social Studies, University of
East Anglia, 1976. 545p. 8 maps. bibliog.

This detailed study of one of the most dynamic sectors of Peruvian agriculture during
the late-19th and early-20th centuries relies heavily upon the letters of Ronald Gordon,
administrator of the British Sugar Company in Cañete in the years 1914-20. A long
introductory essay on the development of the sugar industry, and a shorter piece on
the history of the British Sugar Company, are followed by a reproduction of the letters
themselves.

280 **The export economies: their pattern of development in historical
perspective.**
Jonathan Victor Levin. Cambridge, Massachusetts: Harvard
University Press, 1960. 347p. map. bibliog.

The long chapter on 'Peru in the *guano* age' (p. 27-123) in this classic, general study of
export economies is of enduring importance for an understanding of the rôle of British
and French intermediaries in the transport and marketing of *guano* in the mid-19th
century.

281 **Foreign interests in the War of the Pacific.**
V. G. Kiernan. *Hispanic American Historical Review*, vol 25 (1955),
p. 14-36.

Using British Foreign Office records, this article examines the extent to which Britain
might have used its influence to support Chile in its seizure of the Bolivian port of
Antofagasta in February 1879, an act which led Bolivia to declare war on Chile, with
Peru entering the conflict in support of Bolivia. The conclusion is that, although British
capitalists welcomed and probably encouraged Chilean aggression, the British
government steadfastly remained neutral in the conflict.

282 **The Grace contract, the Peruvian corporation, and Peruvian history.**
Rory Miller. *Ibero-Amerikanisches Archiv*, vol 9, no. 3 (1983),
p. 319-48.

Two of the principal issues which dominate the historiography of British 'economic
imperialism' in Peru are the events which led to the approval of the Grace contract in
1889 and the activities of the Peruvian Corporation, formed by the beneficiaries of the
contract, which operated Peru's railways until 1972. This important revisionist article
suggests that the Corporation was relatively weak and ineffectual, and had little success
in promoting further foreign investment in Peru.

283 **Gran Bretaña y el Perú, 1826-1919: informes de los consules británicos.**
(Great Britain and Peru, 1826-1919: reports of the British consuls.)
Edited by Heraclio Bonilla. Lima: Instituto de Estudios Peruanos,
1975-77. 5 vols.

The reports to the Foreign Office of the British consuls in Peru in the century after
independence paid particular attention to economic and political matters. This
collection is an important work of reference, as a mirror both of conditions in Peru and
of British attitudes towards the country.

284 **Guano y burguesía en el Perú.** (*Guano* and bourgeoisie in Peru.)
Heraclio Bonilla. Lima: Instituto de Estudios Peruanos, 1974. 186p.
bibliog.

Based upon the ideas in Bonilla's doctoral dissertation, this book addressed itself to
the question of why Peru did not derive greater economic benefit in 1840-80 from the
exploitation of *guano*, a commodity owned by the state. It argues that the fundamental
factors were the weakness of the internal market and the peculiar composition of the
ruling class, which abdicated its national responsibilities.

285 **Guano y crecimiento en el Perú del siglo XIX.** (*Guano* and growth in
19th century Peru.)
Shane Hunt. *HISLA. Revista Latinoamericana de Historia Económica
y Social*, vol 4 (1984), p. 35-92.

Traditionally, it has been argued that Peru and the Peruvians were exploited by foreign
interests during the mid-19th century *guano* era. This important revisionist article
demonstrates that the bulk of the profits were retained in Peru, and were used to
generate economic and commercial development.

286 **Historia de la república del Perú, 1822-1933.** (History of the republic of
Peru, 1822-1933.)
Jorge Basadre Grohmann. Lima: Editorial Universitaria, 1984.
7th ed. 10 vols. bibliog.

This monumental compendium, first published in 1939, remains the standard work of
reference for the history of Peru in the century after independence. Its grasp of
political and social issues is particularly impressive.

287 **Historia del movimiento obrero peruano (1890-1977).** (History of the
Peruvian workers' movement [1890-1977].).
Denis Sulmont. Lima: Tarea, 1977. 358p.

Although written from a subjective standpoint – with the declared aim of strengthening
the development of working-class consciousness – this polemical work provides an
interesting survey of trade union activity in Peru since the late-19th century. Like
other studies it recognizes that trade union activity grew out of the rapid economic
growth of the period 1890-1930.

288 **The House of Gibbs and the Peruvian guano monopoly.**
W. M. Mathew. London: Royal Historical Society, 1981. 281p.
bibliog. (Studies in History, 25).

For almost forty years, from 1840, the *guano* trade dominated the commercial and
financial life of Peru, and provided the advanced economies of the world, notably
Britain, with a commodity of great importance for agricultural improvement. During
that period the trade ranked as one of the most important Latin American export
businesses. This book examines the involvement in it of the principal contractor, the
London merchant house of Antony Gibbs & Sons. It does not pretend to be either a
systematic business history of Gibbs or a comprehensive analysis of the effects of the
trade on Peru, although much of its material touches upon these questions; its principal
aim, which is realized, is to analyse both the way in which Gibbs handled the trade,
and the nature and implications of their relationship with the Peruvian government,
the owner of the *guano*.

History. The republican period (1824- .)

289 **Indian integration in Peru: a half century of experience, 1900-1948.**
Thomas M. Davies, Jr.   Lincoln, Nebraska: University of Nebraska
Press, 1974. 2nd ed. 204p. 3 maps. bibliog.

Preceded by a brief discussion of attitudes towards the indigenous population in the
19th century, the bulk of this monograph deals with official attempts to integrate the
Indian into national life in the period up to the presidency of Manuel Odría. It
concentrates upon the actions of the presidency, the congress and political parties, and
attempts to evaluate the sincerity of their respective programmes.

290 **La iniciación de la república.** (The foundation of the republic.)
Jorge Basadre.   Lima: R. & E. Rosay, 1929-30. 2 vols.

This early work by Peru's most respected historian of the 20th century analyses the
political problems of the opening years of the republican period. His thoughtful
suggestions are more detailed than the observations in his later general history,
Historia de la república del Perú, 1822-1933 (q.v.).

291 **The intellectuals and the crisis of modern Peruvian nationalism: 1870-
1919.**
Jesus Chavarría.   *Hispanic American Historical Review*, vol. 50 (1970),
p. 257-78.

The 1870s was a crucial decade owing to the magnitude of Peru's political and
economic problems. During those years articulate social groups, mainly in Lima, began
to discuss critically the country's backward and stagnant institutions. Constituting the
educated élites, they clamoured for political and social change, emphasizing the
paramount need to unify and modernize Peruvian society. This stimulating article
discusses these trends in the period up to 1919, a year in which the emergence of a new
group of intellectuals, whose principal figures were to be José Carlos Mariátegui and
Victor Raúl Haya de la Torre, led to the emergence of a new stage of the crisis of
national identity.

292 **Lanas y capital mercantil en el sur: la casa Ricketts, 1895-1935.** (Wool
and mercantile capital in the south: the Ricketts company, 1895-1935.).
Manuel Burga, Wilson Reátegui.   Lima: Instituto de Estudios
Peruanos, 1981. 215p. bibliog.

The English immigrant, William Ricketts first settled in the southern city of Arequipa
as an employee of a wool exporter. After working for several foreign firms he
established his own company in 1895, and in due course became not only one of the
largest exporters of fine wools but also an importer of finished textiles, liquors,
furniture, metal goods and construction materials. His activities and the reasons for his
prominence are subjected to detailed scrutiny in this study, based upon the company's
archives.

293 **The last conquistadores: the Spanish intervention in Peru and Chile,
1863-1866.**
William Columbus Davis.   Athens, Georgia: University of Georgia
Press, 1950. 386p. bibliog.

The bizarre attempt of Spain – or, at least, of a number of misguided Spanish
individuals – to reconquer Chile and Peru in the 1860s is clearly explained in this

volume. It also gives an insight into general Spanish American attitudes towards European intervention, and the ability of Peru and Chile to defend themselves at a time when the US Civil War ruled out any attempt to invoke the Monroe Doctrine.

294 **Leguía: vida y obra del constructor del gran Perú.** (Leguía: life and work of the builder of a great Peru.)
Manuel E. Capuñay. Lima: Compañia de Impresiones y Publicidad, 1952. 279p.

Leguía (1864-1932) was president of Peru from 1919 until his overthrow, in 1930, by the military revolt led by Luis M. Sánchez Cerro. Found guilty of corruption, he died in captivity. For most of his eleven years in office, a period commonly referred to as the *oncenio*, he presided over rapid economic growth but his relations with organized labour shifted from peaceful co-existence to harsh repression. As the title of this biography indicates, it is a laudatory work, stressing business expansion in the period prior to the onset of the Great Depression of 1929.

295 **Manuel Pardo y Lavalle, su vida y obra.** (Manuel Pardo y Lavalle, his life and work.)
Evaristo San Cristóval. Lima: Editorial Gil, 1945. 730p. bibliog.

Manuel Pardo became president of Peru in 1872, at the age of thirty-seven, as the candidate of the country's first political party, the Civilista (Civilianist) Party. Having earned a fortune from banking, insurance and commerce in his twenties, he embodied the ideal of managerial competence. However, faced with massive economic problems, he suspended service of the foreign debt at the beginning of 1876 and left office later that year; he was assassinated in 1878. This solid biography provides detailed coverage of his career. It is similar in structure to the same author's biography of Luis José de Orbegoso, who served as president in 1835: *El gran mariscal Luis José de Orbegoso* (Lima: Editorial Gil, 1941).

296 **Mercado interno y región: la sierra central, 1820-1930.** (Internal market and region: the central *sierra* 1820-1930.)
Nelson Manrique. Lima: Centro de Estudios y Promoción del Desarrollo, 1987. 280p. map. bibliog.

The traditional historiography of republican Peru has concentrated upon the political society of the national capital. This study shifts the focus from Lima to the central Andes, and examines the ambitious attempts of the region's mineowners, landowners and merchants to promote modernization and development in the period between the foundation of the republic and the War of the Pacific.

297 **La minería peruana y la iniciación de la república, 1820-1840.** (Peruvian mining and the creation of the republic, 1820-1840.)
José Deustua. Lima: Instituto de Estudios Peruanos, 1986. 288p. map. bibliog.

Centred upon an analysis of the mining industry during and immediately after Peru's transition to independence, this book makes an important contribution to the understanding of both the differences and the continuities between the old colonial system and the new republic. It demonstrates that mining production was rapidly reactivated after 1830, thereby demonstrating the survival of an economic dynamism, despite the political instability of the early republican period.

59

History. The republican period (1824- .)

298 **Mineros y campesinos en los Andes.** (Miners and peasants in the Andes.)
Carlos Contreras.   Lima: Instituto de Estudios Peruanos, 1988.
2nd ed. 155p. bibliog.

At the end of the colonial period and during the first decades of the republican period the various mechanisms which had stimulated the recruitment of rural labour for the Andean mining centres disappeared one by one. Deprived of the power given to them over the peasantry by the tribute and *mita* systems, the mineowners had to devise new methods of recruiting labour. This monograph concentrates upon the 19th century, and examines the functioning of the labour market in the central Andes.

299 **Modernization, dislocation, and Aprismo: origin of the Peruvian Aprista party, 1870-1932.**
Peter Klaren.   Austin, Texas: University of Texas Press, 1973. 189p.
2 maps. bibliog.

Founded in 1930, the Partido Aprista Peruano (PAP) was conceived by Victor Raúl Haya de la Torre as the Peruvian counterpart to his Alianza Popular Revolucionaria Americana (APRA), which had been established in Mexico in 1924. Since 1931, it has played a major rôle in Peru's political history, but has tended to draw its strength from the northern part of the country rather than from a broad geographical base. This outstanding monograph examines the Party's roots, arguing that it fed primarily upon those segments of the population in the north coast region who were dislocated and frustrated by the late-19th century development there of a modern export-oriented economic structure, dominated by a dynamic and rapidly expanding sugar industry.

300 **Los movimientos campesinos en el Perú 1879-1965.** (Peasant movements in Peru, 1879-1965.)
Wilfredo Kapsoli.   Lima: Ediciones Atusparia, 1982. 2nd ed. 209p.

This polemical study examines the development of peasant consciousness from a historical perspective. It considers, first, a series of anti-fiscal protests in the period 1879-96, before moving on to the 1920s, when a number of revolts took on a millenarian character. It concludes with a discussion of reformism in the late 1940s, and of revolutionary activity in the period 1956-65.

301 **The origins of the Peruvian labour movement: 1883-1919.**
Peter Blanchard.   Pittsburgh, Pennsylvania: University of Pittsburgh Press, 1982. 214p. bibliog.

The foundations of the modern labour movement in Peru were laid in the period between the end of the war with Chile in 1883 and the famous government decree of January 1919 which established the eight-hour working day. During these years of economic growth and relative political stability, the small but expanding urban and industrial labour force succeeded through both political activity and industrial agitation in forging a class consciousness, and in compelling both employers and governments to respond to its demands. The process is clearly charted in this excellent book.

302 **Perú 1820-1920: un siglo de desarrollo capitalista.** (Peru 1820-1920: a century of capitalist development.)
Ernesto Yepes del Castillo.   Lima: Instituto de Estudios Peruanos, 1972. 367p. bibliog.

This classic application to Peru of the dependency model, which was much in vogue in the early 1970s, is of importance for historiographical reasons rather than as a reliable analysis of the reasons for Peru's failure to industrialize in the 19th century.

303 **The place of the peasantry in the national life of Peru in the nineteenth century.**
Jean Piel.   *Past & Present*, no. 46 (1970), p. 108-33.

Interpretations of rural social relations and changes in land tenure in 19th-century Peru moved forward very quickly in the 1970s, as the opening of hacienda archives to researchers in the wake of agrarian reform allowed them to examine how individual estates had actually functioned. This article very quickly became outdated, particularly because of its stark depiction of a peasantry that was defenceless and ruthlessly exploited. Nevertheless, it is of enduring historiographical importance, and is still frequently cited, as a reflection of the state of research on rural conditions some twenty years ago.

304 **Plantation agriculture and social control in northern Peru, 1875-1933.**
Michael J. Gonzales.   Austin, Texas: University of Texas Press, 1985. 235p. 6 maps. bibliog.

This competent study of the development of the sugar industry on the north coast of Peru, based upon hacienda and plantation records expropriated under the agrarian reform law of 1969, provides a particularly useful analysis of the means employed to obtain labour, both ·by importing indentured Chinese coolies and by recruiting highland peasants.

305 **The popular universities and the origins of Aprismo, 1921-1924.**
Jeffrey L. Klaiber.   *Hispanic American Historical Review*, vol 55 (1975), p. 693-715.

In 1921, Victor Raúl Haya de la Torre, the future leader of the Peruvian Aprista movement, and a number of his fellow students at the University of San Marcos founded the González Prada Popular Universities for workers. The purpose of the centres was to further the aims of the university reform movement by bringing the benefits of culture and learning to the poor and uneducated. When president Leguía suppressed them in 1924 and exiled most of the organizers, Haya and his companions turned their cultural movement into the political organization which led to the formation of the Aprista Party. This article clearly explains the relationship between university reform and political change.

306 **Railways and economic development in central Peru, 1890-1930.**
Rory Miller.   In: *Social and economic change in modern Peru.* Edited by Rory Miller, Clifford T. Smith, John Fisher. Liverpool, England: Centre for Latin American Studies, University of Liverpool, 1976, p. 27-52. (Monograph, 6).

One of the major debates among economic historians studying the 19th century has been about the impact upon South America generally of the building of railways for the export of raw materials. This paper demonstrates that in the Peruvian case the construction of railways was vital to the development of the mining industry, but large areas of the country remained outside of the influence of the railways in 1930, largely because of the expense of feeder transport. Construction of the railways took place ahead of demand, and many investors – Peruvian and foreign – lost money.

307 **Ramón Castilla.**
Rubén Vargas Ugarte.   Buenos Aires: Imprenta López, 1962. 248p.

Castilla became president of Peru in 1845, and initiated a thirty-year period of increased political stability, significant reform, and economic growth, developments which were financed by the profits of the *guano* trade. He stood down from the presidency in 1851, as the constitution required, but returned to office in 1855, serving until 1862. This sound survey of his career is a reliable work of reference.

308 **Religion and revolution in Peru, 1824-1976.**
Jeffrey L. Klaiber.   Notre Dame, Indiana: University of Notre Dame Press, 1977. 259p. bibliog.

The cultural disparity of Peruvian society from the time of independence is examined in this monograph through the lens of religion. It is argued that religious beliefs and practices served as examples of the profound psychological and cultural gap between the educated ruling minority, supported by the formal apparatus of the Catholic Church, and the lower-class Indians, Negroes and *mestizos*, whose popular religion was scorned by the cultural élite. In the 20th century, however, dissident members of the élite succeeded in creating the intellectual climate in which support for revolution could be viewed as compatible with continued membership of the Church.

309 **Un siglo a la deriva: ensayo sobre el Perú, Bolivia y la guerra.** (A century of drift: essays on Peru, Bolivia and the war.)
Heraclio Bonilla.   Lima: Instituto de Estudios Peruanos, 1980. 236p. bibliog.

Many books and articles were published in Peru in 1979-80 to mark the centenary of the outbreak of the War of the Pacific. This was one of the least patriotic and the most perceptive of them, attributing Peru's eventual humiliation at the hands of Chile to a long tradition of military and political incompetence among its ruling class.

310 **Small business in the Peruvian oil industry: Lobitos Oilfields Limited before 1934.**
Rory Miller.   *Business History Review*, vol 56, no. 3 (autumn 1982), p. 400-23.

In the early-20th century, Lobitos Oilfields Limited, a concern founded by British merchants, produced a significant amount of Peru's petroleum output. This article examines its management structure, and explains why it was able to survive as a relatively small independent company in an age of fully-integrated multinationals.

311 **The socavón of Quiulacocha and the steam engine company: technology and capital investment in Cerro de Pasco, 1820-1840.**
José Deustua. In: *Region and class in modern Peruvian history.*
Edited by Rory Miller. Liverpool, England: Institute of Latin
American Studies, University of Liverpool, 1987, p. 35-75.
(Monograph, 14).

This analysis of the recovery of silver production after the wars of independence in Peru's principal mining centre embraces a discussion of the relationship between production and investment in both traditional and modern methods of draining the mines.

312 **South America rediscovered.**
Tom B. Jones. Minneapolis, Minnesota: University of Minnesota
Press, 1949. 285p. map. bibliog.

This entertaining work contains two chapters on the history of Peru in the first fifty years after independence, reconstructed from travelogues (p. 139-70). The tone is set by the opening quotation from a British visitor, who in 1873 described Lima as 'the heaven of women, purgatory of men, and the hell of asses'.

313 **Tacna and Arica: an account of the Chile-Peru boundary dispute and of the arbitrations of the United States.**
William Jefferson Dennis. New Haven, Connecticut: Yale University
Press, 1931. Reprinted, Hamden, Connecticut: Archon Books, 1967.
332p. 6 maps.

Although the victorious Chilean army withdrew from most of Peru in August 1884, the spoils of its success in the War of the Pacific included permanent ownership of Tarapacá, and the continued occupation and administration for ten years of the southern departments of Tacna and Arica. After that interval, according to the 1883 Treaty of Ancón, the people of those departments would determine by plebiscite whether they would remain with Chilean, or revert to Peruvian, sovereignty. In fact, for a variety of reasons, the plebiscite was not held in 1894, and the dispute between the two countries continued until 1929. In that year the Treaty of Lima endorsed the arbitration formula proposed by the United States: Arica remained within Chile, while Peru recovered Tacna. Written in the immediate aftermath of the settlement, this work remains the most satisfactory general account of both the War and the subsequent diplomatic dispute.

314 **The United States and the Andean republics: Peru, Bolivia and Ecuador.**
Fredrick B. Pike. Cambridge, Massachusetts: Harvard University
Press, 1977. 493p. 4 maps. bibliog.

Although this work is intended primarily to contrast the basic value systems and cultural patterns of the Andean republics with those of the United States, it also contains a careful analysis of the historical development of the Andean region as a whole. Its long section on the period between independence and World War II (p. 47-268) provides an excellent coverage of the political history of Peru.

315 **The War of the Pacific and the national and colonial problem in Peru.**
Heraclio Bonilla.   *Past & Present*, no. 81 (1978), p. 91-118.

It is argued in this iconoclastic article, by one of Peru's leading social scientists, that the country's defeat by Chile in the 1879-83 War of the Pacific reflected not only military and naval blunders but also the fundamental absence within Peru of a sense of national identity and purpose. Chile, by contrast, succeeded in uniting the whole of its politically active class in a nationalist crusade.

Population

316 Censo general de la república del Perú formado en 1876. (General
census of the republic of Peru made in 1876.)
Ministerio de Gobierno.   Lima: Imp. del Teatro, 1878. 7 vols.

Peru's first national census, taken on 14 May 1876, showed a total population of
2,699,106. Despite its deficiencies, it is of great value to historians and social scientists.
One of the most important findings was that the bulk of the population (seventy-six per
cent) lived in the *sierra*. By 1940, when the second national census was made, sixty-
four per cent of the population of 6,207,967 lived in the *sierra*. This gradual shift to the
coast continued to be demonstrated in the censuses made in 1961, 1972 and 1981. By
1981, as a consequence of urbanization on the coast, only thirty-seven per cent of the
country's seventeen million inhabitants remained in the *sierra*.

**317 The Indian caste of Peru, 1795-1940: a population study based upon tax
records and census reports.**
George Kubler.   Westport, Connecticut: Greenwood, 1973. 2nd ed.
71p. 20 maps.

Drawn primarily from late colonial census data and 19th-century tax registers, this
incisive study, first published in 1952, provides valuable information on the social and
ethnic composition of the Peruvian population.

318 El norte peruano: realidad poblacional. (The Peruvian north:
population reality.)
Edited by Jose B. Adolph.   Lima: Asociación Multidisciplinaria de
Investigación y Docencia en Población, 1982. 182p.

Although population trends and problems in Peru tend to have common features,
there are also important regional variations. This collection of six essays, originally
prepared for a conference held in Cajamarca in 1981, discusses, with particular
reference to northern Peru, the effects of population growth and migration upon
employment, education, family structures and health care. For a parallel volume on

Population

southern Peru see *El sur peruano: realidad poblacional*, edited by José B. Adolph (Lima: Asociación Multidisciplinaria de Investigación y Docencia en Población, 1983).

319 **The origin and comparability of Peruvian population data, 1776-1815.**
D. G. Browning, D. J. Robinson. *Jahrbuch für Geschichte von Staat, Wirtschaft und Gesellschaft Lateinamerikas*, vol 14 (1977), p. 199-223.

In the late colonial period the Spanish crown made a series of attempts to compile population data for Peru, reflecting partly the prevailing belief that statistical data was intrinsically useful and also the need to update information required for fiscal purposes. This article discusses the 'censuses' prepared between 1776 and 1815, revealing both their shortcomings and their utility. Its general conclusion is they are not sufficiently accurate or reliable to indicate either short-term temporal change or large-scale spatial change in the size and structure of the Peruvian population.

320 **Patterns of urban and regional development in Peru on the eve of the Pacific War.**
Clifford T. Smith. In: *Region and class in modern Peruvian history*. Edited by Rory Miller. Liverpool, England: Institute of Latin American Studies, University of Liverpool, 1987, p. 77-101. (Monograph 14).

Professor Smith provides a perceptive analysis of the data contained in Peru's first national census, made in 1876 during the presidency of Manuel Pardo, and published in 1878. He discusses its deficiencies, before going on to analyse its data on urbanization, regional distribution and occupations.

321 **The people of the Colca valley: a population study.**
Noble David Cook. Boulder, Colorado: Westview, 1982. 100p. bibliog.

This interesting demographic study traces the population history of a discrete geographical section of Peru – the Colca valley in the southern Andes – over a long chronological period, ranging from the initial contact between the European and the Andean native in the early-16th century up to the middle of the 20th century.

322 **Peru: hechos y cifras demográficas.** (Peru: demographic facts and figures.)
Consejo Nacional de Población. Lima: Editorial Universo, 1984. 128p.

During the early-20th century the population of Peru grew slowly but steadily, increasing from a little over three million in 1900 to six million in 1940. Rapid growth began in the 1950s as a result of industrialization and a sharp decrease in mortality. Although the rate of population growth declined from 2.9 per cent in 1961-72 to 2.5 per cent in 1972-81, current projections indicate that by the year 2025 the total population will be in excess of forty million. This excellent work, published by a government agency, describes and explains these trends, making effective use of eighty-four graphs and tables.

323 **La población del Cuzco colonial (siglos XVI-XVIII).** (The population of colonial Cuzco [16th-18th centuries].)
Clemencia Aramburu de Olivera, Pilar Remy S.   Lima: Instituto Andino de Estudios en Población y Desarrollo, 1983. 36p. map. bibliog.

The population of the ancient Inca capital city of Cuzco at the time of conquest is not known, but historians agree that it fell dramatically in the 150 years after 1533, reaching a low point of 13,600 in 1689. Thereafter it increased to an estimated 32,000 in 1786. In the same period the population of its surrounding provinces also increased from 113,000 to 175,000. This brief, incisive work analyses these trends on the basis of a detailed study of baptismal and burial records in the city's ecclesiastical archive.

324 **La población del Perú.** (The population of Peru.)
Oficina Nacional de Estadística y Censos.   Lima: 1974. 346p. 5 maps.

Produced during the most radical phase of the post-1968 revolutionary militarism in Peru, to commemorate UNESCO's declaration of 1974 as 'World Population Year', this wide-ranging official study was prepared in collaboration with the Instituto Nacional de Planificación. Its coverage includes the history of population growth, the composition and distribution of the population, internal migration, and proposed policies to satisfy the basic needs of the increasing number of Peruvians.

325 **La población del Perú 1980-2025: su crecimiento y distribución.** (The population of Peru 1980-2025: its growth and distribution.)
Dirección General de Demografía.   Lima: Oficina de Comunicación, Información e Impresiones, 1984. 68p. 4 maps. bibliog. (Boletín de Análisis Demográfico, no 26).

Although still small by European standards, the population of Peru has increased dramatically since the 1950s, primarily as a consequence of a sharp decrease in mortality rates. Mortality and birth rates are clearly explained in this valuable work, as is the distribution and composition (by age and sex) of the population. On the basis of current trends, it is suggested that the total estimated population is likely to increase from nineteen million in 1984 to twenty-eight million in the year 2000, and to a staggering forty-one million in 2025. During the same period average life expectancy is likely to increase from 58.6 to 72 years.

326 **Población y desarrollo capitalista.** (Population and capitalist development.)
Ricardo Vergara.   Lima: Centro de Estudios y Promoción del Desarrollo, 1982. 139p. bibliog.

Beginning from a basically Marxist view of the relationship between population growth and the development of productive capacity, this neat little volume provides an interesting coverage of the reasons for Peru's rapid population growth since the 1950s, and the increasing concentration of people in Lima and other cities. The factor of fundamental importance, it is suggested, in both urban growth and the disintegration of rural society has been industrial development.

327 **Población y desarrollo en el Perú.** (Population and development in Peru.)
Richard L. Clinton. Lima: Universidad de Lima, Oficina Coordinadora de Investigación Científica. 1985. 207p. bibliog.

Written by a demographic specialist from the University of Oregon, this interesting work provides an analysis of a survey of 170 'leaders of opinion' in Peru about population policy and the possibility of introducing more effective methods of birth-control. Although the reader is invited to reach his own decision about the issue, on the basis of the evidence, the author clearly believes that the 'demographic explosion' in contemporary Peru cannot continue without severe damage being caused to the country's social and political fabric.

328 **Population and development in Peru.**
Clifford T. Smith. London: John Murray, 1988. 58p. 19 maps. bibliog.

Prepared primarily to serve the needs of Advanced Level students of Geography, this book sets a systematic account of the population geography of Peru against the background of Peruvian physical, social and economic environments. It examines Peru's population structure and growth, regional distribution, and patterns of migration, illustrating them by means of a systematic account of the historical and present situations in Peru. It provides a lively, well-informed survey, useful for the general reader.

329 **Problemas poblaciones peruanos.** (Peruvian population problems.)
Edited by Roger Guerra García. Lima: Asociación Multidisciplinaria de Investigación y Docencia en Población, 1980. 411p.

Founded in 1977 to undertake research arising from Peru's rapid population increase, AMIDEP convened a conference of specialist researchers in Tarma in 1979. This collection of eight papers presented at the conference is accompanied by notes of comments made upon them by participants. They range widely across general demography, migration, food production, income distribution, health, education, the rôle of women, and family structures.

330 **Problemas poblaciones peruanos II.** (Peruvian population problems II.)
Edited by Roger Guerra García. Lima: Asociación Multidisciplinaria de Investigación y Docencia en Población, 1986. 402p.

AMIDEP convened the Second National Conference on Population in Tarma in 1985 for seventy Peruvian specialists working in the field of population studies. This collection of nine essays by the country's leading researchers provides excellent coverage of both general demographic trends and of specific problems, including health-care, family structures and nutrition.

331 **Proyeccion de la demografía en el centro y el sur del Perú.**
(Demographic projection for the centre and the south of Peru.)
Alcides Rodríguez Michuy. Lima: Centro Peruano de Investigación Aplicada, 1985. 76p. bibliog.

This detailed analysis of demographic trends in central and southern Peru since 1940 explains the general population structure, mortality, fertility, and patterns of migration.

Immigration and
Internal Migration

332 The African experience in Latin America: 1502 to the present day.
Leslie B. Rout, Jr.   Cambridge, England: Cambridge University
Press, 1976. 404p. bibliog.

The first part of this volume deals with the general process of slavery in colonial Latin America, considering issues such as the slave trade, slave rebellions, and manumission. In the second part, which covers the period since independence, there is specific coverage of Peru (p. 217-26), where slavery survived until 1854. At independence, Peru had approximately 40,000 Negro slaves, and 41,000 free blacks; by the mid-19th century, as a result of earlier restrictions on the slave trade, the number of bondsmen had fallen to 17,000. These were emancipated in 1854, in return for generous payments to slaveholders from the government. The chapter also considers the contribution made by the Afro-Peruvians to national culture.

**333 Chinese bondage in Peru: a history of the Chinese coolie in Peru,
1849-1874.**
Watt Stewart.   Westport, Connecticut: Greenwood, 1970. 2nd ed.
247p. bibliog.

First published in 1951, this is a grim account of the 'coolie trade' which brought some 90,000 Chinese immigrants to Peru in the mid-19th century, mostly by coercion. It succeeds in going beyond mere condemnation of a brutalizing process to explain the social and economic conditions which created it. The coolie immigration was ended in 1874 as a consequence of both national and international condemnation of the high mortality rates, both at sea and upon the plantations where most of the immigrants worked as semi-slaves. In the longer term, some of them and their descendants attained much higher status than they had enjoyed in China, enriching in the process Peruvian culture and cuisine.

334 Cities of peasants.
Bryan Roberts.   London: Edward Arnold, 1978. 207p. bibliog.

Although this general study of the expansion of capitalism in Latin America ranges widely over different countries and disciplinary themes, it draws heavily upon the author's long experience of research in Peru. It examines the general process of migration from the countryside, with particular reference to the ability of the new urban working class to organize itself in pursuit of social and economic improvement. The flavour of life in the cities of Latin America and the immediacy of their problems are both successfully conveyed. The bibliography is excellent.

335 **Conceptos generales sobre la colonización en la montaña peruana.**
(General concepts concerning colonization in the Peruvian *montaña*.)
Raymond E. Crist.   Lima: Centro de Estudios de Población y
Desarrollo, 1969. 16p. (Estudios de Población y Desarrollo, 5).

Although brief, this well-illustrated study provides a useful introduction to the general topic of the colonization of Peruvian Amazonia. It concentrates upon the economic aspects of the process, notably the need to provide improved road links to enable the colonists to market their products, and says little about its impact upon the jungle tribes.

336 **De campesinos a profesionales: migrantes de Huayopampa en Lima.**
(From peasants to professionals: migrants from Huayopampa in Lima.)
Jorge P. Osterling.   Lima: Universidad Católica del Perú, 1980. 203p.
2 maps. bibliog.

The rural community of Huayopampa is located in the province of Huaral, department of Lima, 148 kilometres from the national capital. This interesting study in urban anthropology is less concerned with the process of migration from the community to the city of Lima and its metropolitan area than with the ways in which the migrants adapt to urban life.

337 **East from the Andes: pioneer settlements in the South American heartland.**
Raymond E. Crist, Charles M. Nissly.   Gainesville, Florida:
University of Florida Press, 1973. 166p. bibliog.

This general study of pioneer settlements in the interior of South America concentrates upon case studies of Venezuela and Bolivia. However, Peruvian data is also introduced in a general discussion of the dynamics of internal migration.

338 **Immigration and *mestizaje* in nineteenth-century Peru.**
Mario C. Vázquez.   In: *Race and class in Latin America*. Edited by
Magnus Mörner. New York, Columbia University Press, 1970,
p. 73-95.

European and United States immigrants to Peru in the 19th century tended to retain their racial and cultural identity, whereas the descendants of Negro slaves and Asian immigrants mixed more readily with the local population and intermarried to a large degree. Social and racial mobility was also encouraged by economic development, and by the fact that most immigrants were male. A significant conclusion arising from this study is the suggestion that the usual view of highland Indian communities as closed to outsiders is erroneous.

339 **The Japanese and Peru, 1873-1973.**
Clinton Harvey Gardiner. Albuquerque, New Mexico: University of
New Mexico Press, 1975. 202p. map. bibliog.

Japanese migration to Peru began in 1899, when a party of 790 settlers were landed in
Callao; it was part of a general process begun in 1868, when the first Japanese
emigrants had gone abroad to Hawaii. The process ground to a halt in 1923, following
the dissolution of emigration companies which had transported a total of 17,764
settlers. However, the migrants retained their identity, and according to the 1940
census numbered 17,598, a figure which represented over twenty-eight per cent of
Peru's foreign population. The vast majority lived in the Lima-Callao metropolitan
area, where they were heavily involved in grocery stores, restaurants, and general
merchandise occupations. This detailed study pays particular attention to their harsh
experiences in World War II, when 1,800 Japanese were deported to the United States
to be interned. This process is considered in even greater detail in the same author's
Pawns in a triangle of hate (Seattle, Washington: University of Washington Press,
1981).

340 **Jews in Latin America.**
Jacob Beller. New York: Jonathan David, 1969. 303p.

This general survey of Jews in Latin America includes a chapter entitled, somewhat
fancifully, 'Peru: Jewish life in the land of the Incas' (p. 128-43). The author suggests
that the modern Jewish community numbers 5,000, the majority of whom are resident
in Lima. Most of them, or their parents, arrived after World War I, from East
European countries. They are divided into Sephardic, German and East European
communities, which are united through a Central Committee. As in other countries of
South America, their contributions to cultural and financial life are disproportionately
large in relation to the small size of the Jewish communites in the total population.

341 **La migración a Lima entre 1972 y 1981: anotaciones desde una
perspective económica.** (Migration to Lima between 1972 and 1981:
notes from an economic perspective.)
Francisco Verdara V. Lima: Fundación Friedrich Ebert, 1985. 65p.
bibliog.

This stimulating study begins by demonstrating, on the basis of census data, that
between 1972 and 1981 the rate of growth in the population of Lima was lower than in
the period between 1940 and 1971. It argues that the basic reason for the decline was
not a fall in the birth-rate, but a slowing-down in the rate of migration.

342 **Migración e integración en el Perú.** (Migration and integration in Peru.)
Edited by Henry F. Dobyns, Mario C. Vázquez. Lima: Editorial
Estudios Andinos, 1963. 196p. bibliog.

The twenty-four brief essays in this volume were initially presented as papers at a
symposium held in Lima in 1962. They are divided into five groups, dealing
respectively with general causes of migration, migration to Lima, other cities, the
effects of migration upon highland communities, and general conclusions. Inevitably
some of the findings are now outdated, but the work as a whole provides a good
indication of the state of migration studies in the early 1960s.

343 **Migración en las comunidades indígenas del Perú antes de la reforma agraria.** (Migration in the indigenous communities of Peru before the agrarian reform.)
Hector Martínez.   Lima: Centro de Estudios de Población y Desarrollo, 1970. 15p. (Estudios de Población y Desarrollo, 7).

The agrarian reform legislation introduced in Peru in 1970 was designed in part to promote the opportunities for indigenous communities in the highlands of Peru to become self-sufficient. This interesting study, based upon surveys made among over 900 indigenous communities in 1961-62, explains the need before the reform for many rural inhabitants to move out of their communities – to haciendas, cities and the eastern settlements – because of the pressure of population growth upon community land.

344 **Las migraciones internas en el Perú.** (Internal migration in Peru.)
Hector Martínez.   Lima: Centro de Estudios de Población y Desarrollo, 1968. 15p. bibliog. (Estudios de Población y Desarrollo, 3).

This brief study provides a stimulating introduction to the phenomenon of internal migration in Peru since the late 1940s, explaining in relatively simple terms the demographic, economic, social, cultural and political impact of rapid urbanization.

345 **La modernización y la migración interna en el Perú.** (Modernization and internal migration in Peru.)
Fernando Bertoli, Felipe Portocarrero.   Lima: Instituto de Estudios Peruanos, 1968. 120p.

On the basis of data contained in the national censuses of 1940 and 1961, this study examines the relationships between modernization and internal migration in Peru. Its general conclusions are not particularly surprising, but it is useful to have them confirmed by detailed statistical information. It is suggested, first, that modernization promotes migration, and, second, that the more developed provinces of the country experience greater degrees of both immigration and emigration than under-developed areas.

346 **Peru's invisible migrants: a case study of inter-Andean migration.**
Stephen B. Brush.   In: *Land and power in Latin America: agrarian economics and social processes in the Andes*. Edited by B. S. Orlove, G. Custred. New York: Holmes & Meier, 1980, p. 211-28.

Most works on internal migration deal with movements between rural areas and cities; this interesting study is concerned with the less visible inter-rural migration in the highlands.

347 **Poder blanco y resistencia negra en el Perú.** (White power and black resistance in Peru.)
Denys Cuche.   Lima: Instituto Nacional de Cultura, 1975. 198p. bibliog.

Written by a French sociologist, this somewhat subjective study concentrates upon the social conditions of Peru's Negro population in the period after the 1854 abolition of slavery. It covers issues such as Negro occupations, white racism, discrimination,

Negro social organization, and Negro religion and folklore. Its general conclusion is that Negroes suffered severe social and racial discrimination as a distinctive minority in a class-ridden and racist society.

348 Los polacos en el Perú. (The Poles in Peru.)
Kazimierz Kochanek. Lima: Editorial Salesiana, 1979. 200p. map.

This work does not provide a particularly coherent account of Polish immigration. However, its general coverage of the careers of individual Polish immigrants of note in the 19th and 20th centuries succeeds in presenting a reasonable overview of their contribution to Peruvian economic and cultural life. The size of the Polish community in Peru is not given but it is likely to be closer to the 3,000 in Venezuela than the 120,000 in Argentina.

349 The social history of a provincial town: Huancayo, 1890-1972.
Bryan Roberts. In: *Social and economic change in modern Peru.* Edited by Rory Miller, Clifford T. Smith, John Fisher. Liverpool: University of Liverpool, Centre for Latin American Studies, 1976, p. 136-93. (Monograph, 6).

Most studies of internal migration in Peru have concentrated· upon the transfer of settlers from rural areas to Lima. However, the process has also involved the significant growth of towns and cities in the highlands. In the period covered in this rich study the population of the central Andean town of Huancayo grew from 5,000 to 125,000, making it one of Peru's major urban centres. The analysis explains the relative significance of commerce, industry and the service sector in the growth of distinctively urban occupational groups. It is argued, moreover, that, but for urban growth in Huancayo, the social problems caused by mass migration to Lima and other coastal cities would have been even more profound.

350 Taquile en Lima. (Taquile in Lima.)
José Matos Mar. Lima: Fondo Internacional para la Promoción de la Cultura. 1986. 515p.

Taquile is an indigenous community located on a small island in Lake Titicaca, near the Peruvian frontier with Bolivia. When the author of this book came into contact with the community in 1950, its 640 inhabitants were monolingual Quechua speakers, deeply rooted in traditional social, religious and economic practices. In the mid 1950s, as the community's population grew, migration occurred to various locations, including, inevitably, the national capital. This detailed study is built around the oral testimony of seven Taquile families which settled in Lima. It is a dense and highly suggestive work, which considers both the impact of city life upon migrants from rural areas, and the changes wrought in the city by migration.

351 The 'young towns' of Lima: aspects of urbanization in Peru.
Peter Lloyd. Cambridge, England: Cambridge University Press, 1980. 160p. 4 maps. bibliog.

This discussion of the conditions faced in Peruvian cities by migrants from rural areas is based upon a detailed analysis of Medalla Milagrosa, a community of 100 families in Lima. From it, general conclusions are derived about the reasons for internal migration, and about the poor housing conditions experienced by migrants as a consequence of the failure of government and the private sector to provide low-cost housing. One important finding is that, although self-help enables migrants to build modest houses, there is little scope for their movement out of their 'young towns' into more affluent, middle-class areas: the urban population is doomed, therefore, to be starkly divided in perpetuity.

352 **Yugoslavos en el Perú.** (Yugoslavs in Peru.)
   Zivana Meseldzic de Pereyra.   Lima: Editorial La Equidad, 1985.
   240p. bibliog.

Written by a Yugoslav who arrived in Peru in 1969, this study avoids quantification in favour of an impressionistic survey of Slavs who migrated to Peru in the 19th and 20th centuries, and of their contribution to various areas of economic and cultural activity.

Anthropology

353 **Adaptive responses of native Amazonians.**
Edited by Raymond B. Hames, William T. Vickers. New York:
Academic Press, 1983. 516p. map. bibliog.
The native societies of Amazonia hold considerable fascination for many anthropologists. Much of this interest stems from their endemic warfare, rich cosmologies,
varied social structures, and apparent lack of state-level political organization. Their
ability to manage their environment is also of fundamental importance to the analysis
of Amazonian cultural dynamics. The fifteen essays in this collection are all concerned
with ecological anthropology. They are organized, for obvious reasons, not on the
basis of national identity, which means very little to Amazonian societies, but
according to the major modes of subsistence (cultivation, hunting and fishing),
nutrition, and settlement pattern. Several of the essays deal specifically with groups
located in Peruvian Amazonia: Machiguenga, Huambisa, Aguaruna and Cocamilla.

354 **Alpacas, sheep, and men: the wool export economy and regional society
in southern Peru.**
Benjamin S. Orlove. New York: Academic Press, 1977. 270p. bibliog.
This book examines the Sicuani region in southern highland Peru, and traces the
economic and political conflicts that followed its incorporation into the world wool
economy in the late-19th century. It shows that the export economy engendered local
conflicts, in the countryside between landlord and peasant, and in the town between
landlord and merchant. The general theme is to discover and analyse the
anthropological consequences of the metamorphosis of a closed, isolated, local society
into an open one, intregated into national politics and global economics.

355 **An analysis of co-parenthood (*compradazgo*).**
Sidney Wilfred Mintz, Eric Robert Wolf. *Southwestern Journal of
Anthropology*, vol. 6 (1950), p. 341-68.
Co-parenthood, or spiritual kinship, is one of the most pervasive socio-religious
phenomena in the Andean world. It is frequently arranged at festive occasions, such as

baptism or marriage, and confers mutual rights and obligations upon the recipients. This article remains one of the clearest and most concise explanations of its origins and significance.

356 Andean banditry and peasant community organisation, 1882-1930.
Erick D. Langer. In: *Bandidos: the varieties of Latin American banditry*. Edited by Richard W. Slatta. New York: Greenwood, 1987, p.113-30.

Banditry was widespread among rural communities in Peru in the late-19th and early-20th centuries. This essay examines the phenomenon in terms of community resistance to socio-economic exploitation.

357 Andean kinship and marriage.
Edited by Ralph Bolton, Enrique Mayer. Washington, DC: American Anthropological Association, 1977. 298p. map. bibliog.

The twelve essays in this collection were originally presented at a symposium on Andean kinship and marriage held in Toronto in 1972. They derive from detailed study of communities from the whole central Andean region, from the Peru- Ecuador border to Lake Titicaca. The topics covered include marriage ceremonies, trial marriage, family structure, and the complex issues arising from both actual and fictive kinship.

358 Antiguos dioses y nuevos conflictos andinos. (Ancient gods and new Andean conflicts.)
Enrique González Carre, Fermín Rivera Pineda. Ayacucho: Universidad Nacional de San Cristóbal de Huamanga, 1983. 105p. bibliog.

On the basis of ethnographic and anthropological data gathered in the central Peruvian area around Ayacucho, this study explains modern indigenous views of distant events such as the death of the last Inca emperor of Peru. Using the techniques of oral history, it also makes suggestive observations about the relationship between popular religious beliefs and the social disturbances which appeared in the region in the 1960s.

359 At the crossroads of the earth and the sky: an Andean cosmology.
Gary Dwayne Urton. Austin, Texas: University of Texas Press. 248p. 2 maps. bibliog.

In modern Peru, as in Inca times, astronomical observation continues to be of fundamental importance for Indian communities, particularly for the regulation of the agricultural calendar. Derived from extensive field work in the small village of Misminay, near Cuzco, this ethno-astronomical monograph provides a wealth of data on Andean astronomical systems, and social and cultural variations.

360 Campa cosmology.
Gerald Weiss. *Ethnology*, vol. 11, no. 2 (April 1972), p. 157-72.

The Campa Indians of eastern Peru, who were estimated to number about 30,000 when this article was written, occupy a large territory to the west of the Ucayali river. This study argues that their cosmological thinking, at first sight childishly simple to outsiders, represents an adequate and coherent attempt to make sense out of existence on the basis of the limited information available to them.

361 **Carnival and coca leaf: some traditions of the Quechua ayllu.**
Douglas Gifford, Pauline Hoggarth. Edinburgh, London: Scottish
Academic Press, 1976. 111p. bibliog.

The core of this fascinating volume is an account, written in 1963 by two Quechua speakers, of Indian community life in southern Peru. Their narrative is particularly rich on carnival traditions, healing practices, and rites associated with birth, marriage and death. The original text is published in a mixture of Quechua and Spanish, and is accompanied by a translation into English. The work concludes with an account of field work undertaken by the editors in the early 1970s.

362 **The Casinahua of eastern Peru.**
Edited by Jane Powell Dwyer. Providence, Rhode Island: Brown
University, Haffenreffer Museum of Anthropology, 1975. 238p. map.
bibliog.

The Casinahua Indians of eastern Peru had their first contact with Western culture in the 1940s, although their Brazilian counterparts were contacted by rubber workers and priests at the beginning of the 20th century. This extremely well-illustrated book, based upon museum materials and field work, describes their social organization, rituals, and economic activities.

363 **A community in the Andes: problems and progress in Muquiyauyo.**
Richard N. Adams. Seattle, Washington: University of Washington
Press, 1959. 251p. 3 maps. bibliog.

The mountain community of Muquiyauyo, in the department of Huancayo, was identified in the 1940s by a number of anthropologists as possessing progressive traits. This book, the result of field work carried out in 1949-50 to explore the nature of this progressivism, provides an outstanding description of life in the community, and is particularly rich on the relationships between *mestizos* and Indians.

364 **Ecology and exchange in the Andes.**
Edited by David Lehmann. Cambridge, England: Cambridge
University Press, 1982. 245p. 2 maps. bibliog.

Four of the eight essays in this collection refer specifically to Peru, and two of the general discussions also draw heavily upon Peruvian material. The basic question which they all address is: in what ways has the impact of market penetration and capitalist development on the peasant economy in the Andean countries been shaped by a heritage of political culture and the characteristics of ecology and climate?

365 **Hualcan: life in the highlands of Peru.**
William W. Stein. Ithaca, New York: Cornell University Press, 1961.
383p. 2 maps. bibliog.

The materials upon which this monograph is based were gathered in the early 1950s in the independent, landowning Indian village of Hualcan, located in the mountains of central Peru, between Lima and Trujillo. It provides a fascinating account of the community's internal dynamics, of its social and economic problems, and of the changes being wrought by its gradual incorporation into the Peruvian national political economy.

Anthropology

366 Indians of South America.
Paul Radin. New York: Greenwood, 1942. 324p. bibliog.

This sound general survey gives specific attention to Peruvian anthropology in chapters dealing with the tribes of the Amazon basin (p. 113-37) and the Aymara people of the central Andes (p. 277-96). There are also chapters of a more historical nature on the Quechua people.

367 Inequality in the Peruvian Andes: class and ethnicity in Cuzco.
Pierre L. van den Berghe, George P. Primov.   Columbia, Missouri;
London: University of Missouri Press, 1977. 324p. map. bibliog.

Class and ethnicity are the two most widespread forms of group inequality in large-scale complex societies. However, although class and ethnic differences interact with each other in very complex ways, the two phenomena are qualitatively different, and must be kept analytically distinct. This rich study documents in detail the interplay between those class and ethnic factors that exist in the region of Cuzco.

368 Kuyo Chico: applied anthropology in an Indian community.
Oscar Nuñez del Prado.   Chicago: University of Chicago Press, 1973.
162p. map.

In the mid 1960s the author, who taught in the department of anthropology in the University of Cuzco, directed an applied anthropology project in the nearby impoverished rural community of Kuyo Chico. Its purpose was to modify living conditions by attempting to break down the local power structure, notably the community's dependence upon the district capital of Pisac, through methods adjusted to local customs. The book provides a step-by-step account of the way in which his team went about introducing changes in political and economic organization, education, health and housing.

369 Land and power in Latin America: agrarian economies and social processes in the Andes.
Edited by Benjamin S. Orlove, Glynn Custred.   New York: Holmes & Meier, 1980. 258p. bibliog.

The twelve essays in this volume attempt to explain the relationship between attitudes to agrarian structures and socio-cultural factors in the highlands of Peru. For example, that by Orlove on 'The position of rustlers in regional society: social banditry in the Andes' demonstrates that cattle rustling is dictated by not only economic necessity but also by community resistance to exploitation by powerful, non-Indian landowners.

370 Marriage practices in lowland South America.
Edited by Kenneth M. Kensinger.   Urbana, Illinois; Chicago:
University of Illinois Press, 1984. 297p. map. bibliog.

As befits a series of essays concerning tribal groups who are in most cases ignorant of national boundaries, this volume begins with a general analysis of marriage rules and the definition of marriage in lowland South American societies, by Judith Shapiro (p. 1-30). The editor's discussion of marriage practices among the Casinahua is of particular interest for Peruvianists (p. 221-51).

371 **Moon, sun and witches: gender ideologies and class in Inca and colonial Peru.**
Irene Silverblatt.   Princeton, New Jersey: Princeton University Press, 1987. 266p. bibliog.

Examining the interplay between gender ideologies and political hierarchy, this rich and compelling analysis shows how women were relegated to a secondary rôle in society during both the Inca and Spanish periods in Peru. During the colonial period, those who resisted politically or socially were frequently accused of witchcraft. This study is of major significance to those who wish to understand gender relationships in the modern Andean world.

372 **Mountain of the condor: metaphor and ritual in an Andean *ayllu*.**
Joseph W. Bastien.   Prospect Heights, Illinois: Waveland, 1978. 227p. map. bibliog.

This detailed anthropological study of the Aymara *ayllu*, or community, of Kata focuses on a unique group of diviners and soothsayers. The community of forty-six men and sixty-one women lies north east of Lake Titicaca, near the Bolivian frontier with Peru; it has been visited since pre-Inca times by Indians from a wide area of the central Andes in search of cures and fortune-telling. The valuable analysis provides fascinating data on rituals, beliefs and symbolism, and should be read by any serious student of Andean anthropology.

373 **Nacimiento de una utopia: muerte y resurrección de los incas.** (Birth of a utopia: the death and resurrection of the Incas.)
Manuel Burga.   Lima: Instituto de Apoyo Agrario, 1988. 428p. bibliog.

The attitudes of the indigenous peoples of Peru since the 17th century towards the history of the Inca civilization are examined in this fascinating analysis of documents, oral tradition and folklore. The central theme concerns the way in which immediate post-conquest pessimism about the destruction of the Inca world was transformed into an enduring conviction that the last Inca emperor will be resurrected to restore traditional cultural values.

374 **Native peoples of South America.**
Julian H. Steward, Louis C. Faron.   New York: McGraw-Hill, 1959. 481p.

This superb work of synthesis combines historical analysis with anthropological discussion. The chapter on 'Native central Andean culture of the historic era' (p. 119-73) is particularly impressive.

375 **Pastores de puna.** (Pastoralists of the *puna*.)
Edited by Jorge A. Flores Ochoa.   Lima: Instituto de Estudios Peruanos, 1977. 305p. bibliog.

Since time immemorial a multitude of communities in the high plateau, or *puna*, 4,000 metres above sea level in southern Peru, have built their existence around the grazing of Andean cameloids. The ten essays in this collection, three of them by the editor, examine these Quechua and Aymara pastoral communities from ecological, ethnographic and socio-political standpoints, providing much valuable information about

Anthropology

their social organization, their religious beliefs, and their socio-economic relationships of exchange with agricultural communities.

376 **The peasants of El Dorado: conflict and contradiction in a Peruvian frontier settlement.**
Robin Shoemaker. Ithaca, New York: Cornell University Press, 1981. 265p. map. bibliog.

This anthropological study, based upon field work undertaken in 1973-75, moves away from the traditional highland area to the eastern jungle settlement of Satipo, a town of about 5,000 inhabitants serving as the economic and social centre for a widely scattered population of 38,000. The conclusion moves beyond the bounds of pure anthropology to argue that the principal barrier to Satipo's development lies not in its internal socio-cultural conflicts but in the problem of 'internal colonialism'. This, by producing terms of trade which are unfavourable to the settlers, inhibits progress in the areas of housing, education, health and nutrition.

377 **Peasants, power, and applied social change: Vicos as a model.**
Edited by Henry F. Dobyns, Paul L. Doughty, Harold D. Laswell. Beverly Hills, California; London: Sage, 1964. 237p. bibliog.

Located in the department of Ancash, north of Lima, the Vicos area attracted a great deal of attention in the 1950s as the focus of a collaborative project, undertaken by Peru's National Indian Institute and anthropologists from Cornell University, to improve the standard of living of its few thousand rural highland Indians. The rôle of the anthropologists, apart from furnishing research funds from US foundations, was to employ their skills as data collectors to find out what the Indians themselves wanted, and to advise the various official organizations which became involved of how to develop the project within the framework of current principles of social and cultural change. The editors themselves contributed five of the eight chapters of this volume, which analyses and explains the anthropological significance of the project.

378 **Peasants, primitives, and proletariats: the struggle for identity in South America.**
Edited by David L. Browman, Ronald A. Schwarz. The Hague; Paris; New York: Mouton, 1979. 429p. bibliog.

This collection of essays, the initial versions of which were read at the 1973 International Congress of Anthropological and Ethnological Sciences, deals with the inter-relations of the people of South America and their social institutions. Two of the contributions are concerned exclusively with Peru (p. 125-47, 253-66), and Peruvian issues also feature prominently in several of the general discussions, including that of Xavier Albó on 'The future of oppressed languages in the Andes' (p. 267-88).

379 **Peruvian contexts of change.**
Edited by William W. Stein. New Brunswick, New Jersey: Transaction Books; Oxford: Clio Distribution Service, 1985. 400p. bibliog.

The five anthropological essays in this volume deal with contemporary socio-economic conditions in a country facing enormous problems, without easy access to the wealth needed to alleviate them. Of particular interest is the contribution by Luis Millones

80

(p. 56-123), which focuses on the lumpen proletariat of Lima, the so-called marginal masses, against the historical background of ethnicity.

380 **Resistance, rebellion and consciousness in the Andean peasant world: eighteenth to twentieth centuries.**
Edited by Steve J. Stern. Madison, Wisconsin: University of Wisconsin Press, 1988. 446p. 9 maps. bibliog.

This volume contains a series of essays on Andean rebellion during the last 200 years. The most original and provocative contributions on Peru include analyses by Jan Szeminski and Frank Salomon of the cultural aspects of native resistance in the 18th century, and Heraclio Bonilla's thoughtful critique of recent writings on peasant revolts in the 19th century.

381 **La situación del indígena en América del Sur.** (The situation of the indigenous inhabitants of South America.)
Edited by Georg Grunberg. Montevideo: Tierra Nueva, 1972. 510p.

The twenty chapters in this comprehensive survey of the situation of the indigenous peoples of South America are concerned primarily with lowland societies. Detailed coverage of the groups located in eastern Peru is provided in the contribution of Stefano Varese, which pays particular attention to inter-ethnic relations, linguistics, and the juridical status of tribal groups (p. 157-99).

382 **Sociedad e ideología: ensayos de historia y antropología andinas.**
(Society and ideology: essays on Andean history and anthropology.)
Nathan Wachtel. Lima: Instituto de Estudios Peruanos, 1973. 228p. bibliog.

Four key essays by the leading French specialist on Andean history and anthropology are contained in this volume. Although they focus upon historical themes (the social organization of Inca Cuzco, reciprocity in the Inca state, the destructuration of the Andean world in the colonial period, and acculturation) they are essential reading for the modern anthropologist because of the insight which they provide into indigenous attitudes and mentalities.

383 **Spirits, shamans, and stars: perspectives from South America.**
Edited by David L. Browman, Ronald A. Schwarz. The Hague; Paris; New York: Mouton, 1979. 276p. bibliog.

The collection of papers in this volume deals with the patterns of thought of the populations and cultures of South America, and with their symbolic and expressive aspects. The chapters of particular relevance to Peru include two dealing with psychotropic drugs, and two on medical anthropology (p. 39-62, 149-56, 223-32).

384 **Tobacco and shamanism in South America.**
Johannes Wilbert. New Haven, Connecticut: Yale University Press, 1987. 294p. 8 maps. bibliog.

Tobacco-producing plants, or *nicotanias*, are native to the Americas, and, as such, are widely used, particularly in lowland areas for ritual purposes. This specialized monograph is organized thematically – its principal sections deal with methods of consumption, pharmacology and shamanism – and there are frequent references to the practices of Indians in Peruvian Amazonia.

385 **To defend ourselves: ecology and ritual in an Andean Village.**
Billie Jean Isbell. Austin, Texas: University of Texas Press, 1978.
289p. bibliog.

This impressive monograph explains the cultural relationship between complex socio-
religious rituals and the adaptation of indigenous communities to the needs of their
environment in Andean highland communities. The relationship between ritual and the
agricultural cycle is shown to be particularly close.

386 **To hunt in the morning.**
Janet Siskind. New York: Oxford University Press, 1973. 214p. map.

The Sharanahua Indians live on the upper Purus river of eastern Peru, near the
frontier with Brazil. This detailed anthropological study provides a sympathetic
account of their culture and history, their view of the world, their economic activities,
and their medicinal practices.

387 **Tsewa's gift: magic and meaning in an Amazonian society.**
Michael F. Brown. Washington, DC, London: Smithsonian
Institution Press, 1985. 220p. 3 maps. bibliog.

The Agurana Jivaro Indians of the Alto Rio Mayo in eastern Peru come under detailed
scrutiny in this study of magical practices among the native people of the Upper
Amazon. It is argued that magic makes sense to the Agurana, given their
representations of reality, for they do not think of it as an activity qualitatively
different from religion, mythology, or even practical action.

388 **Urban anthropology in Lima: an overview.**
James M. Wallace. *Latin American Research Review*, vol. 14, no. 3
(1984), p. 57-85.

The city of Lima has been the subject of a relatively large number of anthropological
studies during the last thirty years. However, no ethnography of the entire city has
been attempted, and the research has tended to be concerned with comparatively small
units, such as squatter settlements and the highland migrant. The survey discusses,
within a typological framework, the ethnographic studies which have been carried out,
and attempts to describe and integrate their nature, focus and methods.

389 **Vegetalismo: shamanism among the mestizo population of the Peruvian
Amazon.**
Luis Eduardo Luna. Stockholm: Almquist & Wiksell, 1986. 202p.
map. bibliog.

There has been a general upsurge of interest among anthropologists in recent years in
both shamanism and psychotropic plants. This book provides a detailed analysis of
both phenomena among the *mestizo* inhabitants of the Peruvian Amazon, showing the
clear continuity with respect to shamanism among ethnic groups of the Upper Amazon
area. The most important of these ideas include the belief that some animals and plants
have powerful spirits from which knowledge and power can be derived, and that in
order to learn from plants it is necessary to follow rigorous dietary prescriptions and
sexual segregation.

390 **The warm valley people: duality and land reform among the Quechua Indians of highland Peru.**
Harold O. Skar. Oslo: Universitetsforlaget, 1982. 350p. 5 maps. bibliog.

Built around a detailed analysis of the impact of land reform in the 1970s upon the southern Peruvian Quechua-speaking community of Matapuquio, this monograph makes an important contribution to the general field of social anthropology. It demonstrates, at one level, the real benefits derived by the community from the land reform process, and, more profoundly, the impact of the intrusion of sources of power external to the community upon its traditional principles of dual organization.

391 **Warriors, gods & spirits from Central & South American mythology.**
Douglas Gifford, John Sibick. London: Peter Lowe, 1983. 132p.

Copiously illustrated with dramatic colour pictures, this study of Indian myths is designed for junior readers. It contains a section on Inca mythology, and it also discusses the contemporary beliefs of both highland and lowland Indians in Peru.

392 **Women of the Andes: patriarchy and social change in two Peruvian towns.**
Susan C. Bourque, Kay Barbara Warren. Ann Arbor, Michigan: University of Michigan Press, 1981. 241p. 2 maps. bibliog.

This study is based upon field work undertaken in two remote Peruvian settlements, Mayobamba (with ca. 250 residents) and Chiuchin (with ca. 450 residents), lying on the western slopes of the Andes between Lima and Cerro de Pasco. It presents an ethnographic account of the lives of the women in the communities, and then attempts to relate the authors' findings to general analytic models and theories about women's experiences.

Linguistics

393 **Argot limeña o jerga criolla del Perú.** (The slang of Lima or the creole jargon of Peru.)
Guillermo E. Bendezú Neyra. Lima: Editorial Universo, 1977. 339p. bibliog.

The essential purpose of this work is to present a dictionary of slang which is spoken in the city of Lima. The alphabetical entries are preceded by a somewhat humorous discussion of 'lexical barbarism' and other general characteristics of local speech.

394 **Attitudes towards Spanish and Quechua in bilingual Peru.**
Wolfgang Wölck. In: *Language attitudes: current trends and prospects.* Edited by Roger W. Shuy, Ralph W. Fasold. Washington, DC: Georgetown University Press, 1973, p. 129-47.

Quechua is the largest surviving native language in the Americas, spoken still by an estimated seven million people, the bulk of them in the southern and central Peruvian Andes. This paper describes the results of a socio-linguistic survey of Quechua-Spanish bilingualism upon which the author embarked in 1969. One of the significant findings was that, although Quechua was stigmatized in terms of identifiable social status, there was a great deal of affective native loyalty shown to the language, as measured by testing.

395 **Aula quechua.** (Quechua lecture theatre.)
Edited by Rodolfo Cerrón-Palomino. Lima: Ediciones Signo, 1982. 277p. bibliog.

In 1579, the Spanish viceregal authorities established a chair of Quechua in the Lima University of San Marcos. The majority of the essays in this collection were presented by US and Peruvian scholars at a conference held in 1979 to mark the fourth centenary of the chair's creation. They include synchronic and diachronic linguistic studies, socio-linguistic studies, and discussions of ethno-history and teaching methods. They provide an excellent overview of the state of modern Quechua studies.

396 Ayacucho Quechua grammar and dictionary.
Gary John Parker.   The Hague, Paris: Mouton, 1969. 221p. map. bibliog.

Ayacucho Quechua is spoken by about a million persons in the highlands of the south-central Peruvian departments of Ayacucho, Huancavelica and Apurimac. It is closely related to the Cuzco and Bolivian dialects, spoken to the east and south east, but is quite distinct from the central Peruvian dialects to be found north of Huancavelica. This detailed analysis of Ayacucho Quechua contains a dictionary of 4,000 entries, representing the entire dialect area; the accompanying grammatical description is set in the immediate constituent format, and is oriented toward an exhaustive statement of morphological constructions.

397 Aymara and Spanish in southern Peru: the relationship of language to economic class and social identity.
Michael Painter.   In: *Bilingualism: social issues and policy implications*. Edited by Andrew W. Miracle, Jr. Athens, Georgia: University of Georgia Press, 1983, p. 22-37.

This paper describes aspects of social or ethnic identity and their relationship to economic class in the bilingual setting of the Moho district of southern Peru, where Spanish and Aymara share a complex inter-relationship with the social and economic structure of the district. It makes the interesting point that there are considerable economic advantages to be had from speaking Aymara, particularly as Aymara-speakers who acquire local economic and political power tend to bestow their largesse on people with origins similar to their own.

398 The Aymara language in its social and cultural context: a collection of essays on aspects of Aymara language and culture.
Edited by M. J. Hardman.   Gainesville, Florida: University Presses of Florida, 1981. 317p. bibliog.

The Aymara people, numbering approximately two million, are concentrated in southern Peru and Bolivia. Although they are primarily an agricultural people, there are now considerable numbers of them in Lima. Altogether, about half a million Peruvians speak Aymara. This volume is oriented primarily towards Bolivia, its basic purpose being to explain how the Aymara see themselves, but it is also of relevance for Peruvianists.

399 Contributions towards a grammar and dictionary of Quechua, the language of the Incas of Peru.
Clements R. Markham.   Osnabrück, GFR: Biblio Verlag, 1972. 2nd ed. 223p.

The English geographer Markham undertook prolonged visits to Peru in 1853 and 1860. Unlike many members of the contemporary Peruvian élite, who looked outwards to Europe for cultural inspiration, he took a deep interest in the language and history of the country's indigenous people. His dictionary and study of Quechua grammar, first published in 1864, is a serious work of scholarship, which enables modern scholars to evaluate shifts in the pronunciation and the meaning of words since the mid-19th century.

Linguistics

400 Diccionario Quechua: Cuzco-Collao. (Quecheua dictionary: Cuzco-Collao.)

Antonio Cusihuaman G.   Lima: Ministerio de Educación, 1976. 303p.

The Quechua dialect which is spoken in the department of Cuzco is one of the two most important of the six basic varieties known in Peru; the other is the Quechua of Ayacucho which has a distinctive phonology and lexicon. Prepared by a native Quechua speaker from the Vilcanota valley, this useful, unpretentious dictionary aims to provide a basic guide to the principal words and phrases in current use in the Cuzco-Collao region.

401 Diccionario tri-lingüe Quechua de Cusco: Quechua, English, Castellano.

(Trilingual dictionary of the Quechua of Cuzco: Quechua, English, Castilian.) Esteban Hornberger, Nancy Hornberger.   La Paz, Bolivia: Qoya Rami, 1983. 2nd ed. 598p.

First published in 1978 (Cuzco: Qhapaq Raymi), this tri-lingual dictionary (Quechua-English/Quechua-Spanish) is based upon current Quechua usage in the Cuzco department, and is particularly authoritative on the dialects spoken in its central valleys.

402 Estudios Quechua: planificación, historia y gramática. (Quechua studies: planning, history and grammar.)

David J. Weber Ch.   Yarinacocha, Peru: Ministerio de Educación, Instituto Lingüístico de Verano, 1987. 172p. bibliog. (Serie Lingüística Peruana, no 27).

The Summer Institute of Linguistics is based in Yarinacocha, in the department of Pucallpa. During the last thirty years, it has gradually been entrusted, by the Peruvian state, with broad responsibility for research and teaching in applied linguistics, primarily in the eastern lowlands but also in the highlands. This contribution to a series of volumes on specific languages, written by a US scholar, provides interesting data on language planning, and on the morphology and number system of Quechua.

403 Estudios sobre el español de Lima. (Studies of the Spanish of Lima.)

Rocio Caravedo.   Lima: Universidad Católica del Perú, 1983. 164p. bibliog.

This detailed computer-based study of the contextual variation of the sibilant in the city of Lima is strictly for the specialist in phonetics.

404 Expansión del Quechua: primeros contactos con el castellano. (The expansion of Quechua: the first contacts with Spanish.)

Ibico Rojas Rojas.   Lima: Ediciones Signo, 1980. 131p. bibliog.

The basic aim of the neat synthesis is to outline the factors which led to the expansion of Quechua, to become the dominant indigenous language in Peru by the early-16th century. The conclusion that these factors were primarily economic, military and religious is not particularly original, but the analysis is clear and helpful.

405 **El futuro de los idiomas oprimidos en los Andes.** (The future of the oppressed languages of the Andes.)
Xavier Albó. Lima: Universidad Nacional Mayor de San Marcos, Centro de Investigación de Lingüística Aplicada, 1977. 28p. bibliog. (Documentos de Trabajo, 33).

As the title of this polemical (and influential) paper indicates, its Jesuit author was not impressed by official schemes in Peru and Bolivia in the 1970s to elevate the status of Aymara and Quechua in the bilingual regions of both countries. He argues firmly in favour of the increased use of native languages by the media of social communication, especially radio, in an attempt to convince their speakers that their illiteracy was not a sign of inferiority.

406 **The grouping of South American Indian languages.**
Mary Ritchie Key. Tübingen, GFR: Gunter Narr Verlag, 1979. 170p. 7 maps. bibliog.

The purpose of this book was to provide a general survey of the linguistic work done on South American languages by the late 1970s, and to collect information on current research projects from all the countries except Brazil. It succeeded in its primary task of providing scholars with a source book for further study. In terms of disciplinary range, the discussion concentrates heavily upon phonology rather than grammatical comparisons. There is specific, although not exclusive, discussion of Peru in a long chapter on Andean-equatorial languages (p. 42-83).

407 **Habla la ciudad.** (The city speaks.)
Juan Zevallos (et al.). Lima: Universidad Nacional Mayor de San Marcos, 1986. 174p.

This volume presents oral testimony collected in central Lima by students of the School of Literature of the University of San Marcos in 1986. It throws light upon the daily lives of poor people and their images of themselves and their environment. Its principal significance, however, is that it reveals the 'poetry of current speech', that is the order in which words are used, and the syntactic combinations.

408 **Hablando Quechua con el pueblo.** (Speaking Quechua to the people.)
Juan Antonio Manya Ambur. Cuzco: Instituto Lingüístico y Folklórico Quechua y Aimara, [n.d.]. 48p. map.

The simple, systematic guide to Quechua provides translations of basic words and phrases into Spanish and English. It is designed to provide a grounding in the language for social scientists and other professionals whose work brings them into contact with monolingual Quechua speakers.

409 **Handbook of Amazonian languages: volume 1.**
Edited by Desmond C. Derbyshire, Geoffrey K. Pullum. Berlin, GFR: Mouton de Gruyter, 1986. 642p. map. bibliog.

This volume, the first of a planned series of three on the languages of Amazonia, is intended to increase the accessibility of descriptive and interpretive material relating to their grammatical structure, in the hope that specialists in the mainstream of linguistics will accommodate them in their general surveys of linguistic phenomena. Of particular relevance for Peruvianists is the chapter by Mary Ruth Wise on 'Grammatical characteristics of preAndine Arawakan languages of Peru' (p. 567-642).

Linguistics

410 **Language shift among migrants to Lima, Peru.**
Sarah K. Myers. Chicago, Illinois: University of Chicago,
Department of Geography, 203p. 8 maps. bibliog.

Language is a primary cultural indicator in Peru, as it is in many Latin American countries where miscegenation has been occurring for centuries. This socio-linguistic study is basically a micro-level analysis of the geography of languages, dealing with the cultural implications of how much and in what contexts Quechua-speaking migrants from the Andean highlands use Spanish in Lima.

411 **Las lenguas de los andes centrales.**(The languages of the central Andes.)
Thomas Th. Büttner, translated from the German by Sandra Luz
Franco. Madrid: Ediciones Cultura Hispánica, 1983. 269p. 4 maps.
bibliog.

The aim of this work is to clarify the relationships that exist between the so-called 'central Andean' languages, in particular Quechua and Aymara, but also Haquera and Callahuaya. It goes beyond a merely genetic consideration to examine typologies and spatial aspects, factors of particular significance for the classification of languages that do not have a significant written tradition.

412 **The mutual influences of Spanish and Andean languages.**
M. J. Hardman. *Word*, vol. 33, nos. 1-2 (1982), p. 143-57.

Less than ten per cent of Peru's population are monolingual Quechua speakers, but many more are bilingual in Spanish and Quechua. Inevitably, the latter group finds it impossible to entirely separate the two languages, and words and phrases from each language have invaded the other. This brief but incisive article clearly outlines the process of interchange.

413 **Una nación accoralada: southern Peruvian Quechua language planning
and politics in historical perspective.**
Bruce Mannheim. *Language in Society*, vol. 13, no. 3 (1984),
p. 291-309.

According to the 1972 national census, some two million inhabitants of southern Peru were Quechua speakers. The military government faced this reality thereafter by formally recognizing Quechua as an official language, equal (at least in theory) to Spanish. This article traces both the implications of the change in official attitudes in the 1970s, and the long history of formal and informal discrimination against Quechua.

414 **El negro en el Perú y su transculturación lingüística.** (The Negro in Peru
and his linguistic transculturation.)
Fernando Romero. Lima: Editorial Milla Batres, 1987. 173p. 8 maps.

The basic themes discussed in this work are the ethno-historical aspects of forced Negro migration to Peru in the colonial and early republican periods, and the cultural life of the minority of Negro origin in modern Peru. It concentrates upon speech patterns among the Peruvian communities, mainly small towns on the coast, where the descendants of the country's slave population have had a significant impact on local dialects.

415 **Panorama de la lingüística andina.**
Rodolfo Cerrón-Palomino. *Revista Andina*, vol. 3, no. 2 (Dec. 1985), p. 509-71.
The disciplinary advances in the study of Andean linguistics are explained with admirable clarity in this detailed bibliographical analysis.

416 **Pequeño breviario quechua.** (A brief treatise on Quechua.)
Wolfgang Wölck. Lima: Instituto de Estudios Peruanos, 1987. 101p. bibliog.
Although six different Quechua dialects are spoken in Peru – those of San Martín, Cajamarca, Ancash, Junín, Ayacucho and Cuzco – the German-born author of this work argues that they have a common origin and structure. His study attempts to uncover and describe the structural characteristics of Quechua in general, on the basis of an analytical approach, combining the methodologies of comparative linguistics and linguistic anthropology into what specialists call a 'functional typology'.

417 **Perú: ¿país bilingüe?** (Peru: a bilingual country?)
Alberto Escobar, José Matos Mar, Giorgio Alberti. Lima: Instituto de Estudios Peruanos, 1975. 150p. bibliog.
In 1975, the Peruvian government officially recognized Quechua as a national language, thereby opening up to general scrutiny a number of educational and linguistic problems which hitherto had concerned only a small number of specialists concerned with the marginalization of the speakers of Peru's minority languages. The general thrust of this analysis of former attitudes, current problems and future perspectives, by three such specialists, was an insistence that the recognition of Quechua, welcome though it was, would not in itself create a homogeneous, bilingual society.

418 **Quechua: manual de enseñanza.** (Quechua: teaching manual.)
Clodoaldo Soto Ruiz. Lima: Instituto de Estudios Peruanos, 1979. 444p.
In the mid 1970s the Peruvian government attempted both to elevate the status of Quechua as a national language, and, in practical terms, to encourage the country's Spanish-speaking majority to learn it as a second language. This teaching manual, designed for use by both teachers and students, embraces an explanation of Quechua grammar and vocabulary, and a systematic series of practical lessons. It is based upon the Ayacucho-Chanca dialect, which the author considers to be somewhat easier for the Spanish-speaker to acquire than the Cuzco-Collao variety.

419 **Quechua's loss, Spanish's gain.**
Claire Lefebvre. *Language in Society*, vol. 8 (1979), p. 395-407.
Drawing upon data from the bilingual Cuzco region, this paper illustrates an aspect of the adaptive property of languages, by showing that a loss of function by a language may entail a loss of a particular linguistic distinction. The discussion is somewhat technical, but should be referred to by actual or would-be specialists in linguistics.

Linguistics

420 **El Quechua y la historia social andina.** (Quechua and the social history of the Andes.)
Alfredo Torero.   Lima: Universidad Ricardo Palma, Dirección Universitaria de Investigación, 1974. 240p. map. bibliog.

This superb synthesis is divided into two sections. The first explains the number and the present situation of the languages of the Quechua family and their speakers; the second examines the social factors which have influenced the expansion and contraction of Quechua since pre-conquest times, and considers the broader issue of how any language can be turned from a cohesive social force into a vehicle of social disintegration and ideological penetration if extreme forces use it as a weapon against those who speak it.

421 **El reto del multilingüísmo en el Perú.** (The challenge of multilingualism in Peru.)
Edited by Alberto Escobar.   Lima: Instituto de Estudios Peruanos, 1972. 281p. bibliog.

The ten essays in this collection were all written by specialists on multilingualism in Peru. They seek, first, to explain the extent of multilingualism, and then to examine the pedagogical and psychological implications of the phenomenon. Although the general thrust of the discussion is somewhat subjective – it argues the need for a profound change in official attitudes towards Peru's linguistic diversity – it presents a great deal of valuable objective data.

422 **South American Indian languages: retrospect and prospect.**
Edited by Harriet E. Manelis Klein, Louisa R. Stark.   Austin, Texas: University of Texas Press, 1985. 863p. bibliog.

Knowledge and understanding of South American Indian languages has advanced considerably since 1950 when J. Alden Mason, a specialist contributor to the *Handbook of South American Indians*, described the sub-continent as 'the region of greatest linguistic diversity in the world, and of the greatest ignorance concerning the native languages' (vol. 6, 1950, p. 163). Although several partial classifications have been published since then, this volume represents the first comprehensive attempt to provide both the general and the specialist reader with detailed data on the current status of the Indian languages of South America. The first section contains ten chapters on lowland languages, within which Mary Ruth Wise's discussion of the history and current status of the indigenous languages of lowland Peru (p. 194-223) is of particular relevance.   The second section contains seven chapters on Andean indigenous languages, including Bruce Mannheim's discussion of southern Peruvian Quechua (p. 481-515), and M. J. Hardman's analysis of the relationships between Aymara and Quechua (p. 617-43).

423 **Syntactic modularity.**
Gabriella Hermon.   Dordrecht, The Netherlands; Cinnaminson, New Jersey: Foris, 1985. 265p. bibliog.

Strictly for the specialist in linguistics, this book examines how the modular nature of Government and Binding Theory provides an explanation of the differing properties of non-normative subjects cross-linguistically. It provides a detailed and systematic description of complex constructions in Imbabura Quechua, a dialect of the Ecuadorian highlands and of Huanca Quechua, which is spoken in the Peruvian department of Junín.

424 **Variaciones sociolinguísticas del castellano en el Perú.** (Socio-linguistic variations in the Spanish of Peru.)
Alberto Escobar.   Lima: Instituto de Estudios Peruanos, 1978. 179p. bibliog.

The basic aim of this original analysis is to investigate the nature of the Spanish spoken in a multicultural, multilingual country. The basic conclusion is that it falls into two principal categories: the Spanish spoken by those for whom it is the mother tongue, and the quite distinct version spoken by Quechua and Aymara speakers, who have acquired it as a second language.

Religion

425 **El dios creador andino.** (The Andean creator god.)
   Franklin Pease. Lima: Mosca Azul, 1973. 149p. bibliog.
The idea of a creator god has been fundamental to all Andean religious beliefs since long before the Spanish conquest. Designed for relatively popular consumption, this useful study draws upon both traditional written sources and current myths to explain this central theme, which is of continuing importance to the social and political organization of Andean indigenous communities.

426 **Estructuras andinas del poder: ideología religiosa y política.** (Andean
   power structure: religious ideology and politics.)
   María Rostworowski de Diez Canseco. Lima: Instituto de Estudios
   Peruanos, 1983. 202p. bibliog.
The first part of this complex study analyses the religious, political and military organization of the Inca empire, with particular reference to its major and minor deities, heroes and divine couples; the second part considers the Inca socio-political structure, showing that there, too, dualism was of fundamental importance.

427 **Estudios sobre religión campesina.** (Studies of peasant religion.)
   Manuel M. Marzal. Lima: Universidad Católica del Perú, 1977. 306p.
   bibliog.
The three studies in this stimulating collection, by a well-known Peruvian Jesuit, deal with peasant images of God, indigenous marriage ceremonies, and general religious attitudes among the Peruvian peasantry.

428 **Fishers of men or founders of empire: the Wycliffe bible translators in
   Latin America.**
   David Stoll. London: Zed, 1982. 344p. 6 maps. bibliog.
This somewhat unusual book is basically a critique of the world's largest international organization working with indigenous people, the Summer Institute of Linguistics,

which has been active in Peru for over forty years. It is argued that, although SIL cultivates a non-sectarian, scientific image, its primary purpose is to propagate evangelical Christianity in each community it enters. This policy, especially when it receives government backing, leads to the elevation in each indigenous group of 'believers' who share SIL's convictions, a process which undermines the cohesion of native communities.

429 **'The heart has its reasons': predicaments of missionary Christianity in early colonial Peru.**
Sabine MacCormack. *Hispanic American Historical Review*, vol. 65, no. 3 (Aug. 1985), p. 443-66.

This article discusses Spanish missionary strategies in early colonial Peru, and suggests that the leaders of the Church failed to understand the Indian view that conversion consisted of nothing more than an organic transition rather than a process requiring the wholesale destruction of earlier beliefs and observances. Consequently, the institutional Church was able to relate only to the Spanish minority of the population of Peru, and much of the countryside remained essentially 'pagan'.

430 **Ideología mesiánica del mundo andino.** (Messianic ideology of the Andean world.)
Edited by Juan M.Ossio Acuña. Lima: Ignacio Prado Pastor, 1973. 2nd ed. 477p.

This series of essays, by both Peruvian and foreign anthropologists, is concerned with the continuing influence of memories of the Inca past in messianic religious and protest movements in Peru, from the 16th century to present times.

431 **La iglesia en el Perú: su historia social desde la independencia.** (The Church in Peru: its social history since independence.)
Jeffrey Klaiber Lima: Universidad Católica del Perú, 1988. 530p. bibliog.

The Jesuit author points out in his preface that the steady stream of recent publications on popular religion and liberation theology in Peru has tended to obscure the lack of a reliable, modern history of the Church as an institution. This work partially fills the gap by providing an excellent coverage of its development from the early-19th century until the visit of Pope John Paul II in 1985. Its emphasis is upon the 'social' history of the Church, that is the dynamic relationship which it has enjoyed with Peruvian society, including not only the upper and middle class, but also the popular masses.

432 **La iglesia en Perú y Bolivia: estructuras eclesiásticas.** (The Church in Peru and Bolivia: ecclesiastical structures.)
Isidoro Alonso (et al.) Madrid: Oficina Internacional de Investigaciones Sociales, 1961. 271p. 11 maps.

Published for the International Federation of Catholic Institutes for Social and Socioreligious Research (FERES), this handbook provides a wealth of administrative and organizational data on ecclesiastical structures (for example, parochical boundaries) and on the numbers of clergy and their distribution in Peru.

Religion

433 **Las nuevas sectas en el Perú.** (The new sects in Peru.)
José María Carreras. Lima: Compañia de Jesus, 1983. 79p. bibliog.
This brief critique of 'the new sects' is designed primarily for the use of clergy in Peru, who are called upon to advise confused Catholics about the extent to which they might participate in their worship. The 'sects' which are described and condemned, and which, according to the Jesuit author 'have spread rapidly through our country and have numerous centres not only in Lima but also in the principal cities of our country' include the 'Mahikari' and 'Krishna' movements, and an evangelical group called 'The Children of God'.

434 **Pilgrims of the Andes: regional cults in Cusco.**
Michael J. Sallnow. Washington, DC, London: Smithsonian
Institution Press, 1987. 351p. 10 maps. bibliog.
The ethnographic basis for this study was established during a long period of field work in the Peruvian Andes (1973-74), most of it in the community of Qamawara, province of Calca, in the department of Cuzco. It consists primarily of a study of the sacred landscape of the Andean peasantry, which explains how and why people and resources are periodically mobilized around certain holy objects and sites, and how the religious geography defined by such movements adapts and transforms itself with the passage of time.

435 **Radicalización y conflicto en la iglesia peruana.** (Radicalization and conflict in the Peruvian Church.)
Luís Pasará. Lima: El Virrey, 1986. 172p. bibliog.
The radicalization of a sector of the Peruvian Church during the last three decades is examined and explained in this study by a former member of the National Union of Catholic Students. On the basis of a comparative analysis of radicalization in Brazil, Chile, Argentina, El Salvador and Nicaragua, it is argued that the Peruvian process, which has had significant repercussions for both Church and state, was produced primarily by internal forces of change.

436 **Reflexión sobre la teología de la liberación: perspectivas desde el Perú.**
(Reflections on the theology of liberation: perspectives from Peru.)
Gustavo Gutiérrez (et al.). Iquitos: Centro de Estudios Teológicos de la Amazonia, 1986. 266p.
'Liberation theology' has been a dominant force in the history of the Latin American Church since the Second Conference of Latin American Bishops, held in Medellín (Colombia) in 1968. Drawing on biblical authority and influential words of political and economic analysis, it argued that members of the Church were required to participate actively in the transformation or eradication of the impersonal structures that prevent most Latin Americans from realizing their full human potential or determining their own corporate destinies. In the present work, one of the principal theorists of 'liberation theology' and other Peruvian priests explain its origins and its aims.

437 **Religion, collectivism, and intrahistory: the Peruvian ideal of
     dependence.**
     Fredrick B. Pike. *Journal of Latin American Studies*, vol. 10, no. 2
     (Nov. 1978), p. 239-62.

This complex but significant article discusses the liberation theology movement in
terms of an increasing lower-class rejection of religious beliefs that focus upon 'rewards
in the next world'. It argues that this trend towards the pursuit of individualistic
objectives has been encouraged since the 1960s by the tendency of populist politicians
to abandon the ideal of corporativism in favour of nourishing possessive individualism.

438 **La religión popular en el Perú: informe y diagnóstico.** (Popular religion
     in Peru: report and diagnosis.)
     José Luís González Martínez. Cuzco: Instituto de Pastoral Andina,
     1987. 397p.

Based upon field work and research undertaken between 1979 and 1984, this study
attempts to describe and analyse popular religious manifestations throughout Peru.
The project was vaguely related to the agreement of the Second Conference of Latin
American Bishops, that popular religions should be studied, with the aim of providing
a pastoral ministry more closely related to the religious peculiarities of the people of
the sub-continent.

439 **El sincretismo iberoamericano.** (Iberoamerican syncretism.)
     Manuel M. Marzal. Lima: Universidad Católica del Perú, 1985. 235p.
     bibliog.

Although in the colonial period the majority of the Indians and many of the Negroes of
Latin America were baptised into the Catholic faith imposed by the missionaries, many
groups conserved elements of their original religions as part of their syncretic systems
of belief. This study analyses and compares syncretism by means of a detailed study of
three representative groups in modern Latin America: the Quechuas of Cuzco, the
Mayas of Chiapas (Mexico), and the Negroes of Bahia (Brazil).

440 **A study of the older Protestant missions and churches in Peru and Chile:
     with special reference to the problems of division, nationalism and native
     ministry.**
     Jean Baptiste August Kessler, Jr. Goes, The Netherlands:
     Oosterbaan & Le Cointre, 1967. 369p. 2 maps. bibliog.

This printed version of a doctoral dissertation, presented at the University of Utrecht,
bears the stamp of the deep personal commitment of a missionary who served in Peru
from 1949 until 1958 with the Evangelical Union of South America. It provides a clear,
systematic account of Protestant missionary activity from the early-19th century until
the mid-20th century.

441 **La transformación religiosa peruana.** (The religious transformation of
     Peru.)
     Manuel Marzal. Lima: Universidad Católica del Perú, 1983. 458p.
     bibliog.

In this work, one of the leading authorities on popular religiosity and liberation
theology in contemporary Peru looks back to the colonial period to analyse the

religious transformation wrought in the early years by Spanish missionaries. Its basic theme, supported by a rigorous utilization of anthropological analysis, is that the syncretism identified by previous commentators should be explained in terms of a Catholic-Andean continuum: 'two small half-moons representing aspects of the Catholic system which were never inserted into the indigenous world (for example, a native clergy) and aspects of Andean religions which were never Christianized (for example, the cult of Pachamama)'.

442 **Viracocha: the nature and antiquity of the Andean high god.**
Arthur A. Demarest. Cambridge, Massachusetts: Harvard University, Peabody Museum of Archaeology and Ethnology, 1981. 88p. bibliog.

A brief monograph on the Andean celestial high god of the pre-Conquest era, this draws upon both established interpretations and recent breakthroughs in ethnography, ethno-history, and archaeology to show that this ancient manifold creator and sky deity dominated the state religion of the Tiahuanaco-Huari and Inca horizons.

Social Conditions

443 Agrarian reform and rural poverty: a case study of Peru.
Tom Alberts. Boulder, Colorado: Westview, 1983. 306p. bibliog.

Initiated in 1969 after the establishment of the Velasco Alvarado military government, Peru's programme for agrarian reform was one of the most thorough and enduring in modern Latin America. Based on extensive data for land ownership, income distribution, and agricultural production, this book assesses Peru's experience with development planning since 1950 and discusses efforts to improve the standard of living of its rural population through changes in the agrarian structure.

444 Capitalist development and the peasant economy in Peru.
Adolfo Figuera. Cambridge, England: Cambridge University Press, 1984. 140p.

Although many writers on contemporary Peruvian society recognize that the key to the elimination of rural poverty consists in improving the conditions of the peasantry, who still make up almost a third of the total population, detailed studies of the peasant economy are few and far between. This study, based upon five years of research work among peasant communities in the southern *sierra* provides valuable empirical data on the economic functioning and dynamics of rural society.

445 Class relations in the Andean countryside.
Rodrigo Montoya. *Latin American Perspectives*, vol. 9, no. 3 (1982), p. 62-78.

In this perceptive article, a Peruvian sociologist argues that peasant struggles and land takeovers in the 1960s forced the Peruvian bourgeoisie to tolerate and even sponsor agrarian reform, despite its radicalism, because of fears that resistance would promote even greater disruption of the class system of rural Peru. The discussion also considers the impact upon class relations of the post-1969 agrarian reform programme of the military government.

Social Conditions

446   **Desborde popular y crisis del estado: el nuevo rostro del Perú en la
década de 1980.** (The popular overflow and the crisis of the state: the
new face of Peru in the 1980s.)
José Matos Mar.   Lima: Instituto de Estudios Peruanos, 1984. 111p.

In this wide-ranging analysis of contemporary Peruvian society, one of the country's
leading social scientists offers an optimistic vision of Peru's capacity to free itself from
its Third World status and 'to open its own route towards socialism'. His ideal society
would be based upon pluralism, social justice and a distinctive sense of national unity.

447   **Dilemas de la seguridad social en el Perú.** (Dilemmas of the social
security system in Peru.)
Javier Slodky.   Lima: Fundación Friedrich Ebert, 1985. 134p. bibliog.

This brief study provides a clear analysis of the current social security system in Peru.
It has separate chapters on the system's overall structure, its limitations, health care,
pensions, and contributions. It pays particular attention to administrative problems,
the majority of which, it is argued, are capable of being resolved.

448   **Familia campesina y economía de mercado.** (The peasant family and the
market economy.)
Juan M. Ossio Acuña, Oswaldo Medina García.   Lima: Centro
Regional de Estudios Socio-Económicos, 1985. 239p. bibliog.

Utilizing data collected by anthropological and sociological field work in three peasant
communities in the central Peruvian department of Huancavelica, this book examines
the ways in which the increasing incorporation of the members of peasant families into
market-oriented economic activity affects the structure of family life. One of the
significant conclusions to emerge is that peasants are not merely passive participants in
the national and regional economies, but are capable, in the face of demographic
pressure, of promoting technological improvement in agriculture to enable themselves
to intensify production (in this case of potatoes) and thus take advantage of the
growing urban demand for foodstuffs.

449   **Gender relations, peasant livelihood strategies and migration: a case
study from Cuzco, Peru.**
Sarah A. Radcliffe.   *Bulletin of Latin American Research*, vol. 5, no. 2
(1986), p. 29-47.

This study of the peasant community of Kallarayan, which has 500 inhabitants and is
located above the Vilcanota river valley, provides admirably clear information on the
rôle played by gender ideologies and practices in peasant household livelihood
strategies in contemporary Peru.

450   **Huaylas: an Andean district in search of progress.**
Paul L. Doughty.   Ithaca, New York: Cornell University Press, 1968.
284p. 3 maps. bibliog.

The town of Huaylas, located in a narrow intermontane valley in the department of
Ancash, serves in this study as a test case for the examination of the effects of
modernization in the early 1960s upon Peruvian rural society and small urban centres,
previously articulated into the local rather than the national economy. Particular
attention is paid to the social and economic impact of electrification. The general

conclusion is that modernization was both assisted by and promoted the diminution of social and cultural differences. The book provides fascinating data on small-town society.

451 **Land or death: the peasant struggle in Peru.**
Hugo Blanco.   New York: Pathfinder, 1972. 178p. 2 maps.
In the early 1960s, peasants' protests against their intolerable position at the bottom of Peru's social structure began to be expressed in terms of land invasions, strikes and insurgency. The author of this work, born in Cuzco of a middle-class, *mestizo* family, organized and led peasant struggles in the provinces of La Convención and Lares, in the department of Cuzco. Although understandably written from a subjective standpoint, the account of how and to what extent the rural masses became convinced of the necessity for armed struggle is essential reading for an understanding of the complexities of rural social conditions in this period.

452 **Man and land in Peru.**
Thomas R. Ford.   New York: Russell & Russell, 1955. 176p. map.
bibliog.
This classic study of the evolution of the land system of Peru from pre-Inca days through the colonial period and the republic to the mid-20th century is essential reading for those who wish to understand the social background to agrarian reform in the 1960s and 1970s.

453 **La mujer en los Andes.** (Women in the Andes.)
Edited by June Nash.   Pittsburgh, Pennsylvania: University of Pittsburgh, Centre for Latin American Studies, 1975. 169p. bibliog.
(Estudios Andinos, 12).
This volume contains eight essays on the rôle of women in Andean society. The introductory discussion by Elinor Burkett provides an overview of women in colonial society; the remainder all deal with contemporary social conditions. One of the most interesting contributions is that of Muriel Crespi (p. 151-71), who considers the capacity of peasant women to act as union leaders.

454 **Política social del estado: la seguridad social en el Perú.** (The social policy of the state: social security in Peru.)
Walter Tesch.   Lima: Centro Latinoamericano de Trabajo Social, 1978. 224p. bibliog.
The principal strength of this sound survey of Peru's social security system is its clear analysis of its institutional antecedents, notably the workers' mutual societies which existed prior to the installation in 1936 of a state-run system.

455 **Poverty and problem-solving under military rule: the urban poor in Lima, Peru.**
Henry A. Dietz.   Austin, Texas: University of Texas Press, 1980. 286p. map. bibliog.
This detailed study of the the period between 1968 and 1975, which saw the confluence in Peru of rapid urbanization and a radical military government, provides detailed information on urban social problems in Lima and the methods adopted to tackle

them. It shows how the solution of problems was hampered by the régime's uncertainty about whether they should be tackled by material assistance alone or also by the encouragement of mass political participation.

456 **Producers and reproducers: Andean marketwomen in the economy.**
Florence E. Babb. In: *Women and change in Latin America*. Edited by June Nash, Helen Saffa. South Hadley, Massachusetts: Bergin & Garvey, 1986, p. 53-64.

The case of marketwomen in Andean Peru is used to analyse both the strengths and the shortcomings of current concepts about women's productive and reproductive activities, and their cross-cultural subordination.

457 **Problemática de las poblaciones marginales en el pais.** (The problem of the country's marginal settlements.)
Oscar E. Gómez Peralta. Lima: Grafital S.C.R.L., 1982. 209p.

Written by a medical doctor with wide experience of working in the squatter settlements around Lima, this study illuminates the severe social problems suffered by their inhabitants. It argues strongly for greater co-ordination in the provision of basic services by the many public and private agencies which 'invade the marginal settlements every day, bringing palliatives which are frequently abandoned before they begin' (p. 209).

458 **La realidad económica de los beneficios sociales.** (The economic reality of social benefits.)
Romulo A. Ferrero. Lima: Centro de Estudios Económicos y Sociales, 1957. 31p.

Although now out of date, this clear synthesis provides a good description of the nature, the costs, and the severe limitations of Peru's social security system in the mid 1950s.

459 **La seguridad social en el Perú.** (Social security in Peru.)
Edited by Laura Morales La Torre, Javier Slodky. Lima: Centro de Altos Estudios Sindicales, 1985. 2nd ed. 173p.

In 1984, the Peruvian Centre for Advanced Trade Union Studies and the German-based Friedrich Ebert Foundation organized in Lima a series of debates for workers and union officials on Peru's social security system. The topics covered included the provision of information, health care, pensions and unemployment benefits. This publication reproduces the introductory presentations of specialists in ten separate sessions, and the comments of members of the audiences. Although the format is unusual, it provides a good overview of the strengths and weaknesses of the social security system.

460 **The social matrix of Peruvian indigenous communities.**
Henry F. Dobyns. Ithaca, New York: Cornell University, Department of Anthropology, 1964. 142p. bibliog.

One of the significant reasons for the success of rural development programmes in Peru, supported in the 1960s by Cornell University, was that they sought to base themselves upon an understanding of how rural society actually functioned, rather than upon detailed abstractions. This brief analysis of the internal social dynamics of indigenous communities, derived from detailed field work, is of enduring value.

461 Social security in Latin America: pressure groups, stratification, and inequality.

Carmelo Mesa-Lago. Pittsburgh, Pennsylvania: University of Pittsburgh Press, 1978. 351p. bibliog.

Dedicated to 'the millions of workers and peasants in Latin America who suffer from lack of coverage or poor protection against social risks', this outstanding general survey of social security systems provides both general analysis and a chapter which deals specifically with Peru (p. 113-59). The latter embraces a survey of the historical evolution of Peru's social security system, a description of its current structure and organization, and an evaluation of its inequalities.

462 Social stratification in Peru.

Magali S. Larson, Arlene G. Bergman. Berkeley, California: University of California, Institute of International Studies, 1969. 407p. bibliog.

Although it was published just as the post-1968 military régime was attempting to embark upon large-scale social reform projects, and is, therefore, somewhat dated, this detailed study of the Peruvian social structure constitutes a major work of reference for an understanding of modern society.

463 Squatters and oligarchs: authoritarian rule and policy change in Peru.

David Collier. Baltimore, Maryland: Johns Hopkins University Press, 1976. 187p. map. bibliog.

This important monograph analyses the changed rôle of successive Peruvian governments in the formation of Lima's squatter settlements, from the mid 1940s. Its basic argument is that unplanned urbanization tended to be tolerated as an essential safety-valve, which would enable policy-makers to avoid the necessity for agrarian reform while, at the same time, keeping the socially undesirable migrants at a reasonable distance from the centre of the city of Lima and its attractive suburbs.

Government and Politics

464 **Agriculture, bureaucracy and military government in Peru.**
Peter S. Cleaves, Martin J. Scurrah. Ithaca, New York: Cornell
University Press, 1980. 336p. bibliog.
This work examines the inter-relationship between the armed forces and the
bureaucracy as they carried out the agrarian reform programme introduced by the
Velasco government in 1968.

465 **Alán García: análisis de su gobierno.** (Alán García: an analysis of his
government.)
Enrique Chirinos Soto, (et al.). Lima: Centro de Documentación
Andina, 1986. 316p.
On 28 July 1985, Alán García Pérez succeeded Fernando Belaúnde Terry as president
of the republic. He was the first Aprista to take office as president, and his accession
marked the first transfer of power between two civilian presidents since 1945. The basic
aim of the seven contributors to this volume, the majority of them experienced
Peruvian journalists, was to provide an evaluation of his policies and achievements
during his first year in office. It also provides a valuable retrospective analysis of his
election campaign.

466 **American corporations and Peruvian politics.**
Charles T. Goodsell. Cambridge, Massachusetts: Harvard University
Press, 1974. 272p. bibliog.
In the early 1970s, the Peruvian government expropriated a number of American
companies with large investments in Peru, mainly in extractive industries. This
monograph examines the broader political issues arising from the domination of the
country's foreign investment sector by American capital from the 1920s. It shows how
differential treatment of expropriated corporations in the 1970s (some received
substantial compensation, others did not) was in conformity with a pragmatic
government approach, designed to maintain a delicate *rapprochement* between
nationalist reformers and international capitalists.

467   **Constitución política del Perú.** (Political constitution of Peru.)

F. Bonilla.   Lima: Editorial Mercurio, 1977. 105p.

This volume reproduces the full text of Peru's 1933 constitution (which remained in force until that of 1979 came into effect in 1980), and of subsequent laws which modified and extended it. It also reproduces the brief 'Statute of the Revolutionary Government of the Armed Forces' of 3 October 1968, which provided by decree the legal basis for the military interregnum of 1968-80.

468   **Una democracia en transición: las elecciones peruanas de 1985.** (A democracy in transition: the Peruvian elections of 1985.)

Domingo García Belaúnde.   Lima: Okura Editores, 1986. 2nd ed. 187p.

The Peruvian elections of 1985 attracted considerable international attention, not only because of the success of the young, charismatic Aprista candidate, Alán García, but also because they were conducted freely and fairly, and led to a peaceful, democratic transfer of power. This analysis offers a sound, general survey of the background to them, and of the electoral campaigns.

469   **Diagnosing Peru.**

Luís Pasará.   *Latin American Research Review*, vol. 17, no. 1 (1982), p. 235-43.

Academic and political interest in Peru grew sharply in the 1970s, as the 'Revolutionary Government of the Armed Forces' attempted to introduce radical social and institutional reforms. This review article analyses the state of research on the military régime shortly after the restoration of civilian government.

470   **Los dueños del Perú.** (The owners of Peru.)

Carlos Malpica.   Lima: Ediciones Peisa, 1984. 13th ed. 316p. bibliog.

This very influential study, first published in 1964, presents a detailed analysis of the structure of economic and political power in Peru prior to the 1968 military takeover. It concentrates upon the domestic and foreign owners of mining, fishing and agricultural companies, large commercial groups, and transport companies, with particular reference to their inter-relationships and their political authority. The present edition contains an extensive prologue which sketches the principal changes in the structures of economic and political power arising from the period of military government (1968-80).

471   **The government executive of modern Peru.**

Jack W. Hopkins.   Gainesville, Florida: University of Florida Press, 1967. 141p. bibliog.

The author of this study worked as a 'participant-observer' in the Peruvian bureaucracy in 1964-65, in connection with a technical assistance programme funded by the US Agency for International Development. His empirical analysis of the backgrounds, origins, mobility, and attitudes of a group of senior executives of the government of Peru is valuable primarily because of its scarcity value. It provides a reasonably systematic explanation of how, in the mid 1960s, policy was made and executed by professional civil servants.

472 **Historia de las constituciones del Perú.** (A history of the constitutions of Peru.)
Juan Vicente Ugarte del Pino. Lima: Editorial Andina, 1978. 641p. bibliog.

Like most Latin American countries, Peru has a chequered constitutional history. This solid, reliable guide to its constitutional development in the period up to 1933 deals systematically with the application in viceregal Peru of the constitution of Cádiz of 1812, and with the background to and details of the first republican constitution, that of 1823. New constitutions were introduced in 1826, 1828, 1834, 1836, 1837, 1839, 1855, 1856, 1860, 1867, 1879, and, in the 20th century, in 1920 and 1933. In each case a listing of the principal articles of the code is preceded by a brief analysis of its origins and significance.

473 **José Carlos Mariátegui and the rise of modern Peru, 1890-1930.**
Jesús Chavarría. Albuquerque, New Mexico: University of New Mexico Press, 1979. 247p. bibliog.

This volume examines the career, as a journalist and political organizer in the turbulent period after World War I, of one of the most influential writers Peru has ever produced, and one whose works remain a vital part of Latin American Marxist thought. The annotated bibliography is particularly valuable.

474 **Jueces, justicia y poder en el Perú.** (Judges, justice and power in Peru.)
Luis Pasará. Lima: Cedys, 1982. 226p. bibliog.

This critical analysis of judicial administration in modern Peru argues that it is characterized by inefficiency, corruption and the personal whims of those in authority.

475 **Latin American laws and institutions.**
Albert S. Golbert, Yenny Nun. New York: Praeger, 1982. 573p.

The first section of this work traces the historical and legal development of Latin America, and the second examines internal legal aspects and functions. Although Peru is not dealt with separately, references to its constitutions and laws abound.

476 **Maoism in the Andes: Sendero Luminoso and the contemporary guerrilla movement in Peru.**
Lewis Taylor. Liverpool, England: Centre for Latin American Studies, University of Liverpool, 1983. 40p. bibliog. (Working Paper, 2).

Although brief, this analysis of the origins of the 'Shining Path' movement in Peru is extremely perceptive. It is based upon data gathered during the author's research between January 1980 and September 1982, a period when guerrilla activity was more of an irritant than the major problem which it now represents.

477 **Military reformism and social classes: the Peruvian experience, 1968-80.**
Edited by David Booth, Bernardo Sorj. London: Macmillan, 1983. 210p. bibliog.

The seven substantive essays in this collection, which are preceded by a general introduction written by its editors, focus upon the socio-political dynamics of Peru, and particularly on the nexus between social classes, reform policies and the state, in the period between 1968 and 1980. Chronologically, it tends to concentrate upon the radical phase of the military period (until 1975). The essays were written independently, and they reach divergent conclusions about the significance of the Peruvian experience of the years in question. Nevertheless, they have a certain cohesion, in the sense that they all seek to examine the military-reformist process in Peru in the light of a shared framework of concerns with social theory.

478 **The multinational corporation as a force in Latin American politics: a case study of the International Petroleum Company, Peru.**
Adalberto J. Pinedo. New York: Praeger, 1973. 171p. bibliog.

The seizure of the assets of International Petroleum Company, a subsidiary of the Standard Oil Company of New Jersey, by the Peruvian military government at the end of 1968 was generally regarded as the first clear sign that the new *junta* would promote radical change rather than defend vested interests. This study analyses the background to the nationalization, and in general explains the important rôle played by IPC in Peruvian politics for several decades prior to 1968.

479 **La nueva constitución al alcance de todos.** (The new constitution within reach of all.)
Enrique Chirinos Soto. Lima: Editores Importadores, 1986. 527p. bibliog.

The new constitution of Peru, approved by the constituent assembly on 12 July 1979 and put into effect on 28 July 1980, not only replaced that of 1933 but also formally ended the twelve-year period of military government inaugurated in 1968. In this volume, all 307 articles of the new constitution are reproduced, together with a commentary on each of them from a leading Aprista who played a prominent rôle in the drafting of the document.

480 **El ocaso del poder oligárquico: lucha política en la escena oficial, 1968-1975.** (The end of oligarchic power: political struggle on the official stage, 1968-1975.)
Henry Pease García. Lima: Centro de Estudios y Promoción del Desarrollo, 1977. 313p. bibliog.

This detailed consideration of political change in Peru in the period between 1968 and 1975 concentrates upon division and political conflict within the dominant social class. It is complemented by a valuable bibliography of 1,091 items relating to Peruvian politics during the period under consideration.

481 **Opciones políticas peruanas.** (Peruvian political options.)
Eugenio Chang-Rodríguez. Trujillo, Peru: Editorial Normas Legales, 1987. 2nd ed. 471p. bibliog.

This revised edition of a work first published in 1985 includes an evaluation of the first fifteen months in office of president Alán García. It provides a valuable survey of the history of Peru's political parties from 1871, when the first coherent civilian political party was formed, until the very recent past. Among its somewhat cynical conclusions is the assertion that, whichever party wins an election, power is eventually handed by it to 'autocratic bureaucrats'.

482 **El partido comunista del Perú: Sendero Luminoso.** (The Communist Party of Peru: 'Shining Path'.)
Rogger Mercado U. Lima: Mergrat 1987. 3rd ed. 160p.

The amplified edition of an influential work, first published in 1982, this contains the account of an interview with the leader of 'Shining Path', Abimael Guzmán.

483 **Partidos políticos en el Perú: manual y registro.** (Political parties in Peru: manual and register.)
Alvaro Rojas Samanez. Lima: Ediciones F & A, 1985. 4th ed. 365p. bibliog.

This revised edition of a work first published in 1982, written by a political journalist, provides a somewhat unsophisticated but useful survey of both the history of political parties in Peru, and of current parties and groups. The latter definition includes the 'Shining Path' guerrilla movement, whose origins and activities are analysed in considerable detail (p. 311-51).

484 **Peasant cooperatives and political changes in Peru.**
Cynthia McClintock. Princeton, New Jersey: Princeton University Press, 1981. 410p. bibliog.

This detailed examination of the economic and political structures developed in Peru under the revolutionary military régime of 1968-75 – in particular the self-management structures – assesses their impact on the values and behaviour of the peasantry. It concludes that a new political consciousness did not emerge, but that the experience has enhanced the possibility of dynamic change in the future.

485 **Peruvian democracy under economic stress: an account of the Belaúnde administration, 1963-1968.**
Pedro-Pablo Kuczynski. Princeton, New Jersey; London: Princeton University Press, 1977. 308p. map. bibliog.

An account of the background to the 1968 military revolution, written by an economic adviser to the Peruvian Central Bank during the Belaúnde government, which addresses itself in particular to the question of the efficacy of reformist policies attempted within an orthodox, *laissez-faire* economic model.

486 **The Peruvian experiment: continuity and change under military rule.**
Edited by Abraham F. Lowenthal. Princeton, New Jersey, 1975. 479p. bibliog.

Published just as the most radical period of military-directed change in Peru was drawing to a close, this book represented the first systematic and comprehensive treatment published in any language to evaluate the country's post-1968 'revolution'. It drew upon the expertise of twelve social scientists, two of them Peruvians, with recent and extensive research experience in Peru. Its basic aim was to analyse the evolution of changing public policies against their national background, and to reach an interim assessment of Peru's military régime. The editor's own contribution, entitled 'Peru's ambiguous revolution' reflected the analytical difficulties which radical militarism presented to political scientists, accustomed to equating military interventions in Latin American politics with the protection of conservative interests.

487 **The Peruvian experience considered.**
Edited by Cynthia McClintock, Abraham F. Lowenthal. Princeton, New Jersey: Princeton University Press, 1983. 442p. bibliog.

In the early 1970s, Peru's experiment in radical militarism seemed to many observers to represent an auspicious effort to break the country's cycle of under-development. By 1980, perspectives on the experiment had changed significantly, a point reflected in the presidential election of 18 May, 1980 (the first since 1963), when nearly half of the five million who went to the polls voted for former president Belaúnde, whose overthrow in 1968 had initiated the twelve-year period of military government. The thirteen essays in this volume, written in the main by economists and political scientists (from Peru, the US, the UK and Canada) tend to argue that the experiment failed, if its performance is measured by its goals; if set against the achievements of most other Latin American revolutions, it succeeded in imposing a number of substantial structural changes. This volume provides the best general overview of Peru's experience between 1968 and 1980.

488 **The politics of reform in Peru: the Aprista and other mass parties of Latin America.**
Grant Hilliker. Baltimore, Maryland: Johns Hopkins University Press, 1971. 201p. map. bibliog.

The Peruvian Aprista Party enunciated a revolutionary programme in the 1920s, and sought to achieve power by revolution in the 1930s. In the 1980s, it is a relatively conservative force. The intervening period, particularly the 1950s and 1960s, was one of transition, when it acted opportunistically, and probably just about deserved to be defined as a mass party in favour of reform. This volume provides a reliable survey of its development in the years prior to the beginning of military government in 1968.

489 **The politics of the miraculous in Peru: Haya de la Torre and the spiritualist tradition.**
Fredrick B. Pike. Lincoln, Nebraska; London: University of Nebraska Press, 1986. 391p. bibliog.

In a negative sense, Victor Raúl Haya de la Torre, founder of Peru's Aprista Party, dominated Peruvian political life for nearly fifty years, although it was not until 1978, at the age of eighty-three and a year before his death, that he acquired his first public office, with his election as president of the constituent assembly entrusted with overseeing the transition from military to civilian government. This unusual book suggests that Haya and Aprismo fulfilled an almost religious function by providing the marginal and the afflicted in the Peru of the 1920s and 1930s with a meaningful spiritual brotherhood.

490 **Politics in the altiplano: the dynamics of change in rural Peru.**
Edward Dew. Austin, Texas; London: University of Texas Press, 1969. 216p. 5 maps. bibliog.

This monograph examines political life and change in the remote, impoverished southern highlands of Peru in the 1960s. Based upon field research conducted in 1965 and 1966, it is particularly interesting on geo-political rivalries within the Puno region.

491 **Populism in Peru: the emergence of the masses and the politics of social control.**

Steve Stein. Madison, Wisconsin: University of Wisconsin Press, 1980. 296p. bibliog.

This scholarly and persuasive analysis of Peru's two main populist movements of the 1930s, the APRA and the Sánchez Cerro movements, provides valuable information on the incorporation of the emerging working class into the country's political structure.

492 **Post-revolutionary Peru: the politics of transformation.**

Edited by Stephen M. Gorman. Boulder, Colorado: Westview, 1982. 252p. bibliog.

In 1980, Fernando Belaúnde Terry returned to the office of president from which he had been ousted twelve years earlier, thus ending the longest period of continuous military domination in modern Peru. The nine essays in this work attempt to assess the scope and nature of the social, political and economic changes experienced by the country during the military's revolutionary experiment. Some suggest that, on balance, its effects were positive, even if incomplete; others are more critical. Despite these divergences, the authors tend to agree about issues such as the increased complexity of socio-economic relationships, and the significance of growing lower-class political mobilization and organization.

493 **Power and society in contemporary Peru.**

François Bourricaud, translated by Paul Stevenson. London: Faber & Faber, 1970. 356p. 3 maps.

In this wide-ranging analysis of Peruvian social and political development in the period from 1956 to 1964, first published in French in 1967, detailed attention is paid to the relationships between the military and the oligarchy. The work draws heavily upon Peru's two main newspapers, *La Prensa* and *El Comercio*, and upon literary sources, as reflections of social and political reality.

494 **Pressure groups and power elites in Peruvian politics.**

Carlos A. Astiz. Ithaca, New York; London: Cornell University Press, 1969. 316p. map. bibliog.

Departing from the premise, which was broadly acceptable in the 1960s, that Peru's political processes and institutions had been largely ignored by political scientists, this analysis attempted to both describe the country's institutions and constitutional development, and reveal the underlying factors of continuity and stability obscured by complicated permutations of the political superstructure. The rapid political changes after 1968 meant that many of its findings were quickly outdated, but it remains an excellent guide to the social structure, ideology, and interest groups of the period before the initiation of the radical military régime of 1968-75.

495 **Quien es quien: congreso de la república, 1985-1990.** (Who's who: the congress of the republic, 1985-1990.)
Mario Guimarey, Martin Garay. Lima: Editora Atlantida, 1986. 268p.

Under Peru's bicameral system of government, a sixty-strong elected Senate and a 180-member Chamber of Deputies constitute the Congress of the republic. Lifetime membership of the Senate is also enjoyed by the former constitutional presidents of the republic. This extremely valuable reference work provides a one-page biography, accompanied by a photograph, of each of the sixty-two senators and 180 deputies who took office in 1985.

496 **Revolution from above: military bureaucrats and development in Japan, Turkey, Egypt, and Peru.**
Ellen Kay Trimberger. New Brunswick, New Jersey: Transaction Books, 1978. 196p. bibliog.

The aim of this original study is to provide a methodological analysis of 'unusual' attempts at revolution in the non-Western world. It develops a model of revolution from above by military bureaucrats (as distinct from bourgeois or socialist revolution from below) by comparing the Meiji Restoration of 1868 in Japan, the Ataturk takeover of 1923 in Turkey, Nasser's Egypt, and Peru under the presidency of Velasco Alvarado. A general conclusion is that genuine mass revolutions from below are truly exceptional historical phenomena in Third World countries.

497 **The rise of Sendero Luminoso.**
Colin Harding. In: *Region and class in modern Peruvian history.*
Edited by Rory Miller. Liverpool, England: Institute of Latin American Studies, University of Liverpool, 1987. p. 179-206.
(Monograph, 14).

This chapter traces the development of the 'Shining Path' guerrilla movement from its formation in the 1960s at the University of San Cristóbal de Huamanga through to 1986.

498 **Rural guerrillas in Latin America.**
Richard Gott. Harmondsworth, England: Penguin, 1973. 2nd ed. 637p. bibliog.

A lengthy chapter on Peru, appropriately entitled 'Disaster in Peru' (p. 364-463) describes the background to and the course of the unsuccessful guerrilla campaign of 1965, led by Hugo Blanco, a militant Trotskyist, and Luís de la Puente Uceda. The study as a whole provides a useful context for the evaluation for the Peruvian experience.

499 **Sendero Luminoso: a new revolutionary model.**
James Anderson. London: Institute for the Study of Terrorism, 1987. 87p. bibliog.

Although the author predicted, incorrectly, that the 'Shining Path' guerrilla movement would not become a threat to 'the existence of the Peruvian state', this analysis of the strategic and military aspects of insurgency, based upon first-hand observation, makes a useful contribution to the scanty literature on terrorism.

Government and Politics

500 Seven interpretive essays on Peruvian reality.
José Carlos Mariátegui, translated by Marjory Urquidi.   Austin,
Texas; London: University of Texas Press, 1971. 301p.

Born in 1894 into a lower-middle class family in Moquegua, Mariátegui emerged as
one of Peru's most influential political writers in the 1920s, before his death at the age
of thirty-five. His seven essays on what he defined as 'some essential aspects of
Peruvian reality' were first published in the monthly journals *Mundial* (Lima, 1926-30)
and *Amauta* (Lima, 1920-33) before Mariátegui decided in 1928 to publish them as a
book. He emphasized in his introduction that he was not 'an impartial, objective
critic', but a writer driven by the ambition 'to assist in the creation of Peruvian
socialism'. The pieces range widely across Peru's economic evolution, the Indian, land,
public education, religion, regionalism and centralism, and literature. The translation
into English is excellent.

501 The state and society: Peru in comparative perspective.
Alfred Stepan.   Princeton, New Jersey: Princeton University Press,
1978. 348p. bibliog.

The first part of this book presents a conceptual discussion of the rôle of the state in
various models of political analysis, and a comparative analysis of selected neo-
corporatist régimes in which the state has an important function. In the second part,
some of these concepts are applied in an analysis of the post-1968 attempt to
restructure state-society relations in Peru, when the military attempted to expand the
power of the state apparatus and to use this power in the reconstruction of class,
property, and participation patterns.

502 Struggle in the Andes: peasant political mobilization in Peru.
Howard Handelman.   Austin, Texas; London: University of Texas
Press, 1975. 303p. 7 maps. bibliog.

This examination of the related phenomena of rural unrest and peasant political
mobilization in Peru is particularly interesting in view of the fact that the author's field
work coincided with the announcement, in June, 1969, of extensive land reform; the
first three years of the programme are discussed in the concluding chapter.

503 Las tumbas de Uchuraccay. (The tombs of Uchuraccay.)
José María Salcedo.   Lima: Condor Editores, 1984. 217p.

On 26 January 1983, eight Peruvian journalists and their guide were assassinated in the
remote village of Uchuraccay in the department of Ayacucho. The authorities initially
blamed the atrocity upon 'Shining Path' guerrillas; subsequently, a government
commission of inquiry concluded that it was committed by the villagers, who thought
that the journalists were themselves guerrillas. This inconclusive, but gripping
narrative describes the attempts of another journalist in the first half of 1983 to
discover the truth. Running throughout the narrative is a deep suspicion that the
military authorities in the region were involved in the killings.

Foreign Relations

504 Aggression and history: the case of Ecuador and Peru.
Bryce Wood. Ann Arbor, Michigan: University Microfilms
International, 1978. 310p. 3 maps. bibliog.

This discussion of the Peru–Ecuador boundary dispute is concerned more with its international significance than with the details of either the war of 1941 or its historical antecedents. Nevertheless, its maps are particularly useful in indicating the cartographic aspects of the problem.

505 The boundary dispute between Peru and Ecuador.
Ronald Bruce St. John. *American Journal of International Law*,
vol. 71, no. 2 (April 1977), p. 322-30.

This article argues that, although Ecuador's *de jure* claim to the territory in dispute with Peru is quite impressive, its long *de facto* possession by Peru gives the latter country a much stronger claim in international law.

506 By reason or force: Chile and the balancing of power in South America, 1830-1905.
Robert N. Burr. Berkeley, California; Los Angeles: University of
California Press, 1965. 322p. map. bibliog. (University of California
Publications in History, vol. 77).

The principal value of this detailed study for those interested in Peru is that it places the War of the Pacific and earlier conflicts between Chile and Peru within a very clear framework of Chilean international relations in the 19th century. It demonstrates the superior ability of Chilean leaders to identify and pursue national objectives, and to anticipate Peruvian policies and reactions.

507 **El conflicto militar del Perú con el Ecuador (1941).** (The military conflict between Peru and Ecuador [1941].)
Miguel Monteza Tafur. Lima: Editorial Arica, 1976. 281p. 8 maps.
The author of this detailed account of the Peru–Ecuador conflict of 1941 served during the fighting as a member of the headquarters staff of the Peruvian commander-in-chief, general Eloy Ureta. Although obviously written from a subjective standpoint, it is the best available account of Peru's military tactics in 1941.

508 **Fascist propaganda and the Italian community in Peru during the Benavides regime, 1933-39.**
Orazio A. Ciccarilli. *Journal of Latin American Studies*, vol. 20 (1988), p. 261-88.
In the second half of the 1930s, a propaganda war was waged in Latin America between the Western democracies (the US, the UK and France) and the Axis powers. This article examines the well orchestrated pro-Fascist campaign financed in Peru by the rich Italian community and condoned by the régime of Oscar Benavides between 1933 and 1939. It also considers the impact of Italian influence in Peru upon relations between it and the US.

509 **Historia de los límites del Perú.** (A history of the frontiers of Peru.)
Raúl Porras Barrenechea, Alberto Wagner de Reyna. Lima: Editorial Universitaria, 1981. 200p. 9 maps.
This edition comprises a fascimile reproduction of Porras' book *Historia de los límites del Perú* (Lima: Editorial Rosay, 1930), excluding some of his summaries and bibliographical data, and the text of Wagner de Reyna's study of *Los límites del Perú* (Lima: Editorial Universitaria, 1961), which covered the period from 1930 until 1961. Although the genesis of the book is somewhat unconventional, it serves to bring together two inaccessible works, which jointly provide a very sound coverage of Peru's boundary disputes and relationships with Ecuador, Colombia, Brazil, Bolivia, and Chile.

510 **The impact of U.S. arms transfer policies on relations with Peru: 1945-1978.**
John Leslie Davison. MA thesis, North Texas State University, Denton, Texas, 1979. (Available from University Microfilms, Ann Arbor, Michigan, order no. 79-1313806).
This thesis traces the course of recent US–Peruvian relations, with special emphasis on Peru's arms acquisitions since 1968. It argues that the refusal of the US to provide advanced weapons to Peru, although straining relations with the military government, was in the best hemispheric interests of the US.

511 **Mining and diplomacy: United States interests at Cerro de Pasco, Peru, 1876-1930.**
Charles Harper McArver, Jr. PhD thesis, University of North Carolina, Chapel Hill, North Carolina, 1977. (Available from University Microfilms, Ann Arbor, Michigan, order no. 78-10482).
Mining has always been one of Peru's most important economic activities, and by 1930 US companies dominated the industry. This PhD thesis examines the origins and

growth of the most powerful of these companies, the Cerro de Pasco Copper Corporation, and the impact which its presence in Peru had upon US–Peruvian diplomatic relations during the first three decades of the 20th century.

512 Origins and consequences of the border dispute between Ecuador and Peru.
William P. Avery. *Inter-American Economic Affairs*, vol. 38 (1983), p. 65-77.

Written in the aftermath of armed clashes between Peru and Ecuador in 1981 in the vast Amazonian territory to which both sides lay claim, this article reaches the perhaps predictable conclusion that the limited revival of hostilities was caused by domestic political considerations in each country. An assessment is also made of the negative results of the clash for the already difficult economic co-operation between the two countries within the Andean Pact.

513 Peru and the United States, 1900-1962.
James C. Carey. Notre Dame, Indiana: University of Notre Dame Press, 1964. 243p.

Before this monograph appeared, bilateral relations between the US and Peru had been virtually ignored by writers on foreign policy in 20th-century Latin America, except within the context of general surveys of US relations with South America as a whole. To a large extent, the explanation for this scholarly indifference is that relations between the two countries were relatively harmonious, and no particular incident or problem attracted significant attention until vice-president Richard Nixon was insulted and spat upon when he visited Lima in 1958. However, US business interests had a much sharper focus upon Peru, and one of the merits of this very thorough survey is that it traces not only the policies, relations, and activities of the respective governments but also the relationships between Peru and US private enterprise, and aid organizations.

514 Territorial seas and inter-American relations: with case studies of the Peruvian and U.S. fishing industries.
Bobbie B. Smetherman, Robert M. Smetherman. New York: Praeger, 1974. 121p.

One of the most persistent problems of post-war inter-American relations has been the dispute over boundaries for territorial waters. Peru, like a number of other Latin American nations, now claims a 'territorial sea' extending 200 miles offshore in contradiction to the traditional law of the sea and the wishes of the world's major maritime nations. This study illuminates the complexities (political and economic as well as legal) which lie behind the subject.

515 The United States and Latin American wars, 1932-1942.
Bryce Wood. New York: Columbia University Press, 1966. 519p. 4 maps. bibliog.

During the period covered by this book the assumption that America differed from Europe in being a continent of peace was shattered by three major international conflicts in South America: the Chaco War between Bolivia and Paraguay, the Leticia dispute between Colombia and Peru, and the Marañon question between Ecuador and Peru. This detailed work provides very clear accounts of the origins, details, and settlements of the conflicts, and also evaluates their significance for the 'inter-American system'. Although the focus is upon the inability of the US, as the single great power in the hemisphere, to prevent American states fighting each other, the discussion of Peruvian policies is also very thorough.

516   **U.S. foreign policy and Peru.**
Edited by Daniel A. Sharp.   Austin, Texas; London: University of Texas Press, 1972. 485p.

The fourteen papers in this volume resulted from a series of meetings, held in 1970 in the US, of leaders from business, academe, the Church, labour, media, banking, law, and government to discuss US policy towards Peru. The timing, of course, was significant, for it was clear by 1970 that the radical nature of the military government of Juan Velasco Alvarado was likely to bring it into conflict with US business interests. The meetings were supported by both the US and the Peruvian governments, whose respective views are embraced in official contributions on 'U.S. aid to Peru under the Alliance for Progress' (p. 423-41) and 'Peru's relations with the United States and national development policy' (p. 416-21). The other topics covered include US relations with the Peruvian military, the fisheries dispute, the diplomatic protection of US business in Peru, and US attitudes towards agrarian reform.

517   **Zarumilla-Marañon: the Ecuador-Peru dispute.**
David H. Zook, Jr.   New York: Bookman Associates, 1964. 331p. map. bibliog.

This book provides the most detailed survey in English of the background to and the details of the war of 1941 between Peru and Ecuador over disputed territory in the Zarumilla-Marañon area.

Economy

General

518 **Capitalismo y no capitalismo en el Perú.** (Capitalism and non-capitalism in Peru.)
Rodrigo Montoya. Lima: Mosca Azul, 1980. 331p. 3 maps. bibliog.
This work, which is derived from the author's 1977 doctoral dissertation, uses the records of landowners and merchants in the southern Andes as the primary source for a stimulating general discussion of the relationship between capitalism and the formation of Peruvian society in the century after 1880.

519 **Economía peruana 1985/1986: retos y respuestas.** (The Peruvian economy 1985/1986: challenges and responses.)
Luis Alva Castro. Lima: Instituto de Investigaciones 'Cambio y Desarrollo', 1987. 374p. map. bibliog.
When the Aprista Party took power in Peru in July 1985, with the accession of Alán García to the presidency, it inherited a severe economic crisis, characterized by dramatic falls in personal income, massive price rises, and inflation. This subjective study, written by the country's then prime minister, describes and evaluates the unorthodox economic policies pursued during the first eighteen months of the García presidency, which succeeded in curbing inflation and increasing output.

520 **Government policy and the distribution of income in Peru, 1963-1973.**
Richard Charles Webb. Cambridge, Massachusetts; London: Harvard University Press, 1977. 239p.
This book measures the impact of government policy on the distribution of income in Peru during the Belaúnde presidency (1963-68) and the first five years of the military government headed by Velasco. Both régimes proclaimed the need for redistributive

115

measures, the former concentrating upon schooling and rural development, and the latter upon land reform, industrial reform, and other property transfers. The general findings are, first, that the overall effects of the distributive measures taken throughout the period were mildly progressive, and, second, that the pattern of redistribution under Belaúnde and Velasco was similar, and characterized by redistribution downwards within sectors.

521 **Historia del Banco de la Nación.** (A history of the national bank.)
Carlos Callegari Ramírez. Lima: Centro de Documentación e Información Andina, 1986. 223p. bibliog.

This history of the first banking organization of the Peruvian state covers the period from 1914, when the bank was founded, until 1986. It provides a good general survey of Peru's financial and banking history in the 20th century, and of the 19th-century antecedents.

522 **Historia de los bancos en el Perú. (1860-1879).** (A history of the banks of Peru [1860-1879].)
Carlos Camprubi Alcazar. Lima: Editorial Lumen, 1957. 433p.

During the two decades before the outbreak of the War of the Pacific, Peru experienced a significant period of economic and commercial development, as members of the bourgeoisie began to invest their profits from *guano* and nitrates and the proceeds of the repayment of the internal debt in the development of an impressive financial infrastructure. Although very traditional in its approach, this book provides a reliable survey of the subject of the development of commercial banks in this period.

523 **Inflation and stabilisation in Latin America.**
Edited by Rosemary Thorp, Lawrence Whitehead. London; Basingstoke: Macmillan, 1979. 285p. bibliog.

The issues of inflation and stabilization policy in Latin America attracted considerable debate and research during the 1960s, largely died out in the early years of the 1970s for reasons related to international developments, and again became major topics for debate in the middle of the 1970s. This volume contains six case studies, which review the reactions of six countries to the major adjustment problems thrust upon them. The particularly complex case of Peru, where economic and political problems were closely related in the period 1975-78, is examined in detail by Thorp (p. 110-43); the book as a whole provides the essential context for the evaluation of Peru's problems.

524 **Miners, peasants, and entrepreneurs: regional development in the central highlands of Peru.**
Norman Long, Bryan Roberts. Cambridge, England: Cambridge University Press, 1984. 288p. bibliog.

This is a detailed analysis, by a sociologist and an anthropologist, of the impact of the growth of the mining economy in the highlands of central Peru after 1900 upon social and economic life in the Mantaro valley. It is particularly valuable for its discussion of peasant agriculture and of the reasons for the increasing tendency since 1950 for peasants to migrate to Lima rather than to the mining centres.

525 **Nationalism & capitalism in Peru: a study in neo-imperialism.**
Aníbal Quijano. New York; London: Monthly Review, 1971. 122p.
This tentative examination of the economic policy of Peru's military government from October 1968 until March 1971 seeks to explain economic measures which often seemed to be inconsistent and contradictory.

526 **The other path: the invisible revolution in the Third World.**
Hernando de Soto. New York: Harper & Row, 1989. 271p.
One of the most complex and serious economic issues not only in Peru but also throughout Latin America is the working of the informal market, or the underground economy. The brilliant presentation describes how and on what scale it functions in Peru.

527 **Peru 1890-1977: growth and policy in an open economy.**
Rosemary Thorp, Geoffrey Bertram. London; Basingstoke, England: Macmillan, 1978. 475p. bibliog.
This detailed discussion of economic change since the end of the 19th century argues that 'export-sector bias' was harmful to the economy as a whole. It is based upon copious statistical data.

528 **El Perú heterodoxo: un modelo económico.** (Heterodox Peru: an economic model.)
Daniel Carbonetto (et al.). Lima: Instituto Nacional de Planificación, 1987. 511p. bibliog.
In this major volume, a team of nine economists and political scientists, including Peruvians and representatives of international agencies, seeks to provide short-term answers to Peru's economic crisis of the late 1980s, based upon unconventional economic theories, and the long-term protection of national interests and democratic structures. The text is complex and technical, and is addressed primarily to academics and professionals with a background in economics.

529 **The Peruvian economy: a study of its characteristics, stage of development and main problems.**
Loreto M. Domínguez (et al.). Washington, DC: Division of Economic Research, Pan American Union, 1950. 279p. bibliog.
This is a detailed analysis of economic life on the eve of the industrialization boom of the 1950s.

530 **The Peruvian public investment programme, 1968-78.**
Felipe Portocarrero. *Journal of Latin American Studies*, vol. 14 (1982), p. 433-54.
The huge reform programme embarked upon by the Peruvian military government in 1968 gave a fundamental rôle to state intervention in the economy, and especially to public investment. This article is one of few significant studies which attempts to look beyond short-term economic policy and stabilization attempts to analyse the medium- and long-term aspects of the massive state interventionist policies of the decade after 1968.

Economy. General

531 **Política económico-financiera y la formación del estado: siglo XIX.**
(Economic-financial policy and the formation of the state: the 19th century.)
Javier Tantaleán Arbulu. Lima: Centro de Estudios para el Desarrollo y la Participación, 1983. 316p. bibliog.

This excellent monograph uses the reports of the Peruvian ministers of finance in the 19th century as the major source for a discussion of: the rôle of the state in capital accumulation; the size and significance of the internal debt; and public expenditure.

532 **The political economy of Peru 1956-78: economic development and the restructuring of capital.**
E. V. K. Fitzgerald. Cambridge, England: Cambridge University Press, 1979. 360p. bibliog.

Written as the Peruvian military prepared to restore civilian government after its failure to resolve the country's economic problems, this work looks back to the pre-revolutionary era and attempts, on the basis of statistical analysis, to provide a general picture of the Peruvian political economy during a period of significant social and economic change.

533 **Politics and economics of external debt crisis: the Latin American experience.**
Edited by Miguel S. Wionczek, L. Tomassini. Boulder, Colorado; London: Westview, 1985. 482p. bibliog.

The international debt crisis of Latin America has dominated the region's external economic relations throughout the 1980s, and has also had a major impact on domestic politics as governments have attempted, with varying degrees of enthusiasm, to pursue economic policies which have tended to fall short of debt repudiation. The series of essays in this volume explains the general origins of the crisis and its internal repercussions. The general discussions are complemented by case studies, including the analysis by Robert Devlin and Enrique de la Piedra of 'Peru and its private bankers: scenes from an unhappy marriage' (p. 383-426).

534 **The state and economic development: Peru since 1968.**
E. V. K. Fitzgerald. Cambridge, England: Cambridge University Press, 1976. 127p. bibliog.

The first published account of the 'Peruvian model', whereby the Peruvian military attempted to introduce an economic revolution by following a new development path which it described as 'neither capitalist nor communist', this is enriched by the author's rôle as an economic adviser to Peru during this process.

Trade

535 **Allocation of industry in the Andean common market.**
Jan ter Wengel. Boston, Massachusetts; The Hague; London:
Martinus Nijhoff, 1980. 177p. bibliog.

One of the main problems to be resolved in integration schemes among developing countries is that of the distribution of the resulting benefits. This study of the petrochemical programme of the Andean common market, established by the 1969 Cartagena agreement, shows that the participating countries expect the benefits to be derived mainly from the utilization of the opportunities for industrialization, rather than from the possibilities for increased trade. The problem of the distribution of benefits coincides, therefore, with that of the distribution of the industries made possible by integration among the member countries. This is a complex study, based in part upon theoretical models, which provides valuable data on Peru's rôle in the Andean common market.

536 **The Andean Group: a case study in economic integration among developing countries.**
David Morawetz. Cambridge, Massachusetts; London: Massachusetts Institute of Technology Press, 1974. 171p. map. bibliog.

Many developing countries have turned to economic integration in an attempt to speed up their development. This study analyses some important policy issues involved in economic integration, and examines, in the light of this analysis and the experience of other integration schemes, the Andean Group integration scheme formed by Bolivia, Chile, Colombia, Ecuador, and Peru under the Cartagena agreement of May 1969. It provides a very clear and reliable account of the background to the agreement, and of policies and prospects for transport, the harmonization of economic policies, tariffs, and the distribution of benefits.

537 **Comercio y tendencias del mercado en los productos de la región de la selva peruana.** (Trade and market trends in the products of the Peruvian forest region.)
Eduardo Watson Cisneros. Lima: Universidad Agraria, 1964. 116p. map.

During the 1960s, the Belaúnde administration invested large sums of money in the improvement of road communications with eastern Peru, in the belief that the exploitation of the region's wide range of natural resources could be transformed. This solid, informative work provides reliable statistics for the production and sale of its principal products, including tea, coffee, cotton, fruits, timber, furs, and skins.

538 **Fishing for growth: export-led development in Peru, 1950-1967.**
Michael Roemer. Cambridge, Massachusetts: Harvard University Press, 1970. 208p. bibliog.

From 1950 to 1967, Peru achieved one of the outstanding growth records among the less developed countries, with dramatic increases in gross national product and per

119

capita income. The most notable feature of this growth was the dominant rôle played by primary product exports, within which the most spectacular growth was in fishmeal, a high-protein additive to livestock feeds, manufactured in Peru from anchovy. This monograph provides the best and most detailed account of the development of the fishmeal industry, its place in export trade, its linkages with other sectors of the economy, and its significance, as perceived in 1970, for other primary product export industries in other countries.

539 **The fishing industry of Peru.**
Gerald Eliot. In: *Latin America and the Caribbean: a handbook.* Edited by Claudio Véliz. London: Anthony Blond, 1968, p. 646-51.
The rapid growth of Peru's fishing industry to provide fishmeal for export is described succinctly in this summary, written at the height of the industry's development and before its collapse as a consequence of over-fishing.

540 **Historia de la cámara de comercio de Lima.** (A history of the chamber of trade of Lima.)
Jorge Basadre, Romulo Ferrero. Lima: Santiago Valverde, 1963. 372p.
Published to commemorate the seventy-fifth anniversary of the establishment of Lima's chamber of trade, this solid institutional history falls into two clear parts. The first, written by the historian Basadre, examines the background to the chamber's foundation in 1888, in a period of economic reconstruction imposed by Peru's defeat in the War of the Pacific, and traces its development until 1938; the second part, written by the economist Ferrero, covers the period from 1939 until 1963, and provides a good survey of not only the institutional development but also of Peru's economic development and trade in that period.

541 **Historical contexts of trade and markets in the Peruvian Andes.**
Darrell Eugene La Lone. PhD thesis, University of Michigan, Ann Arbor, Michigan, 1978. (Available from University Microfilms, Ann Arbor, Michigan, order no. 79-07114).
The object of this dissertation is to provide the historical contexts for an understanding of the development of commercial relationships and markets which link Andean highlanders to the regional, national, and world economies. It discusses the major modes of exchange and variations in its organization from Inca times to the present, concentrating in spatial terms upon the Sicuani region of southern Cuzco.

542 **Perú: comercio y desarrollo.** (Peru: trade and development.)
Jaime Quijandría Salmón (et al.). Lima: Centro de Estudios para el Desarrollo y la Participación, 1979. 233p.
In February 1979, ten Peruvian economists presented papers at a national conference of Peruvian representatives at the forthcoming United Nations Conference on Trade and Development (UNCTAD V) meeting, held in Manila. The principal issues addressed in this published version of their discussions include the rôle of United Nations agencies in promoting Third World development, technology transfer, Peru's external debt, and international cooperation in the production and sale of primary products.

543 **El Perú frente a las nuevas tendencias del comercio internacional.** (Peru and the new trends in international trade.)
Edited by Eduardo Ferrero C. Lima: Centro Peruano de Estudios Internacionales, 1984. 328p.

Foreign trade is of vital importance to Peru's development, a point underlined by the fact that in the period 1980-83 it represented more than a third of the country's gross national product. The fifteen papers in this volume, the majority of them by Peruvian economists, cover a range of issues affecting the country's foreign trade, including government policies, commercial relations with the US and the EEC, and regional trade cooperation.

544 **La promoción de exportaciones no tradicionales en el Perú: una evaluación crítica.** (The promotion of non-traditional exports in Peru: a critical evaluation.)
Daniel M. Schydlowsky, Shane J. Hunt, Jaime Mezzera. Lima: Asociación de Exportadores del Perú, 1983. 225p. bibliog.

One of the most intractable problems in the external trade of Latin American countries since World War II has been the recognition that the relatively inelastic international demand for traditional primary products means that an increase in exports usually leads to a fall in prices. Brazil and Colombia attempted to tackle this problem in the 1960s by promoting non-traditional exports, primarily manufactured goods. Peru attempted to follow their example in the 1970s. This rich analysis examines the country's policies for the promotion of non-traditional exports and their results from 1970 until 1981, a period in which their value rose from thirty million to 800 million dollars.

545 **The state and the bourgeosie in the Peruvian fishmeal industry.**
Baltazar Caravedo Molinari, translated by Stephen Gorman. *Latin American Perspectives*, vol. 48, no. 3 (summer 1977), p. 103-21.

By the mid 1970s, the Peruvian fishmeal industry, which had generated almost a third of the country's foreign exchange earnings in 1970-71, was in deep crisis, despite the state's decision in 1973 to nationalize it in the hope of keeping it alive. This article analyses the industry's dynamics in historical perspective, with particular reference to the varying influence of the national bourgeoisie in the development of different sectors.

Industry and mining

546 **Bonanza development: the selva oil industry in Peru 1968-1982.**
George Philip. London: Institute of Latin American Studies, University of London, 1984. 29p. (Working Paper, 12).

Until the installation of a radical military government in 1968, the exploitation of

Economy. Industry and mining

Peru's rich natural resources was largely directed by foreign companies interested primarily in raw material exports. This paper focuses upon the state's attempt after 1968 to take control of the oil industry into its own hands, and the dramatic export-led development of production in the Amazon area.

547 **Burguesía e industria en el Perú, 1948-1956.** (Bourgeoisie and industry in Peru, 1948-1956.)
Baltazar Caravedo Molinari. Lima: Instituto de Estudios Peruanos, 1976. 187p. bibliog.

The relationship between social structure and industrialization is considered in this monograph, with particular reference to the attitudes of Peru's bourgeoisie towards investment. The specific example of Arequipa is considered in the same author's *Desarrollo desigual y la lucha política en el Perú, 1948-1956: la burguesía arequipeña y el estado peruano* (Unequal development and the political struggle in Peru, 1948-1956: the bourgeoisie of Arequipa and the Peruvian state) (Lima: Instituto de Estudios Peruanos, 1978).

548 **La burguesía industrial en el desarrollo peruano.** (The industrial bourgeoisie in the development of Peru.)
Anthony Ferner. Lima: Editorial Esan, 1982. 293p. bibliog.

This monograph, which arises from research undertaken in Lima in 1974-75 for the author's doctoral dissertation, examines the background to and the course of the military's industrialization programme in the 1970s. It argues that this programme was facilitated by the fact that during the previous decade the members of the dominant class interested in industrial and urban development had already begun to distance themselves from the more traditional oligarchic groups which sought to retain Peru's concentration upon the export of primary products.

549 **Crisis and accumulation in the Peruvian mining industry, 1968-1974.**
Elizabeth Dore. *Latin American Perspectives*, vol. 4, no. 3 (summer 1977), p. 77-102.

In 1974-75, the Peruvian military government nationalized with compensation several large foreign companies, including two major US mining companies, the Cerro de Pasco Corporation and the Marcona Mining Company. This polemical article examines the economic background to the expropriations, and its consequences, arguing that 'the nationalizations, instead of representing a blow against capital, have left the capitalists momentarily stronger'. It identifies the process as an attack upon neither imperialism nor capitalism, but as a conspiracy between the Peruvian bourgeoisie and the state to destroy the class-conscious militancy of the miners.

550 **The industrial development of Peru.**
United Nations Department of Economic and Social Affairs. Mexico, DF, 1959. 323p.

Prepared by the secretariat of the Economic Commission for Latin America of the United Nations, at the request of the government of Peru, this extremely detailed survey provides an outstanding coverage of the state of the whole spectrum of Peruvian industry in the late 1950s. The analysis is supported by an impressive array of statistical data on production and investment.

551 **Industrialization and regional development in Peru.**
Hugo Cabieses, Dirk Kruijt, Raúl Lizarraga, Menno Vellinga.
Amsterdam: Centre for Latin American Research and Documentation,
1982. 171p. bibliog.

This study argues that the historical domination of foreign firms over strategic fields of
production created serious sectoral and regional imbalance in the Peruvian economy. It
examines policies pursued in the period from 1968 to 1980 by the military government
to promote regional decentralization of industrial production to zones which were
given priority in successive national development plans. The first part of the analysis
provides an overview of the rôle of the state in the organization of the economy; the
second examines decentralization policies in general; the third and final section
examines the experience of Trujillo in the north and Arequipa in the south as selected
'poles' for industrialization.

552 **Industrialization, industrialists and the nation-state in Peru.**
Fritz Wils. Berkeley, California: University of California, Institute of
International Studies, 1979. 273p. bibliog.

This study of Peruvian industrialists is built around an examination of the impact on
industry of the military government's structural reforms up to 1975. Its evaluation of
the reforms is a positive one, stressing, in contrast to other commentators, their
autonomy with respect to established class interests and their contribution to the
development of a strong state committed to economic growth.

553 **Limits to capitalist development: the industrialization of Peru, 1950-
1980.**
John Weeks. Boulder, Colorado; London: Westview, 1985. 254p.
bibliog.

Rejecting dependency theory as an explanation of under-development, Dr. Weeks
examines Peru's transition from a semi-feudal society to a predominantly capitalist
one, and argues that its failure to achieve greater independence from foreign capital
resulted primarily from internal problems and contradictions.

554 **Metal-mining in Peru: past and present.**
W. F. C. Purser. New York; Washington, DC; London: Praeger.
1971. 329p. 5 maps. bibliog.

This book provides a very solid introduction to the nature, history and importance of
the mines of Peru. Its first section sketches the background of Peru and its mining
history; a second discusses the mines of Peru in production in the modern period; and
a third concentrates upon their economic significance.

555 **The new bourgeoisie and the limits of dependency: mining, class, and
power in 'revolutionary' Peru.**
David G. Becker. Princeton, New Jersey: Princeton University Press,
1983. 419p. bibliog.

This detailed study of the processes of late-capitalist industrialization in export;re-
source-dependent countries concentrates upon Peru's key mining industry in the period
from 1968 to 1980. Apart from its centrality to the Peruvian national economy, mining
is a particularly important sector as a core industry in which three forms of capital

participate: that provided by transnational corporations, that of parastatal enterprises, and that of the 'new bourgeoisie', the ascendant class element in modern Peru.

556 **Oil and politics in Latin America: nationalist movements and state companies.**
George Philip.   Cambridge, England: Cambridge University Press, 1982. 577p. 4 maps. bibliog.

Although primarily intended as a history of the conflict that has been played out in Latin America between the claims of transnational oil companies and those of national sovereignty and state control, this book focuses upon a wide-ranging issue of general relevance to the economist. The nationalization of the International Petroleum Company in Peru in 1968 is considered in some detail (p. 243-57), as is the performance of the state corporation, Petroperú, in running the industry in the period from 1968 until 1980 (p. 429-50).

557 **El trabajo artesanal en los Andes peruanos: el valle del Mantaro.**
(Artisan production in the Peruvian Andes: the Mantaro valley.)
Milagro Luna Ballón, Raúl Galdo Pagaza, Ana Inafuku Yagui.   Lima: Ministerio de Trabajo y Promoción Social, 1983. 233p. 2 maps. bibliog.

Despite a concentration upon ambitious programmes of industrialization during the 1970s, there is a widespread recognition in Peru of the continuing economic and social importance of artisan production, not least as a source of employment capable of preserving the fabric of rural society, and curbing migration to the cities. This excellent study examines and seeks to quantify artisan production, in the central Peruvian Mantaro valley area, of a range of goods, notably silverware, ceramics, textiles, shoes, and furniture.

Agriculture

558 **Achievements and contradictions of the Peruvian agrarian reform.**
Cristóbal Kay.   *Journal of Development Studies*, vol. 18, no. 2 (Jan. 1982), p. 141-70.

This article provides the best short guide to the results of the agrarian reform programme undertaken in Peru by the military régime of 1968-80. It evaluates the process in terms of its contribution to rural development, arguing that land reform is not a sufficient condition for constructive change unless accompanied by proper price, marketing, credit and investment policies. It stresses the importance of understanding the rationality of the pre-existent agrarian system for a successful restructuring of the agrarian economy and society. The contradictions which arose between the state's model and the peasants' model of agrarian reform, as well as those between different types of peasants, are discussed also.

559 **Agrarian reform and peasant economy in southern Peru.**
David Guillet. Columbia, Missouri; London: University of Missouri
Press, 1979. 227p. map. bibliog.

This monograph examines the impact of the post-1968 agrarian reform programme in a
microregion, the Pampa de Anta, of southern Peru, where by 1970 there were thirty-
seven independent communities and seventy haciendas. Essentially, it studies the
participation of peasant beneficiaries in the large co-operative (38,000 hectares) formed
from the expropriation of existing properties between 1971 and 1973. One of its
conclusions is that the reform programme eliminated the power of the region's agrarian
élite, but transferred it not to the peasants but to an 'agrobureaucracy' directly linked
to the national capital.

560 **Agrarian unrest and political conflict in Puno, 1985-1987.**
Lewis Taylor. *Bulletin of Latin American Research*, vol. 6, no. 2
(1987), p. 135-62.

The agrarian reform programme implemented in the southern department of Puno in
the 1970s failed to gratify land hunger and provided scope for recruitment in rural
communities by the recently established left-wing groups. In an attempt to counter this
trend, the managers of co-operatives reluctantly agreed in 1986 to transfer 500,000
hectares of land to peasant communities and freeholders. However, disputes between
communities and co-operatives over further lands continued to create political
instability in an area considered susceptible to infiltration by 'Shining Path' activists.
These problems are explored in this article, which also provides valuable information
on the internal dynamics of the agrarian co-operatives.

561 **The agricultural development of Peru.**
Arthur J. Coutu, Richard A. King. New York; Washington, DC;
London: Praeger, 1969. 183p. bibliog.

Completed on the eve of the agrarian reform programme introduced after the military
intervention of October 1968, this study unintentionally helps to explain why such
reform became a top economic priority, as well as a social and political necessity. It
draws attention to serious structural weaknesses, caused by low investment, and
resulting in inadequate food production. These problems derived from the secondary
priority given to the modernization of agriculture in the 1950s and 1960s.

562 **Agroindustria y transnacionales en el Perú.** (Agro-industry and
transnationals in Peru.)
Jorge Fernández-Baca, Carlos Parodi Zevallos, Fabián Tume Torres.
Lima: Centro de Estudios y Promoción del Desarrollo, 1983. 260p.
bibliog.

Between 1974 and 1982, food production in Peru remained stagnant and prices rose
above the rate of inflation, despite government subsidies and price controls. This study
attempts to explain these trends, on the basis of a detailed analysis of agro-industry,
and focuses in particular on the rôle of international capital in food processing and
marketing.

563 **Aspectos cuantitativos de la reforma agraria (1969-1979).** (Quantitative aspects of the agrarian reform [1969-1979].)
José María Caballero, Elena Alvarez. Lima: Instituto de Estudios Peruanos, 1980. 151p.

This brief but important study provides a wealth of quantitative data on aspects of the agrarian reform programme which some other researchers have not fully understood, including the proportion of lands affected, the extent of land controlled by co-operatives, and the proportion of peasants who benefited from land redistribution.

564 **Desarrollo desigual y crisis en la agricultura peruana, 1944-1969.** (Unequal development and crisis in Peruvian agriculture, 1944-1969.)
Raul Hopkins. Lima: Instituto de Estudios Peruanos, 1981. 209p. bibliog.

Although written at a time when most agricultural economists were debating the results of agrarian reform, this monograph looks back to the twenty-five year period which led up to it. It examines agricultural production and prices, investment, government policies, and the relationship between agriculture and the national economy. In short, it exposes the roots of the agrarian crisis which the reforms attempted to address in the 1970s.

565 **Economía agraria de la sierra peruana antes de la reforma agraria de 1969.** (The agrarian economy of the Peruvian highlands before the agrarian reform of 1969.)
José María Caballero. Lima: Instituto de Estudios Peruanos, 1981. 426p. bibliog.

This impressive study focuses upon the Peruvian highlands, an area where the capitalist development of agriculture in the 20th century has had to adapt to unique natural and social conditions. It analyses the region's structural characteristics on the eve of the 1969 agrarian reform legislation, and provides an economic and statistical survey of population distribution, resources, production and income, as well as an analysis of productive relations and processes of change.

566 **Política económica y agricultura en el Perú, 1969-1979.** (Economic policy and agriculture in Peru, 1969-1979.)
Elena Alvarez. Lima: Instituto de Estudios Peruanos, 1983. 343p. bibliog.

The principal value of this monograph is that it goes beyond a discussion of land, peasants, and production to examine the impact of agrarian policies in Peru upon the production and consumption of foodstuffs. It provides a detailed analysis of price policies, subsidies, taxes, credit and commercialization, and explains that the agrarian problem in Peru cannot be isolated from the global development of the economy.

567 **Priorización y desarrollo del sector agrario en el Perú.** (The prioritization and development of the agrarian sector in Peru.)
Edited by Adolfo Figueroa Arevalo, Javier Portocarrero Maisch. Lima: Universidad Católica del Perú, 1986. 645p.

In July 1985, some two weeks before the initiation of the presidential term of Alán García, twenty specialists on Peruvian agriculture, including both researchers and rural administrators, exchanged ideas on the agrarian policies which the new government might be expected to pursue in the period 1985-90. Their discussions, reproduced in this volume, cover four general themes: the expansion of the agrarian frontier; the relationships between the unit of production and agricultural development; agricultural development in the highlands; and the rôle of the state in agricultural development.

568 **Problems of regional development in Peru.**
C. T. Smith. *Geography*, vol. 53, no. 3 (July 1968), p. 260-81.

The relative importance of agricultural development and reform in the promotion of regional development is clearly explained in this succinct article.

569 **Realidad del campo peruano despues de la reforma agraria: 10 ensayos críticos.** (The reality of the Peruvian countryside after the agrarian reform: 10 critical essays.)
Carlos Amat y León (et al.). Lima: Centro de Investigación y Capitación, 1980. 388p. bibliog.

The ten essays in this collection provide a good general coverage of the impact of agrarian reform upon rural society and economic life in the period which ended with the return of the Peruvian military to barracks in 1980. Particular attention is paid to the inconsistencies and limitations of the reform programme, including the fact that its overall effect was to transfer resources from the rural sector to urban and industrial interests.

570 **La reforma agraria en el Perú.** (Agrarian reform in Peru.)
José Matos Mar, José Manuel Mejía. Lima: Instituto de Estudios Peruanos, 1980. 379p. map. bibliog.

This detailed study offers a global vision of the agrarian reform programme of Peru's military government, analysing its origins, its principal features, and its results. Its point of departure is the significant observation that, except in Cuba, agrarian reform in Latin America before 1969 (in Mexico and Bolivia, for example) had succeeded only when traditional social relationships in the countryside were being attacked by both the peasantry and significant sectors of the bourgeoisie, who sought to channel peasant discontent into the process of modernization, of both agriculture and the state. In Peru, by contrast, modernization and integration were attempted in a society which had seen little agrarian reform, and in which social division was accentuated by ethnic and cultural factors. These considerations, it is argued, help to explain why modernization and integration were only partially secured.

571 **El rol de la selva en el desarrollo agricola del Perú.** (The rôle of the forest in the agricultural development of Peru.)
Chungsuk Cha. Lima: Banco Central de Reserva del Perú, 1969. 2nd ed. 137p. bibliog.

In the 1960s, the eastern forest region of Peru experienced significant agricultural development as a consequence of improvements in communications and production techniques. This study provides a clear coverage of both the production and marketing of the region's resources, and of the potential for further agricultural development, as perceived in 1969.

572 **Self-management and political participation in Peru, 1969-1975: the corporatist illusion.**
Cynthia McClintock.   London; Beverley Hills, California: Sage, 1978. 63p.

This monograph challenges the idea of corporatism by demonstrating that the establishment of self-managed agrarian co-operatives after 1969 reinforced divisions among the peasantry, as those within the co-operatives used their increased political strength to resist further social reform by the state.

573 **Women in Andean agriculture: peasant production and rural wage employment in Colombia and Peru.**
Carmen Diana Deere, Magdalena León de Leal.   Geneva: International Labour Office. 1982. 172p.

The rôle played by women in peasant agriculture in Peru is of fundamental importance. They participate actively not only in field work and animal raising, but also in the processing and marketing of agricultural and animal produce. Moreover, they are also engaged as seasonal labour on large estates and modern commercial farms. However, as this study clearly indicates, their level of economic participation and their status within the family and community are extremely diverse, just as the peasantry itself does not form a homogeneous social grouping.

Transport and Communications

574 **Caminos del Perú.** (Roads of Peru.)
Antonello Gerbi.   Lima: Banco de Crédito del Perú, 1944. 107p.
bibliog.

As with other works by this outstanding Italian scholar, this unusual and perceptive discussion of the state of roads in Peru in the early 1940s, and of the history of communication by road from the pre-conquest period is beautifully written. The brief bibliographical essay contains references to works in Spanish on Inca roads, the colonial postal system, and railway construction in the 19th century.

575 **Cusco: sistemas viales, articulación y desarrollo regional.** (Cuzco: transport systems, their articulation, and regional development.)
Epifanio Baca Tupayachi.   Cuzco: Centro de Estudios Rurales Andinos 'Bartolomé de las Casas', 1983. 68p map.

This brief analysis of the transport network (road, rail and air) in the Cuzco region explains its historical evolution, analyses its articulation with the regional economy, and proposes a number of new projects designed to promote further economic development.

576 **Henry Meiggs: Yankee Pizarro.**
Watt Stewart.   New York: AMS, 1968. 2nd ed. 370p. bibliog.

In 1868, the US engineer, Meiggs, moved from Chile to Peru and was entrusted with the construction of the Arequipa railway. During the next decade he also received contracts to build the Oroya railway, and a series of roads, including those from Arequipa to Puno and Juliaca to Cuzco. Most of the projects were unfinished in 1877 when work ground to a halt because of Peru's virtual bankruptcy. Nevertheless, they eventually provided the infrastructure for Peru's modern transport system. This biography, first published in 1946, provides a sound survey of the career of Meiggs, and of late-19th century Peruvian attitudes towards transport and communications.

129

Transport and Communications

577 **Peru's own conquest.**
Fernando Belaúnde Terry, introduction by David A. Robinson.
Lima: American Studies, 1965. 219p.

This work was first published as *La conquista del Perú por los peruanos* (The conquest of Peru by the Peruvians), (Lima: Ediciones Tawantisuyu, 1959). It is a visionary statement of schemes to water Peru's deserts and colonize its jungles, and it provides an essential aid to an understanding of the ambitious schemes of road construction undertaken by Belaúnde in eastern Peru during his first presidency (1963-68).

578 **Railways of the Andes.**
Brian Fawcett. London: Allen & Unwin, 1963. 328p. map.

In a somewhat unsystematic way this book provides good descriptions, accompanied by photographs, of the principal railway systems of the Andes, including, of course, the southern and central Peruvian lines, the Cerro de Pasco railway, and the Pisco-Ica railway.

579 **Railways of South America.**
George S. Brady, W. Rodney Long. Washington, DC: Government Printing Office, 1926. 2 vols. 9 maps.

This general survey, prepared under the auspices of the US Department of Commerce, provides a clear, unpretentious description of the railway system of each South American country. The chapter on Peru (vol. 2, p. 192-274) covers both the history and the current status of the various lines of the early-20th century, and is complemented by an excellent map.

580 **Transportation and economic development in Latin America.**
Charles J. Stokes. New York; Washington, DC; London: Praeger, 1968. 204p. 12 maps. bibliog.

This general discussion of transport systems in modern Latin America draws upon a number of case studies. That of particular relevance to Peru is the so-called 'Carretera Marginal de la Selva', the notional international road stretching 5,500 kilometres from the Colombian border with Venezuela through eastern Peru to Santa Cruz in Bolivia. The chapter on the project (p. 113-45) summarizes the research undertaken in the 1960s to determine its economic feasibility.

Labour Movement and Trade Unions

581 **Anarquismo y sindicalismo en el Perú.** (Anarchism and syndicalism in
Peru.)
Piedad Pareja. Lima: Rikchay Peru, 1978. 120p. bibliog.
In Peru, as in other Latin American countries, economic growth and industrialization
in the early-20th century led to an intensification of working-class consciousness, and
attempts to organize workers. This brief study concentrates upon the anarchist
movement in Peru in the 1920s, and in particular upon the conflicts between its leaders
and those of other left-wing groups.

582 **Blue-collar workers in Peru.**
David Chaplin. In: *Peruvian nationalism: a corporatist revolution.*
Edited by David Chaplin. New Brunswick, New Jersey: Transaction
Books, 1976, p. 205-25.
Peru's industrial workers represented only five per cent of the country's labour force in
the 1960s, but, despite their small numbers, they were highly organized and received
elaborate and effective welfare and working condition benefits. This paper provides a
succinct description of their organization, political influence, and benefits. For a more
detailed analysis see the same author's *The Peruvian industrial labour force,*
(Princeton, New Jersey: Princeton University Press, 1967).

583 **A case of neo-feudalism: La Convención, Peru.**
E. J. E. Hobsbawm. *Journal of Latin American Studies*, vol. 1 (1969),
p. 31-50.
This illuminating study of the relationships between landowners and tenants in the
province of La Convención, department of Cuzco, from the late-19th century provides
invaluable information on the background to the formation of peasant unions there in
the early 1960s.

584   **Common management strategies in industrial relations: Peru.**
William Foote Whyte.   In: *Industrial relations and social change in Latin America.* Edited by William H. Form, Albert A. Blum. Gainesville, Florida: University of Florida Press, 1965, p. 46-69.

This paper, based upon a series of field studies in several industrial plants in the Lima-Callao metropolitan area (where three-quarters of Peru's manufacturing was concentrated in the 1960s) discusses the strategies employed by executives for the handling of their union-management relations.

585   **Labor and politics in Peru: the system of political bargaining.**
James L. Payne.   New Haven, Connecticut; London: Yale University Press, 1965. 292p. map.

The focus for this study is the politics of organized labour, a definition which embraces labour relations, in modern Peru. Its chronological range is somewhat unusual in that it deals only with the years 1915-19, 1945-48 and 1956-62, periods of 'free government', when labour organizations enjoyed freedom 'to organize, speak, write, demonstrate, and oppose the government'. Despite this self-imposed restriction, the book serves as a valuable introduction to the development of unions and labour relations.

586   **Labour relations and multinational corporations: the Cerro de Pasco Corporation in Peru (1902-1974).**
Dirk Kruijt, Menno Vellinga.   Assen, The Netherlands: Van Gorcum, 1979. 262p. bibliog.

Up until its nationalization in 1974, the Cerro de Pasco Corporation was the largest private employer in Peru, occupying, because of the general importance of mining in the Peruvian economy, a strategic position in the economic and socio-political spheres. This book examines and explains the emergence of its mineworkers in the late 1960s and the early 1970s as the vanguard of a radical political movement, aspiring to accelerate the process of structural transformation initiated in Peruvian society in 1968 by the revolutionary government of the armed forces.

587   **Latifundio y sindicalismo agrario en el Perú.** (The great estate and agrarian syndicalism in Peru.)
Eduardo Fioravanti.   Instituto de Estudios Peruanos, 1976. 2nd ed. 225p. bibliog.

This monograph on peasant unions concentrates upon the valleys of La Convención y Lares, department of Cuzco, in the period from 1958 to 1964, and is constructed around oral and written material collected by the author during field work undertaken in 1969-70. These sub-tropical regions, which experienced an upsurge of peasant agitation in the period under consideration, were characterized by an anachronistic system of seigneurial organization and were inhabited by a peasantry subjected to pre-capitalist relations of production. It is suggested that the organization of peasant unions was fuelled by their desire to own and control the land, and not by the quest for political power.

588   **Miners and national politics in Peru, 1900-1974.**
      Julian Laite.   *Journal of Latin American Studies*, vol. 12 (1980),
      p. 317-40.

This article provides a very thorough analysis of the development of mining unions in central Peru during the 20th century, and of the relationships between unions and governments. It demonstrates that, despite the propensity for expressive violence associated with the miners' culture, their political activities have progressed steadily from informally organized violent confrontation to formal, regulated negotiations between trade union leaders, management and the state.

589   **Reordering disorder: an approach to the analysis of Peruvian industrial relations.**
      Nigel Haworth.   In: *Region and class in modern Peruvian history*.
      Edited by Rory Miller. Liverpool, England: Institute of Latin
      American Studies, University of Liverpool 1987, p. 163-78.
      (Monograph, 14).

This valuable discussion of the Peruvian industrial relations system seeks both to provide an explanation of the paucity of data on the subject and to offer a framework in which the analysis of Peru's fragmented bargaining process may be located.

Statistics

590 **Peru: compendio estadístico 1982.** (Peru: statistical compendium 1982.)
Lima: Instituto Nacional Estadística, 1983. 124p. 2 maps.

This useful summary of statistical information, presented in the form of tables, graphs and figures, provides basic data on Peruvian geography, population, society, trade, finances and related issues. It serves as a handy work of reference for those who do not require statistics in great detail.

591 **Perú: el agro en cifras.** (Peru: agriculture in figures.)
Hector Maletta, Michel Eresue, Volma Gómez, Rosario Gómez de Zea. Lima: Universidad del Pacífico, 1984. 481p.

The period between 1968 and 1980 was one in which the Peruvian state extended and perfected the gathering of statistical data across the whole range of its activities. In the agricultural sector, systematic censuses were taken of participants and resources, and research projects on the social and economic aspects of agriculture multiplied. This volume consists entirely of detailed statistical data on all aspects of agriculture during the period of military government. Many of the series actually begin before 1968 and continue into the early years of the 1980s.

592 **Perú: las provincias en cifras 1876-1981.** (Peru: the provinces in figures.)
Hector Maletta, Alejandro Bardales, Katia Makhlouf. Lima: Ediciones Amidep, [n.d.]. 3 vols. bibliog.

These three outstanding statistical surveys provide comparative data drawn from both Peru's first national census of 1876, and its most recent, of 1981, for each of the country's 150 provinces. The first volume (272p.) deals with statistics concerning population and migration, the second (376p.) with the work force and employment, and the third (215p.) with the agrarian structure. Although the date of publication is not indicated, the inclusion in the bibliography of items published in 1984 suggests 1985 or later.

593 **Peruvian employment statistics since 1940: an evaluation.**
Alison MacEwan Scott. Liverpool, England: Institute of Latin
American Studies, University of Liverpool 1988, 49p. (Working
Paper, 8).

In Latin America, the most reliable sources of data on employment are usually sample
surveys, but these were only introduced in the late 1960s in most countries, and are
therefore of only limited value for long-run analysis. National population censuses go
back much further but are notorious for their unreliability and are bedevilled by
changes in methodology between censuses. These problems produce a scepticism
amongst some scholars which leads them to rule out the use of census data altogether.
Others take the view that the need for long-run information is so pressing that the
laborious task of evaluation and adjustment of figures has to be undertaken. This
paper presents the results of such an exercise for Peru, with particular reference to the
national population censuses of 1940, 1961, 1972 and 1981, and a number of
employment surveys conducted by the Ministry of Labour between 1972 and 1974.

594 **Síntesis de la economía peruana.** (A survey of the Peruvian economy.)
Manuel Fuentes Irurozgui. Lima: Empresa Gráfica Sanmarti, 1950.
268p.

This survey of the Peruvian economy and its development up to 1950 contains a useful
compilation of statistics for the first half of the 20th century.

595 **Statistical abstract of Latin America.**
Los Angeles: University of California, Center of Latin American
Studies, 1955- . annual.

This invaluable compilation, based on official data, provides annual statistics for each
of the twenty countries in Latin America on land tenure, communications, population,
health and education, trade, national accounts and related topics.

Environment

596 Andean ecology and civilization.

Edited by Shozo Masuda, Izumi Shimada, Craig Morris.   Tokyo:
University of Tokyo Press, 1985. 550p. 7 maps. bibliog.

The twenty-three papers in this collection were presented at an inter-disciplinary
conference on Andean ecological complementarity (lowland-highland interaction)
organized in 1983 by the Wenner-Gren Foundation for Anthropological Research.
They deal primarily with the nature and consequences of man-environment interplay
and inter-regional interaction in the Andes from the pre-hispanic to the modern
periods, and they cover a variety of lowland and highland regions from Ecuador to
northern Chile, and from the Pacific coast to the Amazonian jungle. The majority of
the papers concentrate upon Peru, and they are essential reading for those interested
in the creative dynamism between man and environment in the Central Andes.

597 Biogeography and quaternary history in tropical America.

Edited by T. C. Whitmore, G. T. Prance.   Oxford, England:
Clarendon, 1987. 212p. 114 maps. bibliog.

This rich and complex scientific study ranges widely across the soils and vegetation, the
biogeography, and the early history of man in lowland tropical South America.
Although its coverage is thematic rather than regional, it is a work of relevance to
those interested in both environmental change and instability, and the environment in
human perspective in the extensive tropical lowlands of eastern Peru. The bibliography
provides valuable references to additional material available in scientific journals.

598 The environment and native Andean agriculture.

Stephen B. Brush.   *América Indígena*, vol. 40, no. 1 (1980), p. 161-72.

The indigenous crops, animals and agro-pastoral technology of the Andean people,
whose ancestors invented and developed agriculture 6,000 years ago, are adapted to a
precipitous terrain characterized by abrupt climatic variation and the hazards of frost,
drought and erosion. This synthesis argues that native Andean culture has succeeded in
exploiting this environment by the continued use of certain crops, animals and

technologies since prehistoric times without serious degradation of the landscape. However, the pressures of rapid population increase and economic development are producing fundamental changes in the technology of Andean environment. These pressures and changes are described in this article, which explores alternative strategies for protecting and utilizing the agricultural resources of the Andes.

599 Mountain, field, and family: the economy and human ecology of an Andean valley.

Stephen B. Brush.   Pennsylvania, Philadelphia: University of Pennsylvania Press, 1977. 199p. 8 maps. bibliog.

This study derives from a 1970 project, in which the author participated, to investigate late pre-hispanic occupation of the eastern Andes, drawing on archeological, ethno-historical, and ethnographic sources. It focuses upon the village of Uchucmarca in northern Peru, and its physical and social environment. It shows how the village culture, and individual inhabitants, have adapted to the Andean landscape which surrounds them. The natural environment is marked by tremendous diversity, and the adaptations designed to produce enough food to sustain the lives of the villagers are examined in detail.

600 National parks, conservation, and agrarian reform in Peru.

Mary L. Barker.   *Geographical Review*, 70, 1980, p. 1-18.

This article analyses the delicate balance in Peru between environmental protection and agricultural development. There, as in many other relatively poor countries, areas of natural beauty, with populations of rare animal species, are under increasing pressure from the imperative to promote more intensive agricultural production.

601 Plants, man and the land in the Vilcanota valley of Peru.

Daniel W. Gade.   The Hague: Junk, 1975. 240p. 9 maps. bibliog.

Man's symbiosis with plants is the most fundamental material fact of human life on the earth. This monograph may be described as essentially a geography of plant resources in an important Andean valley which has great environmental diversity and a cultural constant, in so far as a non-literate, Quechua-speaking peasantry dominates throughout the zone. Its basic objective is to analyse man's present use of plants, cultivated and wild, within spatial and chronological contexts. This aspect of the man–nature theme is of interest to a variety of disciplinary specialists, including geographers, botanists and anthropologists; the author defines his field of study as 'cultural biogeography'.

602 Prehistoric Andean ecology: man, settlement and environment in the Andes.

Edited by Frédéric-André Engel.   New York: Department of Anthropology, Hunter College, City University of New York, 1980-84. 4 vols.

These four volumes contain the reports of the field research undertaken in Peru between 1965 and 1980 by the Center for the Study of Arid Zones of the National Agrarian University of Peru. The Center, which from 1965 until 1975 was called the Institute of Pre-Columbian Anthropology and Agriculture, specializes in the problems of arid land ecologies. It bases much of its research activity upon the beliefs that archaeology can make an invaluable contribution to modern understanding of the

Environment

environment and to the history of natural resources, and that significant social projections can be made from the study of agricultural techniques developed by pre-Columbian farmers of the Andes. The first volume (1980, 180p.) provides an atlas of archaeological sites in the central Andes; the second (1981, 155p.) concentrates upon the far south of Peru; the third (1983, 185p.) deals with stone typology; and the fourth (1984, 186p.) is concerned exclusively with the problem of man's adaptation to the environment in the Chilca hydrological basin.

Education

603 **Aspectos sociales de la educación rural en el Perú.** (Social aspects of
rural education in Peru.)
Giorgio Alberti, Julio Cotler. Lima: Instituto de Estudios Peruanos,
1972. 149p. bibliog.
Although published in August 1972, five months after the announcement of the radical
programme for educational reform of the military government, this study was prepared
in 1971. Its powerful argument in favour of using rural education to promote social
change anticipated in many ways the reform programme.

604 **Bilingual education: an experience in Peruvian Amazonia.**
Edited by Mildred L. Larson, Patricia M. Davis. Dallas, Texas:
Summer Institute of Linguistics, 1981. 417p. map.
The SIL, although engaged primarily in bible translation and diffusion, has been
deeply involved since the mid 1950s in bilingual education in the eastern lowlands of
Peru. The purpose of this book is to report the results of the experiment over a twenty-
five year period. Section one describes the historical background to the programme;
sections two and three cover its goals and results; section four discusses the preparation
of teaching materials in vernacular languages; and section five relates the programme
to the broader framework of indigenous communities and culture.

605 **Bilingual education success, but policy failure.**
Nancy H. Hornberger. *Language in Society*, vol. 16 (1987), p. 205-26.
In 1977, a bilingual education project began in rural areas of the southern department
of Puno, as a direct result of Peru's 1972 education reform programme. This paper
presents the results of an ethnographic and socio-linguistic study, which compared
Quechua language use and maintenance between a bilingual education school and a
monolingual (Spanish) school. In the former, teacher–pupil language relations
improved dramatically, as community members were encouraged to value and use
Quechua. However, poor planning, including the inappropriate application of the
project in urban areas which were too bilingual for a model aimed essentially at
monolingual Quechua children, created many practical difficulties.

Education

606 **Educational change in Latin America: the case of Peru.**
Beatrice Avalos. Cardiff: University College Cardiff Press, 1978. 92p.
bibliog.

This brief, clear study explains the general relevance of changes in educational systems to meet the challenge of social, political, and economic change, before going on to provide a detailed analysis of the educational reform programme introduced in Peru in 1972.

607 **Human resources, education and economic development in Peru.**
Organisation for Economic Co-operation and Development. Paris: OECD, 1967. 372p.

This report on human resource and educational planning was prepared in 1964 by the Peruvian National Planning Institute with the collaboration of the OECD. Its main purpose was to take the economic and social development targets of Peru as a basis for long-term quantitative and qualitative forecasts of human resources and educational requirements, which would serve as the foundations for a policy of planned educational development. The volume contains a wealth of detail on actual educational provision in 1964.

608 **El magisterio y sus luchas 1885-1978.** (Schoolteachers and their struggles 1885-1978.)
César Pezo del Pino, Eduardo Ballón Echegaray, Luís Peirano Falconi. Lima: Centro de Estudios y Promoción del Desarrollo, 1978. 276p. bibliog.

Although concerned primarily with the struggles of schoolteachers in Peru for proper professional status and conditions since the 1940s, this study also provides a sound coverage of general attitudes towards primary and secondary education since the late-19th century.

609 **Movimiento universitario en el Perú, 1909-1980.** (The university movement in Peru, 1909-1980.)
Antonio Cruz, Neptali Carpio. Lima: Alma Matinal, 1981. 125p. bibliog.

This analysis of the development of universities in 20th-century Peru was written by two young student activists. Although it is a subjective study, it is recommended for those who seek to understand the politicization of university life in modern Peru.

610 **Reforma educativa. Qué pasó?** (The educational reform. What happened?)
Kenneth Delgado Santa Gadea. Lima: Ediciones SAGSA, 1981. 228p. bibliog.

The purpose of this book is to analyse the aims and the application of the educational reform programme of the military government in the 1970s. It describes the background to the new system, and pays particular attention to its results in the field of rural education. Its general and predictable conclusion is that the programme was only partially successful.

Science and Technology

611 **Agricultural technology in developing countries.**
A. L. MacDonald. Rotterdam, The Netherlands: Rotterdam
University Press, 1976. 236p. bibliog.

This book provides a detailed account of the relationship between social factors and
the introduction of modern agricultural techniques in two highland regions of Peru: the
Mantaro valley and the Andahuaylas region.

612 **Crecimiento, industrialización y cambio técnico: Perú 1955-1980.**
(Growth, industrialization and technical change: Peru 1955-1980.)
Máximo Vega-Centeno. Lima: Universidad Católica del Perú, 1983.
349p. bibliog.

The focus of this work is upon the relationship between technology and industrial
development in Peru. It offers both a theoretical framework and a series of empirical
studies of the application of technology in the Peruvian manufacturing sector.

613 **Política tecnológica y seguridad alimentaria en América Latina.**
(Technological policy and food-supply security in Latin America.)
Martin Piñeiro, E. S. Obschatko. Lima: Instituto de Estudios
Peruanos, 1985. 90p. bibliog.

The concept of 'food-supply security' emerged in the 1970s, as international
organizations, faced with a nutritional crisis in many parts of the Third World, sought
to promote the strategic production of basic foodstuffs, such as cereals, meat and milk,
to levels sufficient to cover basic needs without resort to imports. This study examines
the relationship between agricultural technology and increases in food production in
Latin America as a whole. However, much of its data is drawn from the experience of
Peru.

Science and Technology

614 **The role of science and technology in Peruvian economic development.**
Washington, DC: National Academy of Sciences, 1966. 85p.

This report records the issues discussed and the conclusions reached at a Peruvian–US workshop on the rôle of science and technology in Peruvian economic development, held in Paracas, Peru, in 1966. The contents include consideration of the development of science and technology in Peru, and the influence of the scientific community on political decisions affecting development planning.

615 **Tecnología andina y desarrollo regional.** (Andean technology and regional development.)
Ricardo Claverias H. (et al.). Puno: Instituto de Investigaciones para el Desarrollo Social del Altiplano, 1985. 185p.

Prepared by a team of researchers from the universities of Cuzco and Puno, this work argues in favour of using traditional technology and 'popular knowledge' in the Andean highlands as the basis for agricultural and regional development. It suggests that imported technology is often inappropriate to local needs, and also tends to destroy local initiative and independence.

Literature

General

616 The Andes viewed from the city: literary and political discourse on the Indian in Peru, 1848-1930.
Efrain Kristal. New York: Peter Lang, 1987. 240p. bibliog.
This survey of *indigenista* writing includes discussion of the works of Narciso Aréstegui, Manuel González Prada, Clorinda Matto de Turner and Ventura García Calderón.

617 The bridge of San Luis Rey.
Thornton N. Wilder. London: Longman, Green, 1927. 140p.
This novel provides a highly readable, fictional recreation of life in colonial Peru.

618 From oral to written expression: native Andean chronicles of the early colonial period.
Edited by Rolena Klahn Adorno. Syracuse, New York: Maxwell School of Citizenship and Public Affairs, Syracuse University, 1982. 181p. bibliog.
This volume contains six essays by distinguished literary scholars and anthropologists on the transition in early colonial Peru from the pre-Columbian oral tradition to the creation of literary works in Spanish by ethnic Andeans.

619 Guaman Poma: writing and resistance in colonial Peru.
Rolena Klahn Adorno. Austin, Texas: University of Texas Press, 1986. 189p. bibliog.
The famous pictorial history of Peru written for King Philip III of Spain in 1615 by this obscure Indian writer is of enormous importance to scholars from a variety of

143

disciplines, including history and anthropology. The aim of this study is to analyse its language, and 'reconstruct the ways in which a native American translated his experience in the language of the other'.

620 **A history of Peruvian literature.**
James Higgins.   Liverpool, England: Francis Cairns, 1987. 379p. bibliog.

This work concentrates on the 20th century, when Peru has produced an astonishing range of literary material, and international writers such as César Vallejo, José María Arguedas and Mario Vargas Llosa. However, it also provides a valuable context for understanding modern Peruvian literature by examining both the native, Quechua, tradition, and colonial and early republican trends.

621 **Literatura quechua.** (Quechua literature.)
Edited by Edmundo Bendezú Aybar.   Caracas: Bibloteca Ayacucho, 1980. 450p. bibliog.

The collecting and recording of Quechua stories and poetry began in Peru immediately after the Spanish conquest, as the first chroniclers and missionaries struggled to understand the complexities of indigenous culture. It continued throughout the colonial period and the 19th century, reaching a new intensity in the 20th century, with the growth of interest in anthropology, linguistics and folklore. The majority of Quechua tales, even in the modern period, have been written not so much to be read, but to be spoken and heard in the context of non-literary activity, such as singing, dance, agricultural work and religious rituals. This outstanding anthology provides a selection of stories from the Inca, colonial and modern periods, supplemented by a detailed chronological table and an excellent bibliography.

622 **The modern short story in Peru.**
Earl M. Aldrich, Jr.   Madison, Milwaukee: University of Wisconsin Press, 1966. 212p. bibliog.

This work provides a chronological view of the development of the modern short story in Peruvian literature from the time of its introduction at the turn of the present century through to the early 1960s.

623 **The poet in Peru: alienation and the quest for a super-reality.**
James Higgins.   Liverpool, England: Francis Cairns, 1982. 166p.

In spite of adverse cultural conditions, Peru has produced much excellent poetry. This study of six 20th-century poets – César Vallejo, José María Eguren, Carlos Germán Belli, Antonio Cisneros, César Moro and Martín Adán – is designed to introduce their work to a wider public.

624 **Writing for fewer and fewer: Peruvian fiction 1979-1980.**
David O. Wise.   *Latin American Research Review*, vol. 18 (1983), p. 189-200.

Although intended as a review of a number of specific novels published in 1979-80, this essay makes a number of cogent general observations about the publishing industry and its difficulties in Peru.

Novels and poetry in translation

625 Aunt Julia and the scriptwriter.
Mario Vargas Llosa, translated by H. R. Lane. London: Faber & Faber, 1983. 374p.

Set in the Lima of the 1950s, this frank, autobiographical novel is dedicated to the author's first wife, Julia Urquidi Illanes, the aunt Julia of the title, 'to whom this novel and I owe so much'. Those interested in Julia's reaction to the rather unflattering portrait painted of her should see Julia Urquidi Illanes, *Lo que Varguitas no dijo*. (What little Vargas did not tell.) (La Paz: Khana Cruz, 1983).

626 Broad and alien is the world.
Ciro Alegría, translated by Harriet de Onis. New York: Farrar & Rinehart, 1941. 434p.

This classic political novel describes the sufferings of an idealized Indian highland community at the hands of successive generations of exploiters.

627 César Vallejo: an anthology of his poetry.
Edited by James Higgins. Oxford: Pergamon, 1970. 183p. bibliog.

Vallejo is one of the great poets of the Spanish language; he is also one of the most difficult to interpret. Although in this edition the notes have been deliberately kept to a minimum, the introductory essay (p. 1-82) provides a brief analysis of each of the fifty poems in the anthology. The bibliography provides useful references to Vallejo's own works and to books of criticism, most of which are in Spanish.

628 The complete posthumous poetry.
César Vallejo, translated by Clayton Eshelman, José Rubía Barcía. Berkeley, California: University of California Press, 1982. 367p.

This volume contains all the verse written by Vallejo in his latter years, the period in which he produced his finest work.

629 Conversation in the cathedral.
Mario Vargas Llosa, translated by Gregory Rabassa. New York: Harper & Row, 1974. 601p.

This massive and complex novel offers a disenchanted overview of Peruvian society during the period 1948-63. Above all, it exposes the corrupting influence of the Manuel Odría dictatorship, which in its turn is seen as a symptom of deep-rooted ills.

630 Deep rivers.
José María Arguedas, translated by Frances Horning Barraclough. Austin, Texas: University of Texas Press, 1978. 264p.

Arguedas' most accomplished novel, written in Spanish in 1958, explores the clash of Peru's two major cultures through the story of a young boy caught between the Quechua and hispanic worlds.

631 Drums for Rancas.

Manuel Scorza, translated by Edith Grossman. London: Secker & Warburg, 1977. 214p.

Between 1950 and 1962, a number of communities in the central Andes resisted the expansion at their expense of the mighty Cerro de Pasco corporation. This politically realistic novel – Scorza claims to be 'not a novelist so much as a witness' – describes the resistance of the community of Rancas against the enclosure of the traditional pastures enjoyed by its members for grazing their sheep, and the repression which the villagers suffered at the hands of the forces of law and order.

632 The green house.

Mario Vargas Llosa, translated by Gregory Rabassa. London: Cape, 1969. 405p.

Juxtaposing story-lines set in Piura and in Amazonas, this ambitious novel portrays the geographical, cultural and social fragmentation of the Peruvian nation.

633 The newest Peruvian poetry in translation.

Edited by Luis A. Ramos-García, Edgar O'Hara. Austin, Texas: Studia Hispanica, 1979. 69p.

Although modest in size, this text is attractive and important. It provides English translations of selected works of nineteen poets, covering material produced since the early 1960s, and is arranged in chronological order.

634 Peru: the new poetry.

Edited by Maureen Ahern, David Tipton. London: London Magazine Editions, 1970. 128p.

This attractive selection of the works of eleven Peruvian poets, ranging chronologically from Sebastián Salazar Bondy (1924-65) to Mirko Lauer (1947- .) is concerned primarily with material published in the 1960s.

635 The real life of Alejandro Mayta.

Mario Vargas Llosa, translated by A. Macadam. London: Faber & Faber, 1986. 320p.

Fact and fiction are intermingled in this political novel, which charts the sad history of small, left-wing guerrilla groups in Peru during the author's youth. A number of the characters are derived from his personal reminiscences.

636 The spider hangs too far from the ground.

Antonio Cisneros, translated by Maureen Ahern, William Rowe, David Tipton. London: Cape Goliard, 1970. 60p.

This selection of forty poems represents the best work of the leading Peruvian poet of the 1960s generation.

637 The time of the hero.

Mario Vargas Llosa. London: Picador, 1986. 409p.

First published as *La ciudad y los perros* (The city and the dogs)(Barelona: Seix Barral, 1962), this novel of adolescence, set in a Lima military academy, portrays a world which stands as a microcosm of Peruvian society as a whole.

638 **The war of the end of the world.**
Mario Vargas Llosa, translated by Helen R. Lane.   London: Faber &
Faber, 1985.

This powerful historical novel, first published in Spanish (Barcelona: Seix Barral,
1981), is inspired by a real episode in late-19th century Brazil, when a mysterious
prophet gathered into his apocalyptic movement all the damned of the earth –
prostitutes, beggars and bandits – to establish the libertarian paradise of Canudos. The
underlying theme of the book is the fatal attraction of Latin American revolutions.

639 **Yawar fiesta.**
José María Arguedas, translated by Frances Horning Barraclough.
London: Quartet Books, 1985. 200p.

Dating from 1941, Arguedas' first novel portrays the complexities of traditional
Andean society and explores the impact of change on that society.

Folklore

640 **El folklore mágico de Cajamarca.** (The magical folklore of Cajamarca.)
Luís Ibérico Mas. Trujillo: Editorial Moreno, 1980. 213p. bibliog.

This work describes and analyses the popular religious practices of the rural inhabitants of the Cajamarca region of northern Peru. The particular application of popular customs in the field of medicine is discussed in the same author's subsequent, but undated work *El folklore médico de Cajamarca* (Cajamarca: Universidad Nacional de Cajamarca).

641 **El Inca por la Coya: historia de un drama popular en los Andes peruanos.** (History of a popular drama in the Peruvian Andes.)
Luis Millones. Lima: Fundación Friedrich Ebert, 1988. 106p. bibliog.

Each year on 2 September (the feast of Santa Rosa of Lima) the inhabitants of the village of Carhuamayo perform a play in memory of the execution of the Inca emperor, Atahualpa, by Francisco Pizarro. The work explains the origins and the religious and cultural significance of the tradition.

642 **Kay Pacha.**
Bernabé Condori, Rosalind Gow. Cuzco: Centro de Estudios Rurales Andinos 'Bartolomé de las Casas', 1982. 99p.

This bilingual (Quechua and Spanish) translation of a folk-tale of the remote community of Pinchimuro (department of Cuzco) provides a good example of the richness and importance of Andean oral tradition.

643 **The singing mountaineers: songs and tales of the Quechua people.**
Edited by Ruth Stephan. Austin, Texas; London: University of Texas Press, 1957. 203p. bibliog.

Almost half of this volume is devoted to Quechua songs, and a similar proportion to Quechua tales, both collected by the great Peruvian writer, José María Arguedas, who spent his childhood living with Indians in the highlands of Apurimac. They were published in Spanish in 1938 and 1949. The editor's lengthy introduction to the present collection provides a clear and detailed explanation of its importance.

644 **Vicos: las fiestas en la integración y desintegración cultural.** (Vicos: festivals in cultural integration and disintegration.)
Hector Martínez Arellano. *Revista del Museo Nacional* (Lima), vol. 28 (1959), p. 189-247.

Taking the hacienda of Vicos as an example, this article examines its history, and the rôle of festivals in providing its inhabitants with social and cultural cohesion.

Music and Theatre

645 **Apuntes para un diccionario biográfico musical peruano.** (Notes for a
Peruvian biographical dictionary of music.)
Rodolfo Barbacci. *Fénix*, vol. 2, no. 6 (1949), p. 414-510.

This detailed biographical listing, arranged alphabetically, of information concerning
the musical history of Peru was prepared by Barbacci between 1855 and 1866. It
contains references to the colonial period, but is concerned primarily with composers
and artists of the republican era.

646 **The contemporary Peruvian theatre.**
Robert J. Morris. Lubbock, Texas: Texas Tech Press, 1977. 98p.
bibliog.

This brief but incisive study examines, within an historical perspective, the dramatic
productions of those writers who have made substantial contributions to Peruvian
theatre since the end of World War II.

647 **Guía musical del Perú.** (A musical guide to Peru.)
Carlos Raygada. *Fénix*, vol. 12 (1956-57), p. 3-77; vol. 13 (1963),
p. 1-82; vol. 14 (1964), p. 3-95.

The author of these three extensive articles on Peruvian music enjoyed a long career as
a musical critic in Peru from 1925. Composers, instrumentalists, singers and teachers
are covered in these pieces, which together represent the best guide to the musical life
of Peru during the first half of the 20th century.

648 **The new theatre of Peru.**
Arthur Natalla, Jr. New York: Senda Nueva, 1982. 130p. bibliog.

This excellent guide to the modern Peruvian theatre concentrates on the period since
1946, when the establishment of a national theatre company and the government
sponsorship of an annual theatre prize encouraged the emergence of a new generation
of dramatic talents.

Art and Architecture

649   Baroque and rococo in Latin America.

Pál Kelemen.   New York: Dover, 1967. 2nd ed. 2 vols. bibliog.

First published in one volume (New York: Macmillan, 1951), this superb guide to the art and architecture of colonial Latin America concentrates upon Mexico and Peru, which, as the centres of Spanish power and wealth, were particularly important areas for extravagant display. The first volume (269p.) contains the written text; the second (192p.) is devoted entirely to black-and-white plates.

650   Contemporary art in Latin America.

Gilbert Chase.   New York: Free Press; London: Collier-Macmillan, 1970. 292p. bibliog.

This is the best available general introduction to contemporary plastic arts and architecture in Latin America. It covers the period from 1920 until 1970, and deals specifically with Peru (p. 96-112) within a chapter entitled 'Nativism and modernism on the west coast' (p. 96-126).

651   The Cuzco circle.

Leopoldo Castedo.   New York: Center for Inter-American Relations, 1976. 144p.

This catalogue of forty-one paintings of the 17th, 18th and 19th centuries, from Cuzco, exhibited in New York in 1976, contains an outstanding set of photographs and a valuable historical introduction.

652   Folk art of Peru.

Lima: Ministry of Foreign Affairs, Department of Cultural Affairs, 1970. 32p.

A useful introduction to Peruvian popular art and its significance is provided by this brief, well-illustrated guide. The English text is accompanied by a translation into Spanish.

Art and Architecture

653 **A history of Latin American art and architecture from pre-Columbian times to the present.**
Leopoldo Castedo, translated and edited by Phyllis Freeman.
London: Pall Mall, 1969. 320p. 5 maps. bibliog.
This general survey devotes considerable attention to pre-Columbian art and architecture in Peru (p. 69-98), and also covers the baroque architecture of the colonial period (p. 164-77). Its discussion of the republican period is brief, and embraced within thematic chapters.

654 **Introducción a la pintura peruana del Siglo XX.** (An introduction to Peruvian painting of the 20th century.)
Mirko Lauer. Lima: Mosca Azul, 1976. 214p. bibliog.
This work concentrates upon an analysis of the ideas of both the producers and the purchasers of 20th-century Peruvian paintings. It contains useful information on the art market.

655 **Peruvian colonial painting.**
Pál Kelemen. Brooklyn, New York: Brooklyn Museum, 1971. 112p.
This catalogue of an exhibition of Peruvian colonial painting, shown at the Brooklyn Museum in 1971-72, contains a clear and reliable introductory essay, and descriptions and black-and-white photographs of forty-one paintings.

656 **El Perú y el arte.** (Peru and art.)
Manuel González Salazar. Lima: Ediciones San Julián, 1970. 191p.
This valuable volume consists almost entirely of black-and-white photographs, with brief descriptions, of the colonial architecture of Lima.

657 **Pintores peruanos de la república.** (Peruvian painters of the republican period.)
Juan Villacorta Paredes. Lima: Libreria Studium, 1971. 126p.
The principal value of this somewhat pedestrian guide is that it provides brief biographies and descriptions of the paintings of Peru's 19th-century painters, as well as of those of the 20th century.

658 **Pintura y escultura en el Perú contemporáneo.** (Painting and sculpture in contemporary Peru.)
Juan Manuel Ugarte Elespuru. Lima: Ediciones de Difusión del Arte Peruano. 248p. bibliog.
This authoritative guide to the visual arts in contemporary Peru, written by a former director of the National School of Fine Arts, contains excellent black-and-white plates, and a detailed bibliography.

Food and Food Policy

659 **Agricultura y alimentación: bases de un nuevo enfoque.** (Agriculture
and food supply: the bases for a new focus.)
Edited by Manuel Lajo, Rolando Ames, Carlos Samaniego. Lima:
Universidad Católica del Perú, 1982. 536p.

The eighteen contributors to this volume participated in a symposium on agriculture
and food supply held in Chaclacayo in 1979. They address the general issue of
inadequate food production in Peru and, hence, an increasing reliance on imported
foodstuffs. The principal topics covered include the marketing of food products,
consumption, and the proposed changes to government agrarian policies which might
make Peru less reliant upon imports. It is a sad comment upon the gulf between
academic debate and policy implementation that, since 1982, Peru has become more
rather than less reliant upon imported foodstuffs.

660 **Cultivos andinos: alternativa alimentaria popular?** (Andean crops: an
alternative source of popular nutrition?)
Annette Salis. Cuzco: Centro de Estudios Rurales Andinos
'Bartolomé de las Casas', 1985. 89p. bibliog.

As low agricultural productivity, population increase and inflation make 'Western'
foods increasingly inaccessible for Peru's masses, greater attention is being paid by
agronomists to the possibility of encouraging the production and marketing of
traditional Andean food products. This study presents a nutritional and economic
analysis of the advantages to producers and consumers of increasing the production of
the vegetables *quinua*, *kiwicha* and *tarwi* (*lupinus mutabilis*). The bibliography
provides details of a considerable number of relevant items in specialized journals on
agronomy.

661 **De cocina peruana: exhortaciones.** (On the Peruvian kitchen:
exhortations.)
Adián Felipe Mejía, edited by Juan Francisco Valega. Lima: P. L.
Villanueva, 1969. 138p.

Published to mark the twentieth anniversary of Mejia's death, this commemorative
collection of his press articles about Peruvian food provides a light-hearted and, above
all, well-written survey of the delicacies and specialities of Lima's typical creole
recipes.

662 **Hambre nacional y pan ajeno.** (National hunger and foreign bread.)
Manuel Lajo Lazo. Lima: Editorial Pueblo Indio, 1984. 387p. bibliog.

The author has written prolifically since the late 1970s on Peruvian food supply,
nutrition, pricing policies, and related issues. This volume brings together no less than
sixty of his articles and essays, together with a valuable bibliography of works
published between 1969 and 1984 by other specialists on these themes.

663 **Propuesta de un programa de sustitución de trigo importado en base al
desarrollo de la economía agrícola andina.** (A proposal for a programme
to substitute imported wheat by means of the development of the
Andean agricultural economy.)
Javier Tantaleán Arbulú, José Luís Arauguena. *Allpanchis* (Cuzco),
no. 23 (1984), p. 17-56.

The title of this important article is largely self-explanatory. Although predominantly
concerned with agricultural economics, it also provides valuable data on food
preferences and nutritional levels among Peru's population.

664 **The urban bias of Peruvian food policy: consequences and alternatives.**
Marco A. Ferroni. PhD thesis, Cornell University, 1980. (Available
from University Microfilms, Ann Arbor, Michigan, order no.
80-15666).

This detailed analysis of food production and consumption in Peru argues that the
needs of the urban consumer tend, for understandable reasons, to carry more weight
with government and planners than those of the rural producer.

Libraries and Archives

665 **Archivos arequipeños.** (The archives of Arequipa.)
Alejandro Málaga Medina.   Arequipa: Publiunsa, 1980. 101p.
The southern Peruvian city of Arequipa, the third most important urban centre in
colonial Peru, overtook Cuzco in the mid-19th century and since then has been second
only to Lima, politically and economically. Its local archives are, thus, of considerable
importance for historians of the colonial and the republican periods. This guide
describes four major repositories: the parochial archive of Yanahuara, the municipal
archive, the departmental archive, and the archive of the *cabildo eclesiástico*
(ecclesiastical council).

666 **El archivo Tello.** (The Tello archive.)
Carlos Daniel Valcárcel.   Lima: Tipografía Peruana, 1966. 76p.
The extensive collection of books and documents of the eminent Peruvian
archaeologist, Julio Tello, were donated to the library of the University of San Marcos,
when he died in 1947. According to the introduction to this catalogue, they had been
consulted by 1966 by only one researcher, despite their historical and biographical
importance.

667 **Guía del investigador en el archivo arzobispal del Cuzco.** (Research
guide to the archdiocesan archive of Cuzco.)
Juan Bautista Lassegue-Moleres.   Cuzco: Fondo del Libro del Banco
Industrial del Perú, 1981. 76p.
This research guide to the archive of the archdiocese of Cuzco includes brief comments
on its significance for the study of the socio-economic history of the Church in the
Cuzco region, and its impact upon Andean societies.

668 **Research guide to Andean history: Bolivia, Chile, Ecuador and Peru.**
Edited by John J. TePaske.   Durham, North Carolina: Duke
University Press, 1981. 346p.

This outstanding practical guide for researchers, published under the auspices of the
Conference on Latin American History of the United States contains (p. 206-334)
eighteen brief essays on both Peruvian historiography and the country's principal
archives and libraries.

Mass Media

General

669 **Communication policies in Peru.**
Carlos Ortega, Carlos Romero. Paris: UNESCO, 1977. 68p.
This contribution to the series of UNESCO studies on national communication policies examines policies for the mass media in Peru within the broad context of an analysis of public, institutional and professional attitudes towards communication.

670 **Latin American media: guidance and censorship.**
Marvin Alisky. Ames, Iowa: Iowa State University Press, 1981. 265p. bibliog.
The specific analysis of the Peruvian media (p. 67-88) in this useful general analysis of censorship concentrates upon the 1970s, but also refers to earlier attempts to restrict press freedom during the presidencies of Manuel Prado and Manuel Odría.

671 **Mass media reform and social change: the Peruvian experience.**
Rita Attwood, Sergio Mattos. *Journal of Communication*, vol. 32, no. 2 (spring 1982), p. 33-45.
This succinct article surveys relationships between the military and the Peruvian media between 1968 and 1975, and attempts to evaluate their significance for diverging views on the efficiency of structural media changes in national development efforts. Its appended list of references (p. 43-45) will be of considerable assistance to researchers.

672 **El periodismo en el Perú.** (Journalism in Peru.)
Juan Vicente Requejo. Lima: Centro de Documentación e Información Andina, 1986. 142p. bibliog.
This very useful introduction to reporting in Peru includes information on the

circulations of national, local and imported printed media, and a history of national and local radio and television services. It is the best source of objective, up-to-date information on the media as a whole.

673 **Prensa, radio y TV: historia crítica.** (Press, radio and TV: a critical history.)
Juan Gargurevich.   Lima: Editorial Horizonte, 1987. 319p. bibliog.

This excellent general survey of the mass media in modern Peru covers four topics: the history of the press to 1970; the history of broadcasting to 1970; the expropriation and return of the media in the 1970s; and the development of the media under restored civilian government between 1980 and 1984. See, too, the same author's *Radio y comunicación popular en el Perú* (Radio and popular communication in Peru) (Lima: Centro Peruano de Estudios Sociales, 1987), which discusses the preferences of radio audiences in greater Lima, and the impact of communication by radio upon the peasantry.

Newspapers and periodicals

674 **Government-press relations in Peru.**
Marvin Alisky.   *Journalism Quarterly* (winter 1976), p. 661-65.

As the military government of 1968-80 entered a more conservative phase in 1975, following the replacement of general Juan Velasco as president by general Francisco Morales Bermúdez, its relations with the press oscillated. It eased controls in September 1975, but tightened them in 1976, as street rioters protested against inflation. These shifts are clearly explained in this article.

675 **Mito y verdad de los diarios de Lima.** (The myth and the truth about the Lima daily newspapers.)
Juan Gargurevich.   Lima: Editorial Gráfica Labor, 1972. 310p.

Following the installation of the military government in 1968, the issue of media policies acquired much greater importance in Peru. This useful study provides a good critical survey, both of the Lima press in general, and of its relationships with government before and after 1968.

676 **El periodismo en el Perú.** (Journalism in Peru.)
Raúl Porras Barrenechea.   Lima: Instituto Raúl Porras Barrenechea, 1970. 133p.

This useful volume brings together five of Porras' essays, written in the period 1921-57, most of which appeared in obscure journals. Together they provide a good general survey of the history of the press in the 19th and early-20th centuries.

677 **Prensa: apertura y limites.** (The press: freedom and restrictions.)
Luis Peirano (et al.).   Lima: Centro de Estudios y Promoción del
Desarrollo, 1978. 241p.

This study analyses the ways in which the six principal daily newspapers of Lima
(*Correo, Ultima Hora, Expreso, La Cronica, La Prensa* and *El Comercio*) reported
international, political, rural and labour issues between July 1974 and July 1975,
following their expropriation by the state.

Reference Works

678 **The Cambridge encyclopedia of Latin America and the Caribbean.**
Edited by Simon Collier, Harold Blakemore, Thomas E. Skidmore.
Cambridge, England: Cambridge University Press, 1985. 456p.

The coverage of this profusely illustrated, lively and economically priced general work of reference is thematic rather than regional. References to Peru abound.

679 **The Cambridge history of Latin America.**
Edited by Leslie Bethell. Cambridge, England: Cambridge University Press, 1984-86. [5 vols.] maps. bibliog.

Five volumes have been published so far of this monumental work of reference, and three additional volumes are in preparation; they cover the period from pre-conquest times to 1930. The first two volumes, which deal with the colonial period, are organized thematically and refer frequently to Peru; the third has a chapter on Peru and Bolivia from Independence to the War of the Pacific (p. 539-82); the fourth is again thematic; and the fifth has a chapter on 'The origins of modern Peru, 1880-1930' (p. 587-640). It is an essential work of reference.

680 **Handbook of Latin American popular culture.**
Edited by Harold E. Hinds, Jr., Charles M. Tatum. Westport, Connecticut: Greenwood, 1985, 259p. bibliog.

This outstanding survey of popular culture in Latin America provides ten general thematic overviews of popular music and religion, comics, television, sport, photonovels, film, festivals and carnivals, cartoons, and newspapers. Material on Peru is found in each chapter, and the bibliographies for each category also contain specific references to Peruvian sources.

681 **Historical dictionary of Peru.**
Marvin Alisky. Metuchen, New Jersey; London: Scarecrow, 1979.
157p. bibliog.
Although, inevitably, a work of this nature is bound to be selective in its coverage, this is a handy reference tool, particularly for the recent history of Peru.

682 **The Latin America and Caribbean review 1989.**
Saffron Walden, England: World of Information, 1989. 10th ed. 192p.
This annual publication, designed with the needs of business people in mind, provides general articles and discussions of economic issues, which are followed by brief reports on individual countries. It is a useful source of up-to-date information on Peru.

683 **Latin American political parties.**
Robert J. Alexander. New York; Washington, DC; London: Praeger, 1973. 537p. bibliog.
Designed essentially as a reference volume, this book discusses all the important political parties of Latin America in the 20th century, as well as the outstanding ones of the 19th century. It is organized according to types of parties, the principal categories being personalist and traditional, socialist, national revolutionary, Christian democratic, and totalitarian. Within each section the appropriate Peruvian parties are analysed in some detail.

684 **The world of learning 1989.**
London: Europa, 1989. 39th ed. 2,000p.
The section on Peru (p. 1,043-51) in this comprehensive directory of higher education provides details, including addresses and names of administrators, of universities, libraries, archives, museums, learned societies, academies, and similar organizations.

Bibliographies

685 **Accounts of nineteenth-century South America: an annotated checklist of works by British and United States observers.**
Bernard Naylor. London: Athlone, 1969. 80p.

A fifth of the travel books described in this checklist of 320 items are concerned specifically with the Pacific coast (many travellers visited Chile *en route* to Peru), and a number of the general accounts also contain material on Peru.

686 **Bibliografía de la poesía peruana 65/79.** (A bibliography of Peruvian poetry 65/79.)
Jesús Cabel. Lima: Amaru Editores, 1980. 142p.

This useful guide provides a listing of collections of poetry published by Peruvians, in Peru and abroad, in the period from 1965 to 1979. Works published in the period 1980 to 1984 are covered in the same author's *Bibliografía de la poesía peruana 80/84.* (Lima: Ediciones de la Biblioteca Universitaria, 1986).

687 **Bibliografía indígena andina peruana (1900-1968).** (A bibliography of works on the indigenes of the Peruvian Andes [1900-1968].)
Hector Martínez, Miguel Cameo, Jesús Ramírez. Lima: Ministerio de Trabajo y Comunidades, Instituto Indigenista Peruano, 1968. 2 vols.

Much of the abundant material published since 1900 in Peru on indigenous topics has appeared in short-lived journals, theses, occasional papers, and other relatively obscure outlets. Over 1,700 items are listed or described in these two volumes. The second volume contains indexes of authors, places and subjects.

688 **Bibliografía peruana de historia 1940-1953.** (A bibliography of Peruvian history 1940-1953.)
Alberto Tauro. Lima. [n.p.], 1953. 196p.

This detailed, annotated bibliography provides information on 1,214 historical works produced in the period 1940-53. It is indicative of the historiographical emphasis then in vogue that over 400 deal with the pre-hispanic and conquest period, 300 with the colonial era and only 150 with post-independence; there is a separate section on local history.

689   **Bibliografía regional peruana: colección particular.** (A regional bibliography of Peru: a personal collection.)
Carlos Moreyra Paz Soldán.   Lima: Librería Internacional del Perú, 1967. 518p.

This detailed, annotated bibliography, divided into chapters on each of Peru's modern departments, contains references to many obscure local publications.

690   **Bio-bibliografía de José Carlos Mariátegui.** (Bio-bibliography of José Carlos Mariátegui.)
Guillermo Rouillon.   Lima: Universidad Nacional Mayor de San Marcos, Departamento de Publicaciones, 1963. 345p.

Mariátegui was Peru's most influential political thinker of the 20th century. This copious work contains references to many works by and about him.

691   **Europeans in Latin America: Humboldt to Hudson.**
R. A. McNeil, M.D. Deas.   Oxford: Bodleian Library, 1980. 63p.

Produced as the catalogue of mainly 19th-century travel books exhibited at the Bodleian Library in 1980, this work is of enduring value for its bibliographical and biographical information on travellers to Peru, including Alexander von Humboldt himself, Thomas Cochrane, Clements Markham, Paul Marcoy and Roger Casement.

692   **Fuentes historicas peruanas.** (Peruvian historical sources.)
Raúl Porras Barrenechea.   Lima: Instituto Raúl Porras Barrenechea, 1963. 601p.

This classic annotated bibliography of Peruvian history was published posthumously. It derived from the courses taught by the author, who died in 1960, on Peruvian historical sources at the University of San Marcos, Lima; it remains a standard work of reference for researchers.

693   **Fuentes para el estudio del Perú: bibliografía de bibliografías.** (Sources for the study of Peru: a bibliography of bibliographies.)
Gabriel Lostaunau Rubio, Miguel Angel Rodríguez Rea.   Lima: Herrera Márquez, 1980. 500p.

This guide to bibliographical works concerned with Peru deals primarily with material published in Peru. It covers all significant disciplinary areas, and is an essential reference tool for the serious researcher.

694   **Guía bibliográfica para la historia social y política del Perú en el siglo XX (1895-1960).** (A bibliographical guide to the social and political history of Peru in the 20th century [1895-1960].)
Carl Herbold, Jr., Steve Stein.   Lima: Instituto de Estudios Peruanos, 1971. 165p.

This pioneering attempt to provide a bibliographical guide to the history of 20th-century Peru contains detailed descriptions of 102 books and articles, a list of bibliographies, and general discussions of pamphlet literature, biographies and literary sources relevant to the study of social and political themes. It is an essential tool for researchers.

695 **A guide to the music of Latin America.**
Gilbert Chase.   Washington, DC: Pan American Union, 1962. 2nd ed. 411p.

This excellent guide provides both a general introduction to Latin American music and a bibliographical guide to each country. The chapter on Peru (p. 326-45) covers publications up to 1960.

696 **Introducción a las bases documentales para la historia de la república del Perú, con algunas reflexiones.** (An introduction to the documentary sources for the history of the republic of Peru, with some reflections.)
Jorge Basadre Grohmann.   Lima: Villanueva, 1971. 3 vols.

Although not intended, in a technical sense, to serve as a bibliography of Peruvian history, this masterly historiographical appendix to Basadre's *Historia de la república del Perú, 1822-1933*, lists more than 17,000 items relating to Peru since independence in its first two volumes (1,076p.); the third volume (177p.) provides an index of the others. It is a monumental and indispensable work of reference.

697 **Latin American political parties: a bibliography.**
Harry Kantor.   Gainesville: University of Florida Libraries, Reference and Bibliography Department, 1968. 113p. (Bibliographic Series, no. 6).

The section on Peruvian political parties in this useful guide (p. 83-91) is dominated by references to the Aprista Party.

698 **Law and legal literature of Peru: a revised guide.**
David M. Valderrama.   Washington, DC: Library of Congress, 1976. 296p.

This updated guide to the law and legal literature of Peru supersedes the 1947 work (same title and publisher), prepared by Helen L. Clagett.

699 **Manual de estudios peruanistas.** (A manual of Peruvianist studies.)
Ruben Vargas Ugarte.   Lima: Gil, 1959. 4th ed. 449p.

Although inevitably somewhat dated, this remains a useful introductory work to the historiography of Peru.

700 **Perú: una aproximación bibliográfica.** (Peru: a bibliographical essay.)
Franklin Pease.   México DF: Centro de Estudios Económicos y Sociales del Tercer Mundo, 1979. 244p.

This work deals only with works published in Peru, where the first book was published in 1584. It lists 567 items, divided into sections on geography, history, education, economy, society, culture, international relations, and periodicals. Each section begins with a useful general explanation and evaluation of its bibliography.

701 **Peruvian literature: a bibliography of secondary sources.**
David William Foster.   Westport, Connecticut; London: Greenwood, 1981. 324p.

This detailed work of scholarship is divided into two parts: the first deals with general references, classified according to Library of Congress subdivisions; the longer second part consists of thirty-eight sections on individual writers (from Martín Adán to Mario Vargas Llosa). For each author there are separate listings of bibliographies, monographs and dissertations, and critical essays in journals and collections of essays.

702 **Relaciones peruano-ecuatorianas.** (Peruvian-Ecuadorian relations.)
Alejandro San Martín, Rafael Caro.   Lima: Centro Peruano de Estudios Internacionales, 1985. 62p.

This useful guide to publications concerned with Peru's relations with its northern neighbour is divided into sections dealing respectively with material published in Peru, Ecuador, and other countries. A similar guide to material on Peru's relations with Chile and Bolivia is provided by the same authors' and publisher's *Las relaciones del Perú, Chile y Bolivia* (1985).

703 **La religión en el Perú: aproximación bibliográfica 1900-1983.** (Religion in Peru: a bibliographical essay 1900-1983.)
Cecilia Rivera.   Lima: Comisión Evangélica Latinoamericana de Educación Cristiana, 1985. 251p.

Organized chronologically, this work provides details of 1,475 items on Peruvian religion, published since 1900. One indication of the growing interest in the subject is that it begins with two works published in 1900 and ends with twenty-one for 1983. The listing is preceded by a qualitative analysis of the nature of the publications (p. 25-51).

704 **Religiosidad popular en el Perú: bibliografía.** (Popular religiosity in Peru: a bibliography.)
José Luis González, Teresa María von Ronzelen.   Lima: Centro de Estudios y Publicaciones, 1983. 375p.

This valuable bibliography provides an annotated list of 694 works on religious beliefs in Peru, from the colonial period until 1982. It contains a thematic index, with nineteen sections, a geographical index, and an author index.

705 **A tentative bibliography of Peruvian literature.**
Sturgis E. Leavitt.   Cambridge, Massachusetts: Harvard University Press, 1932. 37p.

This pioneering attempt to provide a bibliographical survey in English of Peruvian literature is of enduring value, particularly for its references to relatively obscure 19th-century publications.

Indexes

There follow three separate indexes: authors (personal and corporate); titles of publications; and subjects. Title entries are italicized and refer either to the main titles, or to other works cited in the annotations. The numbers refer to bibliographic entries, rather than page numbers. Individual index entries are arranged in alphabetical sequence.

Index of Authors

A

Adams, J. 74
Adams, R. N. 363
Adolph. J. B. 318
Adorno, R. K. 618-19
Ahern, M. 634, 636
Alarco de Zadra, A. 58
Alba, V. 11
Albert, B. 279
Alberti, G. 417, 603
Alberts, T. 443
Albó, X. 378, 405
Aldrich, Jr., E. J. 622
Alegría, C. 626
Alexander, R. J. 683
Alexander, W. B. 123
Alisky, M. 670, 674, 681
Alonso, I. 432
Alva Castro, L. 519
Alvarez, E. 563, 566
Amat y León, C. 569
Ames, R. 659
Anderson, J. 499
Andrew, K. J. 219
Andrews, J. 80
Andrews, M. A. 125
Anna, T. E. 258
Anton, F. 141
Arauguena, J. L. 663
Aramburú de Olivera, C. 323
Arguedas, J. M. 630, 639
Arnade, C. W. 257
Astiz, C. A. 494
Attwood, R. 671

Avalos, B. 606
Avery, W. P. 512

B

Babb, F. E. 456
Baca Tupayachi, E. 574
Bacon, E. 187
Bacon, F. 60
Bakewell, P. 241
Ballón Echegaray, E. 608
Bankes, G. 152
Barbacci, R. 645
Barcía, J. R. 628
Bardales, A. 592
Barker, M. L. 600
Barraclough, F. H. 630, 639
Barwell, A. 194
Basadre Grohmann, J. 286, 290, 540, 696
Bastien, J. W. 372
Baudin, L. 190
Becker, D. G. 555
Belaúnde-Terry, F. 577
Bell, W. S. 278
Beller, J. 340
Bendezu Aybar, E. 621
Bendezu Neyra, G. E. 393
Bennett, W. C. 142
Benoit, L. J. 117
Benson, E. P. 143, 165
Bergman, A. G. 462
Bernales Ballesteros, J. 235

Bértoli, F. 345
Bertram, G. 527
Bethell, L. 679
Bingham, H. 97, 104
Bird, J. B. 142
Blakemore, H. 28, 678
Blanchard, P. 301
Blanco, H. 451
Blum, A. A. 584
Boehm, D. A. 21
Bolton, R. 357
Bonilla, F. 467
Bonilla, H. 262, 282, 284, 309, 315, 380
Booth, D. 477
Borah, W. W. 223
Borque, S. C. 392
Bourricaud, F. 493
Bowers, W. 85
Bowman, W. 26
Bowser, F. P. 213
Bradford, W. 193
Bradley, P. T. 238
Brady, G. S. 579
Bram, J. 169
Bray, W. M. 146
Briceño y Salinas, S. 56
Brooks, J. 60
Browman, D. L. 378, 383
Brown, J. 115
Brown, K. W. 214
Brown, L. 53
Brown, M. 186
Brown, M. F. 387
Brown, S. 157
Brown, W. 109

Browning, D. G. 319
Brundage, B. C. 174, 184
Brush, S. B. 346, 598-99
Burr, R. N. 506
Büttner, T. T. 411
Burga, M. 292, 373
Burkett, E. 453
Burkholder, M. A. 245
Burland, C. A. 187
Buse, H. 145
Bushnell, G. H. S. 151
Busto Duthurburu, J. A.
de 206

C

Caballero, J. M. 563, 565
Cabel, J. 686
Cabieses, H. 551
Caceda, C. H. 54
Cahill, D. 220
Callegari Ramírez, C. 521
Cameo, M. 687
Campbell, L. G. 240
Camprubi Alcazar, C. 522
Candy, J. 60
Capuñay, M. E. 294
Caravedo, R. 403
Caravedo Molinari, B.
545, 547
Carbonetto, D. 528
Carey, J. C. 263, 513
Carleton, G. W. 86
Caro, R. 702
Carpio, N. 609
Carrasco, P. 178
Carreras, J. M. 433
Carrio de la Vandera, A.
see Concolocorvo
(pseud.)
Carvell, H. de W. 77
Castedo, L. 651, 653
Castro Bastos, L. 9
Cebreros, F. 39
Cerrón-Palomino, R. 395,
415
Cha, C. 571
Chambi, M. 114, 118
Chang-Rodríguez, E. 481
Chaplin, D. 582
Chapman, F. M. 136
Chase, G. 650, 695
Chavarría, J. 291, 473

Chirinos Soto, E. 465, 479
Ciccarilli, O. A. 508
Cisneros, A. 636
Clagett, H. L. 698
Clark, C. A. 62
Claverías, H. R. 615
Cleaves, P. S. 464
Clement, B. A. 64
Cleven, A. N. 275
Clinton, R. L. 327
Cobb, G. B. 247
Cochrane, T. 69
Coe, M. 143
Cole, G. R. F. 90
Cole, J. A. 246
Collier, D. 463
Collier, G. A. 178
Collier, S. 678
Concolocorvo (pseud.) 67
Condori, B. 642
Consejo Nacional de
Pobación 322
Contreras, C. 298
Cook, N. D. 222, 321
Cotler, J. 603
Courret, A. 7
Courret, E. 7
Courte de la
Blanchardière, R. 73
Coutu, A. J. 561
Crespi, M. 453
Cressy-Marcks, V. O. 116
Crist, R. E. 335, 337
Cruz, A. 609
Cuche, D. 347
Cushner, N. P. 236
Cusihuamán, G. A. 400
Custred, G. 346, 369

D

Davies, K. A. 232
Davies, Jr., T. M. 289
Davis, P. M. 604
Davis, W. C. 293
Davison, J. L. 510
Deas, M. D. 691
Deere, C. D. 573
de la Puente Candamo,
J. A. 260
Delgado Santa Gadea, K.
610
Dell, A. 108

Demarest, A. A. 442
Dennis, W. J. 313
Denny, G. G. 157
Derbyshire, D. C. 409
de Soto, H. 526
Deustua, J. 297, 311
Devlin, R. 533
Dew, E. 490
d'Harcourt, R. 157
Dietz, H. A. 455
Dirección General de
Demografía 325
Dixon, P. 1
Dobyns, H. F. 17, 342,
377, 460
Dockstader, F. J. 156
Dollfus, O. 10, 34
Domínguez, L. M. 529
Donnan, C. B. 159, 162
Dore, E. 549
Dorst, J. 134
Doughty, P. L. 17, 377,
450
Duffield, A. J. 89
Duviols, P. 237
Dwyer, J. P. 362
Dyott, G. M. 113

E

Edlin, H. 120
Eliot, G. 6, 539
Engel, F.-E. 602
Enock, C. R. 12, 96
Eresue, M. 591
Escobar, A. 417, 421, 424
Eshelman, C. 628
Espinoza Galarza, M. 40
Europa, 684

F

Faron, L. C. 374
Farrington, I. S. 146
Fasold, R. W. 394
Fawcett, N. 578
Fernández-Baca, J. 562
Ferner, A. 548
Ferrand, Moscati, J. 160
Ferrero C., E. 543
Ferrero, R. A. 458, 540
Ferreyros, C. E. 102

Ferroni, M. A. 664
Figueroa, A. 444, 567
Fini, M. S. 158
Fioravanti, E. 587
Fisher, J. 217, 227, 251, 261, 306, 349
Fisher, R. C. 53
Fittkau, E. J. 121
Fitzgerald, E. V. K. 532, 534
Flores-Galindo, A. 254, 269
Flores Ochoa, J. A. 375
Flornoy, B. 193
Ford, T. R. 452
Form, W.H. 584
Foster, D. W. 701
Fountain, P. 127
Franco, S. L. 411
Freeman, P. 653
Frézier, A. F. 61, 75
Fuentes Irurozgui, M. 594

G

Gade, D. W. 601
Galdo Pagaza, R. 557
Garay, M. 495
García, A. 202
García Belaúnde, D. 468
García Rosell, C. 29
Gardiner, C. H. 339
Gargurevich, J. 673, 675
Garland, A. 19
Garreaud, E. 7
Gasparini, G. 179
Gerbi, A. 574
Gibson, C. 208
Gifford, D. 361, 391
Goddard, A. 190
Golbert, A. S. 475
Gómez, V. 591
Gómez de Zea, R. 591
Gómez Peralta, O. E. 457
Gonzales, M. J. 304
González, J. L. 704
González Carré, E. 358
Gonález Martínez, J. L. 438
González Salazar, M. 656
Goodall, J. D. 122
Goodenough, W. E. 116
Goodland, R. J. A. 119

Goodsell, C. T. 466
Goodspeed T. H. 132
Gorman, S. M. 492, 545
Gott, R. 498
Gow, R. 642
Griffis, C. N. 53
Grossman, E. 631
Gruenberg, G. 381
Guamán Poma de Ayala, F. 243
Guerin Pettus, J. A. 250
Guerra, F. 155
Guerra García, R. 329-30
Guidoni, E. 147
Guillet, D. 559
Guimaray, M. 495
Gunther, J. 3
Gutiérrez, G. 436

H

Haas, J. 148
Haddingham, E. 164
Hall, B. 66
Halsell, G. 13
Hames, R. B. 353
Hamnett, B. R. 265
Handelman, H. 502
Hardenburg, W. E. 111
Harding, C. 497
Hardman, M. J. 398, 412
Heath, E. 1
Helms, A. Z. 72
Hemming, J. 185, 200
Herbold, Jr., C. 694
Hermon, G. 423
Higgins, J. 620, 623, 627
Hilliker, G. 488
Hinds, Jr., H. E. 680
Hobsbawm, E. J. E. 583
Hoffenburg, H. L. 7
Hoggarth, P. 361
Hopkins, J. W. 471
Hopkins, R. 564
Hornberger, E. 401
Hornberger, N. 401, 605
Haworth, N. 589
Humboldt, A. von 65
Humphreys, R. A. 256, 271
Hunt, S. 285, 544
Hyslop, J.182

I

Iberico Mas, L. 640
Illies, J. 121
Inafuku Yagui, A. 557
Instituto Geográfico Militar 48-49
Instituto Geográfico Nacional 46
Instituto Nacional de Estadística 590
Instituto Nacional de Planificación. Asesoría Geográfico 43
Irwin, M. S. 119
Isbell, B. J. 385
Isherwood, C. 98

J

James, P. E. 33
Jaramillo-Arango, J. 133
Jiménez Borja, A. 160
Johnson, A. W. 122
Johnson, G. R. 18
Johnson, W. W. 2
Jones, T. B. 313
Juan, J. 64, 74
Julien, C. J. 176

K

Kantor, H. 697
Kapsoli, W. 300
Karsten, R. 191
Katz, F. 139
Kay, C. 558
Keatinge, R. W. 154
Keith, R. G. 218
Kelemen, P. 649, 655
Kendall, A. 172
Kensinger, K.M. 370
Kessler, Jr., J. B. A. 440
Key, M. R. 406
Kiernan, V. G. 281
King, R. A. 561
Klaiber, J.L. 305, 308, 431
Klaren, P. 299
Kline, W. D. 67
Klinge, H. 121
Kochanek, K. 348
Kosok, P.163

Kristal, E. 616
Kruijt, D. 551
Kubler, G. 317
Kuczynski, P.-P. 485

L

Laite, J. 588
Lajo Lazo, M. 659, 662
La Lone, D. E. 541
Lane, H. R. 638
Langer, E. D. 356
Lanning, E. P. 153
Larson, M. L. 604
Larson, M. S. 462
Lassegue-Moleres, J. B. 667
Laswell, H. D. 377
Lathrap, D. W. 25
Lauer, M. 654
Lavallé, B. 239
Leavitt, S. E. 705
Lefebvre, C. 419
Lehmann, D. 364
Leonard, I. A. 61
León de Leal, M. 573
Levin, J. V. 280
Lewis, H. L. 124
Lizarraga, R. 551
Lloyd, P. 351
Lockhart, J. 209, 234, 252
Lohmann Villena, G. 242
Lombardi, C. L. 44
Lombardi, J. V. 44
Long, N. 524
Long, W. R. 579
López Dominovich, A. 42
López-Mórillas, F. M. 253
Lostaunau Rubio, G. 693
Lothrop, S. 144
Lowe, F. 84
Lowenthal, A. F. 486-87
Lumbreras, L. G. 150
Luna, L. E. 389
Luna Ballón, M. 557
Lynch, J. 268
Lyon, P. J. 179

M

Macadam, A. 635
McArver, Jr., C. H. 511

McClintock, C. 484, 487, 572
MacCormack, S. 429
MacDonald, A. L. 611
MacEwan Scott, A. 593
Mackey, C. J. 159
McNeil, R. A. 691
Magni, R. 147
Makhlouf, K. 592
Málaga Medina, A. 665
Maletta, H. 591-92
Mallon, F. E. 274
Malpica, C. 470
Manelis Klein, H. E. 422
Mannheim, B. 413
Manrique, B. 296
Manya Ambur, J. A. 408
Marcoy, P. (pseud.) 79
Marett, Sir R. 14
Margolies, L. 179
Mariátegui, J. C. 500
Markham, C. R. 76, 137, 399
Martín, L. 197, 221, 250
Martin, P. F. 22
Martínez, H. 343-44, 687
Martínez Arellano, H. 644
Marzal, M. M. 427, 439, 441
Mason, J. A. 140, 422
Masuda, S. 596
Masur, G. 267
Mathew, W. M. 272, 288
Mathison, G. F. 68
Matos Mar, J. 350, 417, 446, 570
Mattos, S. 671
Maw, H. L. 78
Mayer, E. 357
Means, P. A. 205, 211
Medina García, O. 448
Meggers, B. J. 150
Mejía, A. F. 661
Mejía, J. M. 570
Mejía Baca, J. 101
Mercada U., R. 482
Mesa-Lago, C. 461
Meseldzic de Pereyra, Z. 352
Metford, J. C. J. 266
Métraux, A. 180
Meyer de Schauensee, R. 128
Mezzera, J. 544

Michener, C. K. 103
Miller, J. 82
Miller, L. E. 106
Miller, R. 261, 272-73, 277, 283, 306, 310-11, 320, 349, 497, 589
Miller, R. R. 216
Millones, L. 379, 641
Ministerio de Gobierno 316
Ministerio de Guerra 27
Ministry of Foreign Affairs 652
Minkel, C. W. 33
Mintz, S. W. 355
Miracle, Jr., A. W. 397
Mörner, M. 195, 338
Montemayor, J. de 71
Monteza Tafur, M. 507
Montoya, R. 445, 518
Moore, J. P. 215
Moore, S. F. 188
Morales de la Torre, L. 459
Morawetz, D. 536
Moreyra Paz Soldán, C. 689
Morote Solari, F. 41
Morris, C. 596
Morris, R. J. 646
Morrison, T. 166
Murphy, R. C. 130, 136
Murra, J. V. 170, 175
Myers, S. K. 410

N

Nash, J. 453
Natella, Jr., A. 648
National Academy of Sciences 614
Naylor, B. 685
Niedergang, M. 24
Niles, B. 110
Nun, Y. 475
Nuñez del Prado, O. 368
Nyrop, R. F. 16

O

Oficina Nacional de Estadística y Censos 324

O'Hara, E. 633
O'Leary, D. F. 255
O'Phelan Godoy, S. 249
Organization for Economic
    Co-operation and
    Developoment 607
Orlove, B. S. 346, 354, 369
Ortega, C. 669
Orzero Villegas, V. H. 54
Osborne, C. M. 157
Ossio Acuña, J. M. 430,
    448
Osterling, J. P. 336
Otte, E. 234
Owens, R. J. 15

P

Padden, R. C. 253
Painter, M. 397
Pareja, P. 581
Pareja P. S., J. 31
Parker, G. J. 396
Parker, W. B. 23
Parodi Zevallos, C. 562
Pasará, L. 435, 469, 474
Payne, J. L. 585
Pearse, A. 6
Pease, F. 63, 243, 425, 700
Pease García, H. 480
Peck, A. S. 112
Peck, G. W. 81
Peirano, L. 677
Peirano Falconi, L. 608
Pendle, G. 4
Peñaherrera del Aguila, C.
    32, 38
Pezo del Pino, C. 608
Philip, G. 546, 556
Piedra, E. de la 533
Piel, J. 303
Pike, F. B. 6, 198, 314,
    437, 489, 515
Piñeiro, M. 613
Pinelo, A. J. 478
Pizarro, H. 234
Pizarro, P. 211
Platt, D. C. M. 272
Platt, R. R. 18
Poma, G. 212
Porras Barrenechea, T. 63,
    210, 509, 676, 692
Portocarrero, F. 345, 530

Portocarrero Maisch, J.
    567
Pozorski, S. 148
Pozorski, T. 148
Prance, G. T. 597
Prescott, W. H. 207
Primov, G. P. 367
Proctor, R. 83
Prodgers, C. H. 95
Pulgar Vidal, J. 30
Pullum, G. K. 409
Purser, W. F. C. 554

Q

Quijandría Salmón, J. 542
Quijano, A. 525

R

Rabassa, G. 629, 632
Radcliffe, S. A. 449
Radin, P. 366
Ramírez, J. 687
Ramírez, S. E. 248
Ramos-García, L. A. 633
Raygada, C. 647
Reátegui, W. 292
Reiche, M. 166
Reid, J. W. 160
Reinhard, J. 167
Remy S., P. 323
Renwick, A. M. 118
Reparaz, G. de 55
Requejo, J. V. 672
Revel, J. 170
Reynolds, B. 212
Reynolds, S. 212
Ribeiro Ibañez, D. 57
Richardson, V. L. 7
Rick, J. W. 168
Rivera, C. 703
Rivera Pineda, F. 358
Roberts, B. 334, 349, 524
Robinson, D. A. 20, 577
Robinson, D. J. 319
Rodríguez Michuy, A. 331
Roemer, M. 538
Rojas Rojas, I. 404
Rojas Samanez, A. 483
Romero, C. 669
Romero, E. 35

Romero, F. 414
Rosaldo, R. I. 178
Rostworowski de Diez
    Canseco, M. 426
Rouillon, G. 690
Rout, Jr., L. B. 332
Rowe, J. H. 230
Rowe, W. 636
Ruiz, H. 133

S

Saint-Cricq, L. *see*
    Marcoy, P. (pseud.)
St. John, R. B. 505
Salcedo, J. M. 503
Salis, A. 660
Sallnow, M. J. 434
Salomon, F. 380
Samaniego, C. 659
San Cristóval, E. 295
Sandeman, C. 126, 138
Sanmarti, P. 37
San Martín, A. 702
Savoy, G. 192
Scarlett, P. C. 92
Schaedel, R. 144
Schneebaum, T. 107
Schwabe, G. H. 121
Schwarz, R. A. 378, 383
Schweinfurth, C. 131
Schydlowsky, D. M. 544
Scorza, M. 631
Scurrah, M. J. 464
Seebee, F. 93
Shapiro, J. 370
Sharp, D. A. 516
Sheed, R. 24
Shimada, I. 596
Shoemaker, R. 376
Shuy, R. W. 394
Sibbick, J. 391
Silverblatt, I. 371
Silvester, H. 183
Sioli, H. 121
Siskind, J. 386
Sitwell, S. 100
Skar, H. O. 390
Skidmore, T. E. 678
Skinner, J. 70
Slatta, R. W. 356
Slodky, J. 447, 459
Smetherman, B. B. 514

Smith, A. 87
Smith, C. T. 28, 306, 320, 328, 349, 568
Smyth, W. 84
Snow, D. 143
Sorj, V. 477
Soto Ruiz, C. 418
Soustelle, J. 183
Spalding, K. 229
Spruce, R. 129
Squier E. G. 88
Stark, L. R. 422
Steele, A. R. 224
Stein, S. 491, 694
Stein, W. W. 365, 379
Stepan, A. 501
Stephan, R. 643
Stern, S. J. 244, 380
Stevenson, P. 493
Steward, J. H. 374
Stewart, W. 333, 576
Stierlin, H. 171
Stokes, C. J. 580
Stoll, D. 428
Stonier, K. L. 44
Sulmont, D. 287
Sutcliffe, T. 91
Swanson, E. H. 146
Sykes, J. 99
Szeminski, J. 380

T

Tamayo Herrera, J. 196
Tantalean Arbulu, J. 531, 663
Tatum, C. M. 680
Tauro, A. 688
Tax, S. 144
Taylor, L. 270, 277, 476, 560
Taylor, M. 59
Temple, E. 94
TePaske, J. J. 64, 668
ter Wengel, J. 535
Tesch, W. 454
Thorp, R. 523, 527
Tibesar, A. 225, 264
Tipton, D. 634, 636
Tomassini, L. 533
Toor, F. 114
Tord, L. E. 50, 52
Torero, A. 420

Trimberger, E. K. 496
Tschiffely, A. F. 201
Tume Torres, F. 562

U

Ubbelohde-Doering, H. 186
Ugarte del Pino, J. V. 472
Ugarte Elespuru, J. M. 658
Ulloa, A. de 64, 74
Ulloa y Sotomayor, A. 276
United Nations Department of Economic and Social Affairs 550
Urquidi, M. 500
Urton, G. D. 359

V

Valcárcel, C. D. 259, 666
Valderrama, D. M. 698
Valega, J. F. 661
Vallejo, C. 628
Van Den Bergh, H. 181
van den Bergh, P. L. 367
Varese, S. 381
Vargas Llosa, M. 625, 629, 632, 635, 637-38
Vargas Ugarte, R. 71, 307, 699
Varner, J. G. 204, 231
Varner, J. J. 204
Vásquez Ayllón, A. 51
Vázquez, M. C. 338, 342
Vázquez de Espinosa, A. 61-62
Vega-Centeno, M. 612
Véliz, C. 6
Vellinga, M. 551, 586
Verdara V., F. 341
Vergara, R. 326
Vickers, W. T. 353
Villacorta Paredes, J. 657
Von Hagen, V. W. 135-36, 161, 177, 189, 207
von Hanstein, O. 194
von Ronzelen, T. M. 704

W

Wachtel, N. 170, 212, 382
Wallace, A. R. 129
Wallace, J. M. 388
Warren, K. B. 392
Watson Cisneros, E. 537
Webb, R. C. 520
Weber Ch., D. J. 402
Weeks, J. 553
Wehrlich, D. P. 199
Weiss, G. 360
Whitaker, A. P. 228
Whitehead, L. 523
Whitimore, T. C. 597
Whyte, W. F. 584
Wilbert, J. 384
Wilder, T. N. 617
Wilgus, A. C. 275
Willey, G. 144
Wils, F. 552
Wilson, F. 273
Winkleman, B. 149
Wionczek, M. S. 533
Wirth, J. D. 178
Wise, D. O. 624
Wise, M. R. 409
Wölck, W. 394, 416
Wolf, E. R. 355
Wood, B. 504, 515
Woodcock, G. 105
Woods, K. 190
World of Information 682
Wright, M. R. 8
Wyse, E. 149

Y

Ybarra, T. R. 5
Yepes del Castillo, E. 302

Z

Zamora, M. 233
Zárate, A. de 203
Zevallos, J. 407
Zimmerman, A. F. 226
Zook, Jr., D. H. 517
Zuidema, R. T. 173

Index of Titles

A

Accounts of nineteenth-century South America: an annotated checklist of works by British and United States observers 685

Across South America: with an account of a journey from Buenos Ayres to Lima by way of Potosí, with notes on Brazil, Chile and Peru 97

Adaptive responses of native Amazonians 353

Adventures in Peru 95

African experience in Latin America: 1502 to the present day 332

African slave in colonial Peru 213

Aggression and history: the case of Ecuador and Peru 504

Agrarian reform and peasant economy in southern Peru 559

Agrarian reform and rural poverty: a case study of Peru 443

Agricultural development of Peru 561

Agricultural technology in developing countries 611

Agricultura y alimentación: bases de un nuevo enfoque 659

Agriculture, bureaucracy and military government in Peru 464

Agroindustria y transnacionales en el Perú 562

Alán García: análisis de su gobierno 465

Allocation of industry in the Andean common market 535

Alpacas, sheep, and men: the wool export economy and regional society in Southern Peru 354

Amauta 500

Amazon jungle: green hell to red desert . . . 119

Amazon task force 1

American corporations and Peruvian politics 466

Analysis of Inca militarism 169

Anarquismo y sindicalismo en el Perú 581

Ancient American civilizations 139

Ancient burial patterns of the Moche Valley, Peru 159

Ancient civilizations of Peru 140

Ancient Peruvian textiles 141

Andean culture history 142

Andean ecology and civilization 596

Andean group: a case study in economic integration among developing countries 536

Andean kinship and marriage 357

Andean past: land, societies, and conflicts 195

Andean Times 53

Andean republics: Bolivia, Chile, Ecuador, Peru 2

Andes and the Amazon: life and travel in Peru 96

Andes of southern Peru: geographical reconaissance along the seventy-third meridian 26

Andes viewed from the city: literary and political discourse on the Indian in Peru, 1848-1930 616

Anthropological history of Andean polities 170

Antiguos dioses y nuevos conflictos andinos 358

Archivos arequipeños 665

Archivo Tello 666

Arequipa artística y monumental 50

Arequipa y el sur andino: ensayo de historia regional (siglos XVIII-XX) 269

Argot limeña o jerga criolla del Perú 393

Art inca et ses origines: de Valdivia a Machu Picchu 171

Aspectos cuantitativos de la reforma agraria (1969-1979) 563

Aspectos sociales de la educación rural en el Perú 603

Aspects of Inca architecture: description, function and chronology 172

Atlas del Perú 42

Atlas histórico geográfico y de paisajes peruanos 43

Atlas of ancient America 143

Atlas of plant life 120

At the crossroads of the earth and sky: an Andean cosmology 359

Aula Quechua 395

Aunt Julia and the

173

scriptwriter 625
Ayacucho Quechua
grammar and history
396
Aymara language in its
social and cultural
context: a collection of
essays on aspects of
Aymara language and
culture 398

B

Bandidos: the varieties of
Latin American
banditry 356
Bandits and politics in
Peru: landlord and
peasant violence in
Hualgayoc 1900-30
270
Baroque and rococo in
Latin America 649
Bibliografía de la poesía
peruana 65/79 686
Bibliografía de la poesía
peruana 80/84 686
Bibliografía indígena
andina peruana
(1900-1968) 687
Bibliografía peruana de
historia 1940-1953 688
Bibliografía regional
peruana: colección
particular 689
Bilingual education: an
experience in Peruvian
Amazonia 604
Bilingualism: social issues
and policy implications
397
Bio-bibliografía de José
Carlos Mariátegui 690
Biogeography and ecology
in South America 121
Biogeography and
quaternary history in
tropical America 597
Birds of Chile and adjacent
regions of Argentina,
Bolivia and Peru 122
Birds of the ocean: a
handbook for

voyagers . . . 123
Bolívar and the war of
independence 255
Bonanza development: the
selva oil industry in
Peru 1968-1982 546
Bourbons and brandy:
imperial reform in
eighteenth century
Arequipa 214
Bridge of San Luis Rey 617
British consular reports on
the trade and politics
of Latin America,
1824-1826 271
Broad and alien is the
world 626
Burguesía e industria en el
Perú, 1948-1956 547
Burguesía industrial en el
desarrollo peruano 548
Business imperialism
1840-1930: an inquiry
based on British
experience in Latin
America 272
Butterflies of the world 124
By reason or force: Chile
and the balancing of
power in South
America, 1830-1905
506

C

Cabildo in Peru under the
Bourbons 215
Cabildo in Peru under the
Hapsburgs 215
Calendario turístico 51
Cambridge encyclopedia of
Latin America and the
Caribbean 678
Cambridge history of Latin
America 679
Caminos del Perú 574
Capitalismo y no
capitalismo en el Perú
518
Capitalist development and
the peasant economy
in Peru 444
Carnival and coca leaf:

some traditions of the
Quechua ayllu 361
Casinahua of eastern Peru
362
Catálogo de nombres
geográficos del Perú 27
Censo general de la
república del Perú
formado en 1876 316
Ceque system of Cuzco: the
social organization of
the capital of the Inca
173
César Vallejo: an anthology
of his poetry 627
Chinese bondage in Peru: a
history of the Chinese
coolie in Peru,
1849-1874 333
Chronicle of colonial
Lima: the diary of
Josephe and Francisco
Mugaburu, 1640-1697
216
Cities of peasants 334
Ciudad y los perros 637
Civilizations of ancient
America 144
Colonial travellers in Latin
America 61
Comercio y tendencias del
mercado en los
productos de la región
de la selva peruana 537
Commercial relations
between Spain and
Spanish America in the
era of free trade,
1778-1796 217
Common management
strategies in industrial
relations: Peru 584
Communication policies in
Peru 669
Community in the Andes:
problems and progress
in Muquiyauyo 363
Compendium and
description of the West
Indies 62
Complete posthumous
poetry 628
Conceptos generales sobre
la colonización en la

montaña peruana 335
Condor and the cows 98
Conflicto militar del Perú con el Ecuador (1941) 507
Conquest and agrarian change: the emergence of the hacienda system on the Peruvian coast 218
Conquest of the Incas 200
Conquista del Perú por los peruanos 577
Constitución política del Perú 467
Contemporary art in Latin America 650
Contemporary Peruvian theatre 646
Contributions towards a grammar and dictionary of Quechua, the language of the Incas of Peru 399
Conversation in the cathedral 629
Coricancha (garden of gold): being an account of the conquest of the Inca empire 201
Crecimiento, industrialización y cambio técnico: Peru 1955-1980 612
Crisis and decline: the viceroyalty of Peru in the seventeenth century 219
Crónicas del Cuzco 52
Cronistas del Perú (1528-1650) y ostros ensayos 63
Cultivos andinos: alternativa alimentaria popular? 660
Culturas precolombinas: Nazca 160
Cusco: sistemas viales, articulación y desarrollo regional 575
Cuzco: a journey to the ancient capital of Peru . . . 76

Cuzco circle 651

D

Daily life in Peru under the last Incas 190
Daughters of the conquistadores: women of the viceroyalty of Peru 221
De campesinos a profesionales: migrantes de Huayopampa en Lima 336
De cocina peruana: exhortaciones 661
Découverte et la conquête de Pérou d'après les sources originales 202
Deep rivers 630
Defence of community in Peru's central highlands: peasant struggle and capitalist transition, 1860-1940 274
Democracia en transición: las elecciones peruanos de 1985 468
Demographic collapse: Indian Peru, 1520-1620 222
Desarrollo desigual y crisis de la agricultura peruana, 1944-1969 564
Desarrollo desigual y la lucha politica en el Perú, 1948-1956 . . . 547
Desborde popular y crisis del estado: el nuevo rostro del Perú en la década de 1980 446
Desert kingdoms of Peru 161
"Detached recollections" of General D. F. O'Leary 256
Diccionario geográfico del Perú 29
Diccionario quechua:

Cuzco-Collao 400
Diccionario tri-lingüe Quechua de Cusco: Quechua, English, Castellano 401
Dilemas de la seguridad social en el Perú 447
Dios creador andino 425
Discourse and political reflections on the kingdom of Peru 64
Discovery and conquest of Peru 203
Dogs of the conquest 204
Don Nicolás de Piérola: una época de la historia del Perú 276
Drums for Rancas 631
Dueños del Perú 470

E

Early ceremonial architecture in the Andes 162
Early trade and navigation between Mexico and Peru 223
East from the Andes: pioneer settlements in the South American heartland 337
Ecology and exchange in the Andes 364
Economía agraria de la sierra peruana antes de la reforma agraria de 1969 565
Economía peruana 1985/1986: retos y respuestas 519
Economic organization of the Inka state 175
Educational change in Latin America: the case of Peru 606
Emergence of the republic of Bolivia 257
Empire of the Inca 174
L'empire socialiste des Inka 190
Ensayo político sobre el reino de la Nueva

España 65
Essay on the Peruvian
cotton industry,
1825-1920 278
Essay on the Peruvian
sugar industry
1880-1920 279
Estructuras andinas del
poder 426
Estudios Quechua:
planificación, historia
y gramática 402
Estudios sobre el español
de Lima 403
Estudios sobre religión
campesina 427
Europeans in Latin
America: Humboldt to
Hudson 691
Everyday life of the Incas
172
Expansión del Quechua:
primeros contactos con
el castellano 404
Export economies: their
pattern of development
in historical
perspective 280
Extracts from a journal
written on the coasts of
Chile, Peru, and
Mexico in the years
1820, 1821, 1822 66

F

Fall of the Inca empire and
the Spanish rule in
Peru: 1530-1780 205
Fall of the royal
government in Peru
258
Familia campesina y
economía de mercado
448
Family in Peru 99
Fishers of men or founders
of empire: the Wycliffe
bible translators in
Latin America 428
Fishing for growth: export-
led development in
Peru, 1950-1967 538

Flight of the condor: a
wildlife exploration of
the Andes 125
Flowers for the king: the
expedition of Ruiz and
Pavon and the flora of
Peru 224
Fodor's South America 53
Folk art of Peru 652
Folklore mágico de
Cajamarca 640
Folklore médico de
Cajamarca 640
Forgotten river: a book of
Peruvian travel and
botanical notes 126
Franciscan beginnings in
colonial Peru 225
Francisco de Toledo, fifth
viceroy of Peru,
1569-1581 226
Francisco Pizarro: el
marqués gobernador
206
From oral to written
expression: native
Andean chronicles of
the early colonial
period 618
Fuentes históricas peruanas
692
Fuentes para el estudio del
Perú: bibliografía de
bibliografías 693
Futuro de los idiomas
oprimidos en los
Andes 405

G

Geografía del Perú: las
ocho regiones
naturales del Perú 30
Geografía del Perú:
manual 31
Geografía general del Peru:
sintesis 32
Golden wall and mirador:
travels and
observations in Peru
100
Government and society in

colonial Peru: the
intendant system
1784-1814 227
Government executive of
modern Peru 471
Government policy and the
distribution of income
in Peru, 1963-1973 520
Gran Bretaña y el Perú,
1826-1919: informes
de los consules
británicos 283
Gran guía turística del Perú
54
Gran mariscal Luis José
de Orbegoso 295
Great mountains and
forests of South
America 127
Green house 632
Grouping of South
American Indian
languages 406
Guaman Poma: writing
and resistance in
colonial Peru 619
Guano y burguesía en el
Perú 284
Guía bibliográfica para la
historia social y
política del Perú en el
siglo XX 694
Guía del investigador en el
archivo arzobispal del
Cuzco 667
Guide to Peru: handbook
for travelers 55
Guide to the birds of South
America 128
Guide to the music of Latin
America 695

H

Habla la cuidad 407
Hablando Quechua con el
pueblo 408
Hacia el pais de las
orquideas 102
Hambre nacional y pan
ajeno 662
Handbook of Amazonian

languages: volume 1
409
Handbook of Latin
American popular
culture 680
Handbook of South
American Indians 422
Hatunqolla: a view of Inca
rule from the Lake
Titicaca region 176
Heirs of the Incas: a book
about Peru 103
Henry Meiggs: Yankee
Pizarro 576
Highway of the sun 177
Historia de la cámara de
comercio de Lima 540
Historia de la república del
Perú, 1822-1933 286,
290, 696
Historia de las
constituciones del Perú
472
Historia del Banco de la
Nación 521
Historia del indigenismo
cuzqueño: siglos
XVI-XX 196
Historia del movimiento
obrero peruano
(1890-1977) 287
Historia de los bancos en el
Perú (1860-1979) 522
Historia de los límites del
Perú 509
Historical contexts of trade
and markets in the
Peruvian Andes 541
Historical dictionary of
Peru 681
History of Latin American
art and architecture
from pre-Columbian
times to the present 653
History of Peruvian
literature 620
History of the conquest of
Peru 207
Hombre del Marañon: vida
de Manuel Antonio
Mesones Muro 101
House of Gibbs and the
Peruvian guano
monopoly 288

Hualcan: life in the
highlands of Peru 365
Huancavelica mercury
mine 228
Huarochirí: an Andean
society under Inca and
Spanish rule 229
Huaylas: an Andean
district in search of
progress 450
Human resources,
education and
economic development
in Peru 607

I

Ideología mesiánica del
mundo andino 430
Iglesia en el Perú: su
historia social desde la
independencia 431
Iglesia en Perú y Bolivia:
estructuras
eclesiásticas 432
Impact of U.S. arms
transfer policies on
relations with Peru,
1945-1978 510
Inca and Aztec states
1400-1800:
anthropology and
history 178
Inca architecture 179
Inca concept of sovereignty
and the Spanish
administration in Peru
208
Inca land: explorations in
the highlands of Peru
104
Inca por la coya: historia
de un drama popular
en los Andes peruanos
641
Incas 180
Incas and other men:
travels in the
Andes 105
Incas and their
industries 181
Inca: the life and times
of Garcilaso de la

Vega 231
Independencia en el
Perú 262
Indian caste of Peru,
1795-1940: a
population study based
upon tax records and
census reports 317
Indian integration in Peru:
a half century of
experience, 1900-1948
289
Indians of South America
366
Industrial development of
Peru 550
Industrialization and
regional development
in Peru 551
Industrialization,
industrialists and
the nation-state in
Peru 552
Inequality in the Peruvian
Andes: class and
ethnicity in Cuzco 367
Inflation and stabilisation
in Latin America 523
Iniciación de la república
290
Inkawasi: the new
Cuzco 182
Insecurity of British
property in Peru.
Imprisonment of a
British subject.
Contempt of British
authority. Bad faith
and fraud in the
administration of the
law. Persecution
endured in the attempt
to obtain justice. An
appeal to the
representatives of the
British nation by
Henry de Wolfe
Carvell 77
Inside South America 3
In the wilds of South
America: six years of
exploration in
Colombia, Venezuela,
British Guiana, Peru,

Bolivia, Argentina, Paraguay, and Brazil 106
Introducción a la pintura peruana del siglo XX 654
Introducción a las bases documentales para la historia de la república del Perú, con algunas reflexiones 696
Introducción al Perú 145
Itinerario general del Perú 56

J

Japanese and Peru, 1873-1973 339
Jews in Latin America 340
José Carlos Mariátegui and the rise of modern Peru, 1890-1930 473
Journal of a passage from the Pacific to the Atlantic, crossing the Andes in the northern provinces of Peru, and descending the river Marañon, or Amazon 78
Journey across South America from the Pacific Ocean to the Atlantic Ocean 79
Journey from Buenos Ayres, through the provinces of Cordova, Tucuman, and Salta, to Potosí, thence by the deserts of Caranja to Arica, and, subsequently, to Santiago de Chili and Coquimbo, undertaken on behalf of the Chilian and Peruvian Mining Association in the years 1825-26 80
Jueces, justicia y poder en el Perú 474

K

Kay Pacha 642
Keep the river on your right 107
Kingdom of the sun: a short history of Peru 197
Kuyo Chico: applied anthropology in an Indian community 368

L

Labour relations and multinational corporations: the Cerro de Pasco Corporation in Peru (1902-1974) 586
Lanas y capital mercantil en el sur: la casa Ricketts, 1895-1935 292
Land and people of Peru 4
Land and power in Latin America: agrarian economies and social processes in the Andes 346, 369
Land of the Incas 183
Land or death: the peasant struggle in Peru 451
Landowners in colonial Peru 232
Language, authority and indigenous history in the "Comentarios reales de los Incas" 233
Language shift among migrants to Lima, Peru 410
Lands of the Andes: Peru and Bolivia 5
Language attitudes: current trends and prospects 394
Last conquistadores: the Spanish intervention in Peru and Chile, 1863-1866 293
Latifundio y sindicalismo agrario en el Perú 587
Latin America 33
Latin America and the Caribbean review 1989 682
Latin America and the Caribbean: a handbook 6, 539
Latin American history: a teaching atlas 44
Latin American laws and institutions 475
Latin American media: guidance and censorship 670
Latin American political parties 683
Latin American political parties: a bibliography 697
Law and legal literature of Peru: a revised guide 698
Lazarillo: a guide for inexperienced travellers between Buenos Aires and Lima 1773 67
Leguía: vida y obra del constructor del gran Perú 294
Lenguas de los andes centrales 411
Letters and people of the Spanish Indies: the sixteenth century 234
Life, land and water in ancient Peru 163
Lima: la ciudad y sus monumentos 235
Lima: guía de calles 45
Límites del Peru 509
Limits to capitalist development: the industrialization of Peru, 1950-1980 553
Lines to the mountain gods: Nazca and the mysteries of Peru 164
Literatura quechua 621
Llama land: east and west of the Andes in Peru 108

Lo que Varguitas no dijó 625

Lord of Cuzco: a history and description of the Inca people in their final days 184

Lords of the land: sugar, wine and Jesuit estates of colonial Peru, 1700-1767 236

Lutte contre les religions autochtones dans le Pérou colonial: "l'extirpation de l'idolatrie" entre 1532 et 1660 237

M

Machupicchu, Cuzco-Perú 57

Magisterio y sus luchas 1885-1978 608

Making of the past: the New World 146

Man and land in Peru 452

Manual de estudios peruanistas 699

Manuel Pardo y Lavalle, su vida y obra 295

Maoism in the Andes: Sendero Luminoso and the contemporary guerilla movement in Peru 476

Mapa planimétrico de imagenes de sátelite 46

Mapa vial del Perú 47

Marquis et le marchand: les luttes de pouvoir au Cuzco (1700-1730) 239

Marriage practices in lowland South America 370

Melbourne, and the Chincha islands; with sketches of Lima and a voyage round the world 81

Memoirs of General Miller in the service of the republic of Peru 82

Men of Cajamarca: a social and biographical study of the first conquerors of Peru 209

Mercado interno y región: la sierra central, 1820-1930 296

Mercurio Peruano 70

Metal-mining in Peru: past and present 554

Migración a Lima entre 1972 y 1981: anotaciones desde una perspective económica 341

Migración e integración en el Perú 342

Migración en las comunidades indígenas del Perú antes de la reforma agraria 343

Migraciones internas en el Perú 344

Military and society in colonial Peru 1750-1810 240

Military reformism and social classes: the Peruvian experience, 1968-80 477

Minería peruana y la iniciación de la república. 1820-1840 297

Mineros y campesinos en los Andes 298

Miners of the red mountain: Indian labour in Potosí, 1545-1650 241

Miners, peasants, and entrepreneurs - regional development in the central highlands of Peru 524

Mining and diplomacy: United States interests at Cerro de Pasco, Peru, 1876-1930 511

Ministros de la audiencia de Lima (1700-1821) 242

Mito y verdad de los diarios de Lima 675

Mochica: a culture of Peru 165

Modern history of Peru 198

Modern short story in Peru 622

Modernización y la migración interna en el Perú 345

Modernization, dislocation, and Aprismo: origin of the Peruvian Aprista party, 1870-1932 299

Monuments of civilization: the Andes 147

Monuments of the Incas 185

Moon, sun and witches: gender ideologies and class in Inca and colonial Peru 371

Mountain, field, and family: the economy and human ecology of an Andean valley 599

Mountain of the condor: metaphor and ritual in an Andean 'ayllu' 372

Movimiento universitario en el Perú, 1909-1980 609

Movimientos campesinos en el Perú 1879-1965 300

Mujer en los Andes 453

Multinational corporation as a force in Latin America politics: a case study of the International Petroleum Company, Peru 478

Mundial 500

Mystery of the Nazca lines 166

N

Nacimiento de una utopia: muerte y resurrección de los incas 373

Narrative of a journey across the cordillera of the Andes, and of a

residence in Lima and
other parts of Peru, in
the years 1823 and
1824 83
Narrative of a journey from
Lima to Para, across
the Andes and down
the Amazon 84
Narrative of a visit to
Brazil, Peru, and the
Sandwich Islands
during the years 1821
and 1822 68
Narrative of services in the
liberation of Chili,
Peru and Brazil from
Spanish and
Portuguese domination
69
Nationalism & capitalism
in Peru: a study in
neo-imperialism 525
Native peoples of South
America 374
Naval adventures during
thirty-five years service
85
Nazca lines: a new
perspective on their
origin and meaning
167
Negro en el Perú y su
transculturación
linguistica 414
New bourgeoisie and the
limits of dependency:
mining, class, and
power in
'revolutionary' Peru
555
Newest Peruvian poetry in
translation 633
New theatre of Peru 648
Nineteenth century South
America in
photographs 7
Nombre del Perú 210
Norte peruano: realidad
poblacional 318
Notes of a botanist on the
Amazon & Andes 129
Nueva constitución al
alcance de todos 479
Nueva corónica y buen

gobierno 243
Nuevas sectas en el Perú
433

O

Ocaso del poder
oligárquico: lucha
política en le escena
oficial, 1968-1975 480
Oceanic birds of South
America . . . 130
Oil and politics in Latin
America: nationalist
movements and state
companies 556
Old and the new Peru 8
On the royal highway of
the Inca: civilizations
of ancient Peru 186
Opciones políticas
peruanas 481
Origins and development of
the Andean state 148
Origins of the Peruvian
labour movement:
1883-1919 301
Other path: the invisible
revolution in the third
world 526
Our artist in Peru. Leaves
from a sketch book of
a traveller during the
winter of 1865-6 86

P

Paisajes natural y cultural
del Perú 9
Partido comunista del
Perú: Sendero
Luminoso 482
Partidos políticos en el
Perú: manual y
registro 483
Pastores de puna 375
Past worlds: the Times atlas
of archaeology 149

Pawns in a triangle of hate
339
Peasant cooperatives and
political changes in
Peru 484
Peasants of El Dorado:
conflict and
contradiction in a
Peruvian frontier
settlement 376
Peasants, power, and
applied social change:
Vicos as a model 377
Peasants, primitives, and
proletariats: the
struggle for identity in
South America 378
People of the Colca valley:
a population study 321
Peoples and cultures of
ancient Peru 150
Pequeño breviario quechua
416
Periodismo en el Perú 672
Periodismo en el Perú 676
Pérou 10
Pérou: introduction
géographique a l'étude
du developpement 34
Peru 11
Peru 12
Peru 13
Peru 14
Peru 15
Peru 151
Peru: a country study 16
Peru: a cultural history 17
Peru: a short history 199
Peru and the United States,
1900-1962 513
Peru as it is: a residence in
Lima and other parts
of the Peruvian
republic, comprising
an account of the
social and physical
features of that
country 87
Peru before Pizarro 152
Peru before the Incas 153
Perú: carta nacional 48
Perú: comercio y desarrollo
542
Perú: compendio

estadístico 1982 590

Peru 1890-1977: growth
and policy in an open
economy 527

Peru 1821-1960: división
política completa 36

Perú 1820-1920: un siglo
de desarrollo
capitalista 302

Perú: el agro en cifras 591

Perú: el libro del viajero 58

Perú frente a las neuvas
tendencias del
comercio internacional
543

Peru from the air 18

Peru: hechos y cifras
demográficas 322

Perú heterodoxo: un
modelo económico 528

Peru in four dimensions 20

Peru in 1906 and after, with
a historical and
geographical sketch 19

Peru in pictures 21

Peru in the guano
age . . . 89

Peru: incidents of travel in
the land of the Incas 88

Perú: las provincias en
cifras 1876-1981 592

Peru of the twentieth
century 22

Perú: ¿país bilingüe? 417

Perú y el arte 656

Peru: the new poetry 634

Perú: una aproximación
bibliográfica 700

Perú: una nueva geografía
35

Peru under the Incas 187

Peru's Indian peoples and
the challenge of
Spanish conquest:
Huamanga to 1640 244

Peru's own conquest 577

Peruvian adventure 109

Peruvian colonial painting
655

Peruvian contexts of
change 379

Peruvian democracy under
economic stress: an
account of the

Belaúnde
administration,
1963-1968 485

Peruvian economy: a study
of its characteristics,
stage of development
and main problems
529

Peruvian employment
statistics since 1940: an
evaluation 593

Peruvian experiment:
continuity and change
in military rule 486

Peruvian experiment
reconsidered 487

Peruvian industrial labour
force 582

Peruvian literature: a
bibliography of
secondary sources 701

Peruvian pageant 110

Peruvian prehistory: an
overview of pre-Inca
and Inca society 154

Peruvian Times 53

Peruvians at home 90

Peruvians of today 23

Pilgrims of the Andes:
regional cults in Cusco
434

Pintores peruanos de la
república 657

Pintura y escultura en el
Perú contemporáneo
658

Plantation agriculture and
social control in
northern Peru,
1875-1933 304

Plant hunters in the Andes
132

Plants, man and the land in
the Vilcanota valley of
Peru 601

Población del Cuzco
colonial (siglos
XVI-XVIII) 323

Población del Perú 324

Población del Perú
1980-2025: su
crecimiento 325

Población y desarrollo
capitalista 326

Población y desarrollo en
el Perú 327

Poder blanco y resistencia
negra en el Perú 347

Poet in Peru: alienation
and the quest for a
super-reality 623

Polacos en el Perú 348

Política económica y
agricultura en el Perú,
1969-1979 566

Política
económica-financiera y
la formación del
estado: siglo XIX 531

Política social del estado: la
seguridad social en el
Perú 454

Política tecnológica y
seguridad alimentaria
en América Latina 613

Political economy of Peru
1956-78: economic
development and the
restructuring of capital
532

Politics and economics of
external debt crisis: the
Latin American
experience 533

Politics of a colonial
career: José Baquíjano
and the audiencia of
Lima 245

Politics of reform in Peru:
the Aprista and other
mass parties of Latin
America 488

Politics of the miraculous
in Peru: Haya de la
Torre and the
spiritualist tradition
489

Politics in the altiplano: the
dynamics of change in
rural Peru 490

Population and
development in Peru
328

Populism in Peru: the
emergence of the
masses and the politics
of social control 491

Post-revolutionary Peru:

the politics of transformation 492

Potosí mita, 1573-1700: compulsory Indian labor in the Andes 246

Potosí y Huancavelica: bases económicas 1545-1640 247

Poverty and problem-solving under military rule: the urban poor in Lima, Peru 455

Power and property in Inca Peru 188

Power and society in contemporary Peru 493

Prehistoric Andean ecology: man, settlement and environment in the Andes 602

Prehistoric hunters of the high Andes 168

Prensa: apertura y límites 677

Prensa. radio y TV: historia crítica 673

Present state of Peru 70

Pressure groups and power élites in Peruvian politics 494

Priorización y desarrollo del sector agrario en el Perú 567

Problemas poblaciones peruanos 329

Problemas poblaciones peruanos II 330

Problemática de las poblaciones marginales en el país 457

Promoción de exportaciones no tradicionales en el Perú 544

Provincial patriarchs: land tenure and the economics of power in colonial Peru 248

Proyección de la demografía en el centro y el sur del Perú 331

Pueblos del Perú 37

Putumayo: the devil's paradise 111

Q

Quechua: manual de enseñanza 418

Quechua y la historia social andina 420

Quien es quien: congreso de la república, 1985-1990 495

R

Race and class in Latin America 338

Radicalización y conflictos en la iglesia peruana 435

Radio y comunicación popular en el Perú 673

Railways of the Andes 578

Railways of South America 579

Ramón Castilla 307

Realidad del campo peruano despues de la reforma agraria 569

Realidad económica de los beneficios sociales 458

Real life of Alejandro Mayta 635

Realm of the Incas 189

Rebellions and revolts in eighteenth century Peru and Upper Peru 249

Reflexión sobre la teología de la liberación: perspectivas desde el Perú 436

Reforma agraria en el Perú 570

Reforma educativa. Qué pasó? 610

Region and class in modern Peruvian history 273, 277, 309, 320, 497, 589

Relaciones del Perú, Chile y Bolivia 702

Relaciones de viajes de los siglos XVII y XVIII 71

Relaciones peruano-ecuatorianas 702

Relación história del viaje que hizo, a los reynos del Perú y Chile el botánico D. Hipólito Ruiz en el año de 1977 hasta el de 1788, en cuya época regresó a Madrid 133

Relation of the discovery and conquest of the kingdoms of Peru 211

Religion and revolution in Peru, 1824-1976 308

Religión en el Perú: aproximación bibliográfica 1900-1983 703

Religión popular, en el Perú: informe y daignóstico 438

Religiosidad popular en el Perú: bibliografía 704

República del Perú: mapa político 49

Research guide to Andean history: Chile, Ecuador and Peru 668

Resistance, rebellion and consciousness in the Andean world: eighteenth to twentieth centuries 380

Reto del multingüísmo en el Perú 421

Revolución y contrarrevolución en México y el Perú: liberalismo, realeza y separatismo (1800-1824) 265

Revolution from above: military bureaucrats and development in Japan, Turkey, Egypt, and Peru 496

Rol de la selva en el desarrollo agrícola del

Perú 571
Role of science and
    technology in Peruvian
    economic development
    614
Royal commentaries of the
    Incas 231, 233
Rural guerrillas in Latin
    America 498

S

San Martín, the liberator
    266
Scholars and schools in
    colonial Peru 250
Search for the apex of
    America: high
    mountain climbing in
    Peru and Bolivia,
    including the conquest
    of Huascaran, with
    some observations on
    the country and people
    below 112
Seguridad social en el Perú
    459
Self-management and
    political participation
    in Peru, 1969-1975:
    the corporatist illusion
    572
Sendero Luminoso: a new
    revolutionary model
    449
Seven interpretive essays
    on Peruvian reality 500
Siglo a la deriva: ensayo
    sobre el Perú Bolivia y
    la guerra 309
Silent highways of the
    jungle 113
Silver mines and silver
    miners in colonial
    Peru, 1786-1824 251
Simón Bolívar 267
Sincretismo iberoamericano
    439
Singing mountaineers:
    songs and tales of the
    Quechua people 643
Síntesis de la economía
    peruana 594

Síntesis geográfica del Perú
    38
Síntesis geográfica general
    del Perú 39
Situación del indígena en
    América del Sur 381
Sixteen years in Chile and
    Peru from 1822 to
    1839 91
Social and economic
    change in modern
    Peru 306, 349
Social matrix of Peruvian
    indigenous
    communities 460
Social security in Latin
    America: pressure
    groups, stratification,
    and inequality 461
Social stratification in Peru
    462
Socialist empire: the Incas
    of Peru 190
Sociedad y ideología:
    ensayos de historia y
    antropología andinas
    382
South America and Central
    America: a natural
    history 134
South America and the
    Pacific: comprising a
    journey across the
    pampas and the
    Andes, from Buenos
    Ayres to Valparaiso,
    Lima and Panama 92
South America
    rediscovered 312
South America: the green
    world of the naturalists
    136
South American dictators
    during the first century
    of independence 275
South American handbook
    60
South American Indian art
    156
South American Indian
    languages: retrospect
    and prospect 422
South American survival: a
    handbook for the

independent traveller
    59
South American zoo 135
Spanish American
    revolutions, 1808-1826
    268
Spanish Peru, 1532-1560:
    a colonial society 252
Species of birds of South
    America and their
    distribution 128
Spider hangs too far from
    the ground 636
Spirits, shamans, and stars:
    perspectives from
    South America 383
Squatters and oligarchs:
    authoritarian rule and
    policy change in Peru
    463
State and economic
    development: Peru
    since 1968 534
State and society: Peru in
    comparative
    perspective 501
Statistical abstract of Latin
    America 595
Struggle in the Andes:
    peasant political
    mobilization in Peru
    502
Study of the older
    Protestant missions
    and churches in Peru
    and Chile: with special
    reference to the
    problems of division,
    nationalism and native
    ministry 440
Sur peruano: realidad
    poblacional 318
Syntactic modularity 423

T

Tacna and Arica: an
    account of the Chile-
    Peru boundary dispute
    and of the arbitrations
    of the United States
    313
Taquile en Lima 350

Tales of Potosí: Bartolomé
Arzans de Orsua y
Vela 253
Tecnología andina y
desarrollo regional 615
Tentative bibliography of
Peruvian literature 705
Territorial seas and inter-
American relations:
with case studies of the
Peruvian and U.S.
fishing industries 514
Textiles anciens et leurs
techniques 157
Textiles of ancient Peru and
their techniques 157
Three worlds of Peru 114
Time of the hero 637
Tobacco and shamanism in
South America 384
To defend ourselves:
ecology and ritual in
an Andean village 385
To hunt in the morning 386
Toponimia quechua del
Perú 40
Totalitarian state of the
past: the civilization of
the Inca empire in
ancient Peru 191
Trabajo artesanal en los
Andes peruanos: el
valle del Mantaro 557
Transformación religiosa
peruana 441
Transportation and
economic development
in Latin America 580
Travelling impressions in,
and notes on, Peru 93
Travels from Buenos Ayres
by Potosí to Lima 72
Travels in Peru and India
while superintending
the collection of
chinchona plants and
seeds in South
America, and their
introduction into India
137
Travels in various parts of
Peru 94
Travels of Ruiz, Pavon,
and Dombey in Peru

and Chile (1777-1788)
133
Tsewa's gift: magic and
meaning in an
Amazonian society 387
Tumbas de Uchuraccay 503
Tupac Amaru II – 1780 254
20 Latin Americas 24
Two against the Amazon
115

U

United States and Latin
American wars,
1932-1942 515
United States and the
Andean republics:
Peru, Bolivia and
Ecuador 314
U.S. foreign policy and
Peru 516
Upper Amazon 25
Up the Amazon and over
the Andes 116
Urban bias of Peruvian
food policy:
consequences and
alternatives 664

V

Variaciones
sociolingüísticas del
castellano en el Perú
424
Vegetalismo: shamanism
among the mestizo
population of the
Peruvian Amazon 389
Viajes por el Perú centro y
sur 117
Vilcabamba: lost city of the
Incas 192
Viracocha: the nature and
antiquity of the
Andean high god 442
Vision des vaincus: les
indiens du Pérou
devant la conquête
espagnol, 1503-1570
212

Visión geopolítica del Perú
41
Vision of the vanquished:
the Spanish conquest
of Peru through Indian
eyes, 1530-1570 212
Voyage to Peru performed
by the Conde of
St. Malo, in the years
1745, 1746, 1747, 1748
and 1749 73
Voyage to South America
74
Voyage to the South Sea,
and along the coasts of
Chile and Peru, in the
years 1712, 1713 and
1714 75

W

Wanderer in Inca land 138
Wanderings in the Peruvian
Andes 118
Warm valley people:
duality and land
reform among the
Quechua Indians of
highland Peru 390
War of the end of the world
638
Warriors, gods & spirits
from Central & South
American mythology
391
Weavers of ancient Peru
158
Women and change in
Latin America 456
Women of the Andes:
patriarchy and social
change in two
Peruvian towns 392
Women in Andean
agriculture: peasant
production and rural
wage employment in
Colombia and Peru
573
World of learning 1989 684
World of the Inca 193
World of the Incas: a

socialistic state of the past 194

Y

Yawar fiesta 639

'Young towns' of Lima: aspects of urbanization in Peru 351

Yugoslavos en el Perú 352

Z

Zarumilla-Marañon: the Ecuador-Peru dispute 517

Index of Subjects

A

Adán, Martín (poet) 623,
  701
Administrative structure
  36, 39, 42-43, 47 see
  also History
Agriculture 274, 277-79,
  304, 333, 369, 375,
  448, 452, 524, 558-73,
  591-92, 600, 611, 613,
  615, 663
  agrarian reform 274,
    303, 343, 390, 443,
    445, 464, 502, 516,
    520, 558-61, 563-66,
    569-70
  colonial 213-14, 218,
    232, 236, 248
  19th century 274,
    277-79, 303-04
  prehistoric 139, 168, 173,
    598, 602
Aguaruna Indians 353
Agurana Indians 387
Alegría, Ciro (novelist)
  626
Alliance for Progress 516
Almagro, Diego de 202
Amazon 1, 25, 54, 65, 79,
  84, 111, 115-16, 119,
  129, 335, 389, 409,
  512, 546, 596, 632
American Geographical
  Society 177
American Museum of
  Natural History 106
Anarchist movement 581
  see also Trade Unions;
  Workers
Ancash 377, 416, 450
Andahuaylas 611
Andean Pact 512, 535-36
Andes mountains 25-26,
  112, 117, 125, 134,
  139, 144, 148
Anglo-Peruvian College
  118
Antarctic 41

Anthropology 153, 170,
  175, 243, 336, 353-92,
  416, 441, 448, 601-02
  banditry 356, 369
  cosmology 360
  ethnicity 367
  ethnoastronomy 359
  kinship 355, 357
  rituals 372, 384-85, 387
Antofagasta 281
Antony Gibbs & Sons 272,
  288
Aprista party 299, 305,
  465, 468, 479, 488,
  491, 519, 697
Apurimac 1, 396
Arana, Julio César 111
Archaeology 88, 145-46,
  159, 170, 176, 182,
  186, 191, 442, 599,
  602, 666
Architecture 50, 649-50
  19th century 653
  colonial 235, 649, 653,
    656
  contemporary 650
  Inca 100, 146, 171-72,
    179, 185
  pre-Inca 162, 165
Archives 665-68, 684
Arequipa 9, 18, 106, 117,
  211, 214, 232, 269,
  292, 547, 551, 576, 665
Arestégui, Narciso 616
Argentina 98, 348, 435
Arguedas, José María
  (novelist) 620, 630,
  639, 643
Arica 80, 313
Art 649-58
  bibliography 658
  19th century 651, 657
  colonial 651, 655
  contemporary 650, 654,
    657-58
  popular 652
  pre-Columbian 156, 653
Atahualpa 209, 252, 641
Atlantic 78, 84

Atlases
  see Maps and atlases
Ayacucho 82, 117, 244,
  358, 396, 400, 416, 418
  see also Huamanga
Aymara 366, 372, 375,
  397-98, 405, 422, 424
  see also Linguistics

B

Bacon, Francis 60
Banks 113, 521-22
Baquíjano, José 245
Bates, Henry Walter 129
Belaúnde Terry, President
  Fernando 3, 465, 485,
  487, 492, 520, 537, 577
Belli, Carlos Germán
  (poet) 623
Benavides, President
  Oscar 508
Bibliographies 334, 415,
  473, 480, 621, 658,
  662, 685-705
  see also Subjects by
  name, e.g. Literature
Bio-bibliographies 690
Biogeography 597, 601
Birds 121-22, 127-28, 130,
  136, 138
Blanco, Hugo 498
Bolívar, Simón 255-57,
  266-67
Bolivia 80, 89, 94-95, 98,
  176, 195, 249, 251,
  253, 257, 269, 281,
  337, 350, 398, 509,
  515, 536, 570, 702
Booth Steamship Company
  113
Boundary disputes 44, 89,
  255, 267, 313, 504-07,
  509, 514, 516-17
  see also Foreign
  relations; War of the
  Pacific

Brazil 69, 119, 129, 386,
  435, 439, 509, 544
British Embassy 14
British Library 133
British Navy 66, 77-78,
  84-85
British Sugar Company 279
Brooklyn Museum 655
Buenos Aires 67, 72, 103,
  251
Butterflies 123

C

Cádiz 72
Cajamarca 209, 269, 318,
  416, 640
Calca 434
Callahuaya 411
Callao 65, 81, 217, 339,
  584
Campa Indians 360
Cañete 279
Canning, George 271
Canudos 638
Carhuamayo 641
Carrasco, Pedro 178
Carrio de la Vandera,
  Alonso 67
Cartagena 115, 535-36
Casement, Roger 111, 691
Casinahua Indians 362, 370
Castilla, President Ramón
  307
Censorship 670
Cerro de Pasco 87, 126,
  251, 311, 511, 549,
  578, 586, 631
Chaclacayo 659
Chaco War 515
Chambi, Martín
  (photographer) 114,
  118
  see also Photographs
Chanchamayo valley 18
Chapman, Frank Michler
  136
Chavín culture 141
Chicago Natural History
  Museum 131
Chilca 602
Chile 66, 69,80, 85, 89, 91,
  93, 122, 127, 281, 293,
  309, 313, 315, 435,

506, 509, 536, 576,
  596, 685, 702
Chimú culture 161, 163
Chinchona 137
Chinese 304, 333
Chronicles 63
Church 96, 220-21, 225,
  236-37, 264, 308, 429,
  431-32, 435-36, 667
Churches (buildings) 50,
  52, 235
Cisneros, Antonio (poet)
  623, 636
Coca 361
Cocamilla Indians 353
Cochrane, Thomas 263,
  691
Colca valley 18, 321
Colombia 98, 115, 255,
  257, 267, 436, 509,
  516, 536, 544, 580
Compradazgo 355
Condorcanqui, José
  Gabriel 254
  see also Túpac Amaru
Conference of Latin
  American Bishops
  436, 438
Convents 52, 221, 235
Cooking 115, 333, 661
  see also Food
Córdoba 231
Cornell University 377, 460
Cotton 278
Courret, Aquiles
  (photographer) 7
Courret, Eugenio
  (photographer) 7
Cuba 570
Culture 17, 24-25, 332-33,
  680
  see also History
Cuzco 9, 76, 100, 116-17,
  183-84, 186, 196, 200,
  203, 214, 231, 254,
  269, 323, 367, 382,
  396, 400, 416, 418-19,
  434, 451, 541, 574,
  576, 583, 642, 651,
  665, 667

D

de las Heras, Bartolomé
  María 264
Departments 36, 39, 689
Dictionaries
  geographical 29
  historical 681
  Quechua 396, 399-401
Digby, Adrian 144
Diplomacy see Foreign
  relations; History

E

Ecology 9, 119, 353, 364,
  375, 385, 596, 599, 602
  see also Environment
Economy 354, 375, 444,
  448, 450, 518-73, 575,
  594, 614
  debt crisis 533, 542
  industry 520, 535,
    546-57, 582, 584,
    588-89, 612
  inflation 523
  informal 526
  investment 530
  see also Agriculture;
    Banks; Fishing
    industry; History;
    Minerals and mining;
    Trade
Ecuador 64-65, 98, 129,
  195, 423, 504-05, 507,
  509, 512, 515, 517,
  536, 596, 702
Education 520, 603-10
  bilingual 417-18, 604-05
Eguren, José María (poet)
  623
El Salvador 435
Environment 385, 596-602
  see also Ecology
Ethnography 25, 358, 375,
  388, 414, 434, 599, 605
Ethnohistory 175, 243,
  395, 599
Evangelical Union of
  South America 440
Expeditions 1, 26, 192
Exploration and travel 1,
  5, 61-118, 685, 691

Extremadura 206

F

Fauna 106, 121, 125, 135,
138, 600
Festivals 355, 361, 621, 644
First World War 340, 473
Fishing industry 6, 515-16,
538-39, 545
Flora 106, 120, 125-26,
131-32, 137-38, 224,
601
Folklore 347, 621, 640-44
Food and food policy 659-
64
bibliography 662
production 448, 561-62,
566, 613, 659-60
see also Cooking
Foreign relations 293, 313,
315, 504-17, 702
see also Boundary
disputes; War of the
Pacific
France 508
Franciscan Order 225
French Academy of
Sciences 74
Frézier, Amadée 61

G

García Calderón, Ventura
616
Gargía Pérez, President
Alán 465, 468, 481,
519, 567
see also Aprista party
Garcilaso de la Vega 231,
233
Garreaud, Emilio
(photographer) 7
Gazetteers 37, 40
Geography 26-49, 328,
590, 601
González Prada, Manuel
616
Gordon, Ronald 279
Government and politics
464-503, 556
bibliography 480

congress 495
constitutions 467, 472,
479
judicial administration
474
laws 475
populism 491
see also History; Political
parties
Grace contract 282
Great Depression 294
Griffis, C. N. 53
Guamán Poma de Ayala,
Felipe 212, 243
Guano 89, 272, 280,
284-85, 288, 307, 522
Guayaquil 255, 267
Guerrilla movements 476,
498, 503, 635
see also Sendero
Luminoso
Guzmán, Abimael 482
see also Sendero
Luminoso

H

Hakluyt Society 76
Hamburg 72
Haquera 411
Hawaii 339
Haya de la Torre, Victor
Raúl 291, 299, 305,
489
see also Aprista party
Health and welfare 318,
329-31, 351, 368
Heath, Edward 1
Historiography 188, 207,
260, 668, 699
History 195-315, 321
administrative 215, 227,
240, 242
bibliographies 199, 688,
692, 694, 696
colonial 67, 69-75, 170,
205, 213-54, 319
conquest 76, 140,
149-51, 178, 184, 193,
200-12, 641
cultural 197, 305, 308
diplomatic 293, 313, 315
economic 111, 213-14,

216-19, 227-28, 230,
232, 238, 241, 245,
248, 251, 253, 272-74,
278-80, 282-85, 287,
294-99, 306-07,
310-11, 333
independence 66, 82-83,
85, 245, 255-68
intellectual 224, 233,
239, 250
political 265, 269,
275-76, 286, 290-91,
295, 305, 309, 314
religion 220, 225, 308
republican 198, 269-315,
696
social 213, 216, 220-22,
227, 229-30, 234,
239-46, 252-54, 270,
286, 289, 291, 301,
308, 319, 321, 332-33,
338
see also Individuals by
name, e.g. Pizarro,
Francisco; Topics by
name, e.g. Great
depression
Hualcan 365
Hualgayoc 65
Huallaga river 126
Huamanga 244, 497
see also Ayacucho
Huambisa Indians 353
Huancavelica 74, 228, 247,
396, 448
Huancayo 116-17, 274,
349, 363
Huaral 336
Huaylas 450
Huayopampa 336
Human geography 34, 38
Humboldt, Alexander von
691

I

Ica 578
Immigration 222, 304,
332-33, 338-40,
347-48, 352
Incas 22, 40, 76, 88, 100,
104, 141, 146-47,
150-51, 161, 169-96,

189

Incas *cont'd*
200-12, 222, 231, 371,
373, 392, 621, 641
architecture 179, 185
art 171
economy 175, 181, 230
religion 426
roads 177, 186, 574
society 187-88, 190-91,
194, 208, 382
state organization 178,
190
India 137
Indians 6, 99, 103, 107,
183, 216, 218, 221,
229, 233, 237, 252,
308, 317, 338, 343, 460
Amazon 79, 111, 335,
353, 360, 362, 366,
370, 384
bibliography 687
indigenismo 196, 616
integration 289
literature 243, 618-21,
642
oral traditions 358, 373,
618, 642-43
songs 643
see also Anthropology;
Aymara; Linguistics;
Prehistory; Quechua
Industrialization 322, 326,
547-48, 581
see also Economy
Inflation 660, 674
International Congress of
Americanists 144
International Congress of
Anthropological and
Ethnological Sciences
378
International Petroleum
Company 478, 556
Iquitos 113, 116, 126
Italians 508

J

Japanese 339
Jews 340
Journalism 54, 672
Juan Fernández island 91
Juliaca 576

Junín 416, 423

K

Kallarayan 449
Kata 372
Kew Gardens 138
Kiwicha 660
Kuyo Chico 368

L

La Convención 451, 583,
587
Languages *see* Linguistics
Lake Titicaca 106, 350,
357, 372
La Paz 94
Lares 451, 587
Lauer, Mirko (poet) 634
Law 698
see also Government and
politics
Leguía, President Augusto
B. 23, 113, 294
Leticia 515
Libraries 666, 668, 684
Lima 4, 7, 9, 67, 70, 76,
81, 93, 99, 116, 206,
217, 225, 234, 258,
269, 312, 326, 336,
340, 349, 388, 393,
398, 403, 407, 410,
455, 463, 513, 524,
540, 548, 584, 656, 665
Linguistics 381, 393-424,
605
Amazonian 409
bibliography 415
bilingualism 394, 397,
405, 410, 412-13,
417-19, 424
multilingualism 421
slang 393
Spanish 403, 407, 424
see also Aymara;
Quechua
Literature 493, 616-40, 642
bibliographies 686, 701,
705
Lobitos Oilfields Limited
310

Lothrop, Samuel 144

M

Machiguenga Indians 353
Machu Picchu 57, 97, 146,
185
Madrid 64, 74
Malaya 111
Manila 542
Mantaro valley 524, 557,
611
Maps and atlases 42-49,
143
Marañon river 101, 515,
517
Marcona Mining Company
549
Marcoy, Paul 691
see also Saint-Cricq,
Laurent
Mariátegui, José Carlos
291, 473, 500, 690
Maritime rights 41, 514
Markham, Clements 691
Matapuquio 390
Matto de Turner, Clorinda
616
Medellín 436, 438
Media 669-77
Medicine 361, 383, 386,
640
Meiggs, Henry 576
see also Railways
Mercurio Peruano 70
Mexico 235, 265, 439, 570,
649
Migration (internal) 222,
318, 324, 326, 328-29,
331, 334-37, 341-46,
349-51, 410, 524
see also Immigration
Military 199, 240, 262, 413,
443, 445, 455, 469-70,
477-79, 483, 485-88,
492, 501, 503, 516,
525, 530, 532, 534,
546, 548-49, 551-52,
558-61, 569-70, 591,
603, 610, 637
and media 670-71,
674-75
Miller, William 82

Minerals and mining 65,
466, 511, 524, 546,
549, 554-56, 586, 588,
colonial 72-74, 228, 241,
246-47, 251, 253
19th century 87, 89, 94,
297-98, 306, 311
see also Nitrates; Oil;
Silver
Ministry of Labour 593
Misminay 359
Missions and missionaries
70, 107, 236, 429, 440
Moche valley 159
Mochica culture 160-61,
165
Moho 397
Mollendo 18, 106
Monroe Doctrine 293
Montemayor, Juan de 71
Moquegua 500
Morales Bermúdez,
President Francisco
674
Moro, César (poet) 623
Muquiyauyo 363
Murphy, Robert Cushman
136
Museums 684
Music 645, 647
bibliography 695
composers and artists
(biographies) 645

N

National Agrarian
University 602
National Geographic
Society 104
National Indian Institute
377
National parks 47
National Planning Institute
607
National School of Fine
Arts 658
National Union of Catholic
Students 435
Nazca culture 160, 164,
166-67
Negroes 213, 216, 221,
252, 308, 332, 338,
347, 414, 439
see also Slavery
New Spain 223, 225
see also Mexico
New York 651
Nicaragua 435
Nitrates 89, 522
Nixon, Richard 513
Nordenflycht, Thaddeus
von 72
Novels 624, 635, 638
in translation 625-26,
629-32, 635, 638-39

O

Ocopa 116
Odría, President Manuel
105, 289, 629, 670
Oil 310, 478, 556
Ollantaytambo 100, 185
Orbegoso, President Luis
José 295
Orchids 102
Oroya 576

P

Pachita river 84
Pacific 75, 80, 123, 126,
596, 685
Pampa de Anta 559
Paracas 614
Paraguay 515
Pardo, President Manuel
295, 320
Pardo y Barreda, President
José 8, 19
Peasantry 300, 303-04,
334, 354, 364, 380,
427, 434, 444, 448-49,
451, 453, 484, 502,
558-60, 563, 566, 572-
73, 583, 587, 601
Peninsular War 82
Peru-Bolivia
Confederation 94, 261
Peruvian Amazon Rubber
Company 111
Peruvian Central Bank 485
Peruvian Corporation 282
Peruvian Times 53
Petroperú 556
Philip III (King of Spain)
619
Philip V (King of Spain)
64, 75
Photographs 7-8, 19, 21,
43, 52, 57, 110, 112,
114, 117-18, 122, 138,
147, 152, 156, 183,
185, 189, 578, 651,
655-56
see also Photographers
by name, e.g.
Chambi, Martín
Physical geography 32, 34,
38
Piérola, President Nicolás
de 276
Pinchimuro 642
Pisco 578
Piura 9, 632
Pizarro, Francisco 200,
202, 206, 209, 211,
252, 641
Pizarro, Hernando 210,
234
Pizarro, Pedro 211
Place names 40
Poetry 627, 633-34, 636
in translation 627-28,
633-34, 636
bibliographies 686
Quechua 621
Poles 348
Political parties 481, 483,
488, 683, 697
see also Parties by name,
e.g. Sendero
Luminoso
Politics
see History; Government
and politics
Population and
demography 218-19,
222, 316-31, 448, 591,
660
censuses 316-17, 319-20,
341, 345, 592-93
Potatoes 448
Potosí 65, 72, 94, 241, 246,
251, 253
Prado, President Manuel
670

Prehistory 139-94, 442, 602
  ceramics 142, 160, 171,
    181
  irrigation 163
  metalwork 142, 160
  textiles 141-42, 157-58,
    160, 171, 181
Press 493, 670, 672-77
Pucallpa 402
Puno 106, 117, 269, 490,
  560, 576, 605
Purus river 386
Putumayo river 111

Q

Qamewara 434
Quechua 40, 350, 361, 366,
  375, 390, 394-96,
  399-402, 404-05, 408,
  411-13, 416-20,
  422-24, 601, 605, 630,
  642-43
  see also Linguistics
Quinua 660

R

Radio 13, 405, 672-73
Railways 282, 306, 574-76,
  579
  see also Transport and
    communications
Reiche, María 166
Religion 96, 308, 347, 358,
  425-42, 621, 640-41
  bibliographies 703-04
  liberation theology
    436-37, 441
  new sects 433
  pre-Columbian 164-65,
    167, 425, 430, 442
  shamanism 164, 384, 389
  syncretism 439, 441
  see also History
Richardson, Villroy L.
  (photographer) 7
Ricketts, Charles Milner
  271
Ricketts, William 292
Rio de Janeiro 111
Riou, E. 79

Rivers 78
  see also Rivers by name,
  e.g. Putumayo river
Royal Geographical
  Society 76, 96, 116
Royal Institute of
  International
  Affairs 15
Royal Library of
  Copenhagen 243
Rubber 111
Ruiz, Bartolomé 202

S

Sacsahuamán 185
Saint-Cricq, Laurent 79
Salazar Bondy, Sebastián
  (poet) 634
Sánchez Cerro, Luis M.
  294, 491
San Martín (department)
  416
San Martín, José de 66, 69
  85, 263, 266
Santa Cruz 580
Satipo 376
Schaedel, Richard 144
Science and technology
  611-15
Sculpture 658
Second World War 339
Sendero Luminoso 476,
  482-83, 497, 499, 503,
  560
Sevilla 210
Sharanahua Indians 386
Sicuani 354, 541
Silver 65, 72, 80, 87, 223,
  228, 247, 251, 311
Slavery 213, 216, 332, 338,
  347, 414
  see also Negroes
Slavs 352
Social conditions 443-63,
  582
  social security 447, 454,
    458-59, 461
Society 431, 445-46, 451,
  460, 462, 477, 480,
  493-94, 518, 547-48,
  555, 590
  see also History; Social

  conditions
  Society of Jesus 71, 236
Sociology 448
Spain 66, 82, 85, 217, 219,
  234, 258-59, 262, 293
Statistics 39, 590-95
Sugar 248, 279, 299, 304
Summer Institute of
  Linguistics 402, 428,
  604

T

Tacna 313
Taquile 350
Tarapacá 313
Tarma 273
Tarwi 660
Technology see Science
  and technology
Television 13, 672-73
Tello, Julio (archaeologist)
  666
Theatre 646, 648
Tobacco 384
Toledo 211
Toledo, Francisco de 246
Tourism 5, 55, 58-60
Trade 535-45, 590
  colonial 73, 75, 217, 223
  19th century 354
Trade Unions 287, 294,
  301, 453, 459, 581-89
  see also Workers
Transport and
  communications 22,
  113, 273, 335, 537,
  571, 574-80, 669
  see also Railways
Treaty of Ancón 313
Treaty of Lima 313
Trujillo 365, 551
Tumbes 9
Túpac Amaru 200, 249

U

Ucayali river 18, 84, 360
Uchucmarca 599
Uchuraccay 503
United Nations 542, 550
United States of America

88, 313-14, 339,
510-11, 513-16
embassy 107
Universities 305, 609, 666,
684
University of California
Botanical Garden 132
University of Cambridge
109
University of Cuzco 368,
615
University of Oregon 327
University of Oxford 138
University of Princeton 178
University of Puno 615
University of San Cristóbal
de Huamanga 497
University of San Marcos
305, 395, 666, 692
University of Stanford 178
University of Utrecht 440
Urbanization 316, 320,
326, 334, 336, 342-44,
349-51, 455, 463, 548
Ureta, General Eloy 507

V

Vallejo, César (poet) 620,
623, 627-28
Vargas Llosa, Mario
(novelist) 620, 625,
629, 635, 638, 701
Vázquez de Espinosa,
Antonio 61-62
Velasco Alvarado,
President Juan 443,
464, 496, 516, 520, 674
Venezuela 337, 348, 580
Vicos 377, 644
Vicuña 168
Vilcabamba 192, 200
Vilcanota valley 400, 449
Viracocha 442

W

War of the Pacific 89, 93,
281, 296, 309, 313,

315, 506, 540, 679
War of the Spanish
Succession 75
Willey, Gordon 144
Women 329, 371, 453, 456,
573
Wool 292, 354
Workers 305, 334, 459,
491, 549, 581-582, 586
see also Trade Unions

Y

Yale Peruvian expeditions
26, 104
Yanahuara 665
Yarinacocha 402
Yurimaguas 126

Z

Zarumila 517

Map of Peru

This map shows the more important towns and other features.

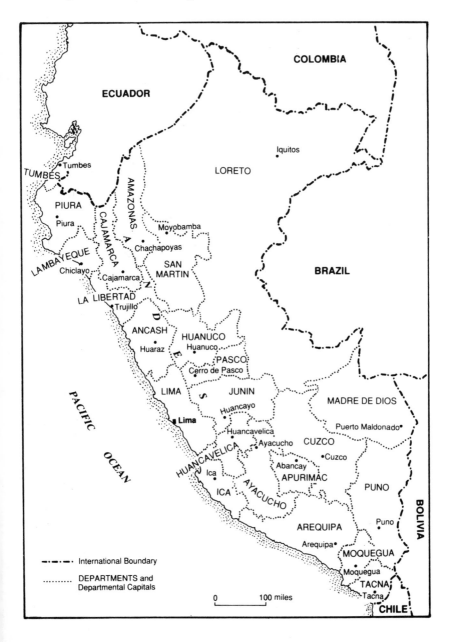

DATE D

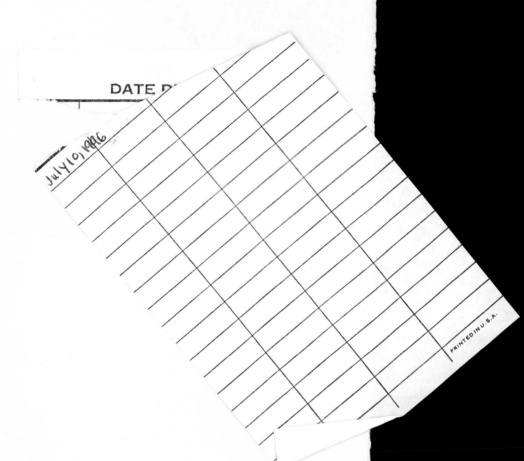

July 10, 1986